ROSARY MEDITATIONS

ROSARY MEDITATIONS

A Lawyer Examines the Evidence

(For Catholics and for Protestants, Too)

ROBERT M. RANDOLPH, KM

PALUXY PRESS

Copyright ©2017 Robert M. Randolph, KM. All rights reserved.

No part of this book may be reproduced, stored in a retrieval system, or transmitted by any means, electronic, mechanical, photocopying, recording, or otherwise, without written permission from the copyright holder.

Published by Paluxy Press.

For ordering information, please visit www.RosaryMeditations.com.

For special discounts for bulk purchases, please call (432) 940-0336 or email info@rosarymeditations.com.

Cover design and composition by Jennings Design, LLC.

ISBN 13: 978-0-9983822-0-3 (Hardcover edition)
ISBN 13: 978-0-9983822-1-0 (Paperback edition)
ISBN 13: 978-0-9983822-2-7 (Case laminate hardcover color edition)
ISBN 13: 978-0-9983822-3-4 (Case laminate hardcover black and white edition)
ISBN 13: 978-0-9983822-4-1 (eBook edition)

LCCN: 2016920280

Printed in the United States of America.

For my "Fathers in the Faith,"
Msgr. Jeffrey N. Steenson, D. Phil. (Oxford), P.A.,
Dr. James Patrick, Th. D. (Trinity, Toronto),
Wallace K. Tomlinson, M.D.,
and Jonathan G. Kerr, J. D.

LIST OF ILLUSTRATIONS

Frontispiece — *The Virgin Annunciate,* detail, Antonello da Messina (?1430–1479), c. 1476–77. Panel, 45 x 34.5 cm. Palazzo Abbatelli, Palermo, Italy. **Photo credit: Mondadori Portfolio/Antonio Quattrone/Art Resource, NY**

10 — *Ecce Ancilla Domini! (The Annunciation),* Dante Gabriel Rossetti (1828–1882), 1849–1850. Oil on canvas, 72.4 x 41.9 cm. Purchased 1886. Tate Gallery, London. **Photo credit: Tate, London/Art Resource, NY**

22 — *Visitation,* Pietro Perugino (1448–1523), Accademia Gallery, Florence. **Photo credit: Scala/Ministero per i Beni e le Attività culturali/Art Resource, NY**

34 — *The Nativity,* John Singleton Copley (American, 1738–1815), about 1776. Oil on canvas, 62.23 x 76.2 cm (24 1/2 x 30 in.) Museum of Fine Arts, Boston. Ernest Wadsworth Longfellow Fund. 1972.981. **Photograph © 2016 Museum of Fine Arts, Boston**

48 — *Simeon and Anna in the Temple,* Rembrandt Harmensz van Rijn (1606–1669), 1628. Oil on oak, 55.5 x 44 cm. Inv. 88. Hamburger Kunsthalle, Hamburg. **Photo credit: bpk Bildagentur / Hamburger Kunsthalle/Elke Walford/Art Resource, NY**

64 — *Christ among the Doctors,* Bernardino Luini (c.1475–1532), probably about 1515–1530. Oil on poplar, 72.4 x 85.7 cm. Holwell Carr Bequest, 1831 (NG18). National Gallery. **Photo credit: © National Gallery, London/Art Resource**

74 — *Baptism of Christ in the Jordan River,* Giotto di Bondone, (1266–1336), ca. 1305. Fresco, post 2001 restoration. Scrovegni Chapel, Padua. **Photo credit: Alfredo Dagli Orti/Art Resource, NY**

80 — *The Marriage at Cana,* Luca Giordano (1634–1705). Museo Nazionale di Capodimonte, Naples. **Photo credit: Alinari/Art Resource, NY**

86 — *The Raising of Lazarus,* Duccio di Buoninsegna, 1310–1311. Tempera and gold on panel, 17 1/8 x 18 1/4 in. (43.5 x 46.4 cm). APx 1975.01. Kimbell Art Museum, Fort Worth, Texas. **Photo credit: © Kimbell Art Museum**

112   *Transfiguration* (post-restoration), Girolamo Savoldo, c.1480–before 1548. Inv. 930. Uffizi Gallery Museum, Florence. **Photo credit: Scala/Ministero per i Beni e le Attività culturali/Art Resource, NY**

118   *Last Supper,* Pietro Annigoni, 1984. Fresco, 520 x 310 cm. Refectory of the Friary of the Basilica of Saint Anthony, Padua. **Photo credit: © Foto G.Deganello/Messaggero S.Antonio Editrice**

138   *Seizure of Christ,* Anthony van Dyck (1599–1641), 1620–1621. Oil on canvas, 3.44 x 2.53 m. Museo del Prado, Madrid. **Photo credit: © Museo Nacional del Prado/Art Resource, NY**

146   *Christ before Pilate,* Jacopo Robusti Tintoretto (1518–1594). Schola di San Rocco, Venice. **Photo credit: Scala/Art Resource, NY**

162   *Christ before Pilate,* Luca Girodano (1634–1705), 1650–1655. Oil on panel, 17 7/8 x 27 1/4 inches (45.4 x 69.2 cm). John G. Johnson Collection, 1917. Philadelphia Museum of Art, Philadelphia. **Photo credit: The Philadelphia Museum of Art/Art Resource, NY**

172   *The Way of the Cross: Station 10, Christ Is Stripped of His Garments,* Giandomenico Tiepolo, (1727–1804). Oil on canvas, 100 x 70 cm. Sacristy, S. Polo, Venice. **Photo credit: Cameraphoto Arte, Venice/Art Resource, NY**

182   *Crucifixion,* Pietro Annigoni, 1983. Fresco. Chapel of Blessings, Basilica of Saint Anthony, Padua. **Photo credit: © Foto G. Deganello/Messaggero S. Antonio Editrice**

204   *The Supper at Emmaus,* Jacopo Bassano (Jacopo dal Ponte), c.1538. Oil on canvas, 39 5/8 x 50 5/8 in. (100.6 x 128.6 cm). APx 1989.03. Kimbell Art Museum, Fort Worth, Texas; acquired with the generous assistance of a gift from Mildred Sterling Hedrick. **Photo credit: © Kimbell Art Museum**

230   *Ascension of Christ,* Benvenuto Tisi Garofalo (1481–1589). Galleria Nazionale d'Arte Antica, Rome. **Photo credit: Scala/Ministero per i Beni e le Attività culturali/Art Resource, NY**

248   Pentecost window, Max Svabinsky, 1933–1935. Stained glass window in the Chapel of St. Ludmila, Southern Aisle of the St. Vitus Cathedral. St. Vitus Cathedral, Prague. **Photo credit: Sites & Photos/Art Resource, NY**

260	*The Assumption of the Virgin*, attributed to Paolo Veronese (Italian, 1528–1588), c. 1548. Oil on canvas. Oval: 31 1/8 x 22 in. (79 x 55.9 cm). Framed: 37 3/4 x 28 15/16 in. (95.9 x 73.5 cm). The David and Alfred Smart Museum of Art, the University of Chicago; Gift of the Samuel H. Kress Foundation. **Photo credit: Photograph © 2016 courtesy of The David and Alfred Smart Museum of Art, the University of Chicago**
276	*Coronation of the Virgin*, Fra Angelico (1387–1455), c.1450. From the doors of the Silver Cabinet. Museo di S. Marco, Florence. **Photo credit: Nicolo Orsi Battaglini/Art Resource, NY**

CONTENTS

LIST OF ILLUSTRATIONS ix
PREFACE 1

I. THE JOYFUL MYSTERIES 9
   A. The Annunciation 11
      1. Mary: education and family. 11
      2. Where? 12
      3. The angel and his greeting 14
      4. The angel's announcement 15
      5. Mary's question. 16
      6. The angel's answer 16
      7. Mary's fiat 17
      8. Mary's conception 17
      9. Mary's marriage to the Holy Spirit 18
     10. Anne's doubt 20

   B. The Visitation 23
      1. Mary's pregnancy; travel to Ain Karem 23
      2. Zechariah's encounter with Gabriel 24
      3. Mary greets Elizabeth; John's recognition 28
      4. Anne sees Elizabeth's pregnancy. 28
      5. Elizabeth's greeting to Mary. 28
      6. Magnificat 29
      7. Zechariah, Elizabeth, Mary, and Anne; signs of the Messiah . . 30
      8. John's birth and circumcision. 30
      9. Zechariah's prophecy (Song of Zechariah) 31
     10. Mary and Anne return to Nazareth 32

   C. The Nativity 35
      1. Joseph and his family 35
      2. Anne tells Joseph; his dream; Mary moves in . . . 38
      3. Roman order for census. 40
      4. Travel to Bethlehem; housed in a stable. 41
      5. Enrollment 43
      6. Jesus' birth 44
      7. Shepherds in the field. 44

   8. Angel appears to shepherds 45
   9. Shepherds find Jesus 46
   10. Jesus' circumcision 47

  D. The Presentation 49
   1. The laws of purification and presentation 49
   2. Mary's purification; entry into the temple 50
   3. Simeon recognizes Jesus; Nunc dimittis 51
   4. Anna 53
   5. Magi in Jerusalem and Bethlehem 53
   6. The "star"; date of Jesus' birth 56
   7. Departure of the Magi 59
   8. Joseph's dream; the flight into Egypt 60
   9. Holy Innocents 60
   10. Holy Family in Egypt; their return 62

  E. Finding the Child Jesus in the Temple 65
   1. Jesus' education 65
   2. Annual parents' conference at Passover 67
   3. Jesus and John are told 67
   4. Confirmation of Jesus and John 68
   5. Jesus is told by his Father to stay 68
   6. Jesus stays behind 68
   7. Jesus questions the rabbis 69
   8. Jesus is lodged in the temple 69
   9. Mary and Joseph return and find Jesus 70
   10. Jesus was on his Father's business; return to Nazareth 70

II. THE LUMINOUS MYSTERIES 73

  A. The Baptism 75
   1. John in the wilderness 75
   2. John begins his ministry 75
   3. Baptism of repentance 76
   4. "Behold the Lamb of God" 76
   5. Jesus' baptism 76
   6. Manner of baptism 77
   7. Holy Spirit descends on Jesus 77
   8. "This is my beloved Son" 78
   9. John encourages his disciples to follow Jesus 78
   10. John's late understanding of Jesus' ministry 78

B. The Wedding at Cana 81
   1. Whose wedding. 81
   2. Who was present?. 81
   3. Mary intercedes with Jesus 82
   4. Jesus' response 82
   5. Mary determines time and place of first miracle 83
   6. "Do whatever he tells you" 83
   7. Jars are filled with water. 84
   8. Water turns to wine. 85
   9. Effect of miracle on company present. 85
  10. Miracle strengthens disciples 85

C. The Proclamation of the Gospel 87
   1. Jesus draws disciples to him and chooses apostles 87
   2. Jesus taught us how to pray. 93
   3. Jesus taught us how to think 95
   4. Jesus taught us how to live 97
   5. Jesus taught us how to forgive 98
   6. Jesus taught us our duty to the state 99
   7. Jesus had the gift of healing. 100
   8. Jesus raised the dead .102
   9. Jesus exercised dominion over the natural world 105
  10. Jesus declared himself to be God 107

D. The Transfiguration 113
   1. Which mountain? 113
   2. Peter, James, and John 113
   3. Timing: Jesus sets his face toward Jerusalem 114
   4. Jesus goes aside to pray 114
   5. Jesus appears in his divinity. 114
   6. Moses and Elijah appear to Jesus 114
   7. Why?. 115
   8. Peter encourages prophets to stay. 115
   9. "This is my beloved Son; listen to him" 116
  10. Peter, James, and John as witnesses; a dynastic claim 116

E. Institution of the Eucharist 119
   1. Jesus safeguards the Last Supper 119
   2. Who was present?. .120
   3. On what day was it held? 120

  4. "This is my body"...................124
  5. Jesus washes their feet...................124
  6. Jesus knew his betrayer...................125
  7. Jesus' teachings...................126
  8. "This is my blood"; transubstantiation;
    the miracles at Lanciano and Bolsena.........126
  9. Closing hymn...................134
  10. The road to Gethsemane...................134

III. The Sorrowful Mysteries 137

A. The Agony in the Garden 139
  1. Jesus prays the first time...................139
  2. Jesus prays the second time...................140
  3. Jesus prays the third time...................140
  4. Jesus sweats blood and his skin
    becomes more sensitive to pain............141
  5. "Whom do you seek?"; "I am He"; Judas' betrayal.......141
  6. Peter and apostles defend Jesus...................142
  7. Jesus halts resistance; apostles scatter...................143
  8. The last miracle; healing a Gentile...................143
  9. Jesus alone arrested...................144
  10. Courage of the apostles...................144

B. The Scourging at the Pillar............... 147
  1. Pre-trial discovery at Annas' house; John and Peter;
    Sanhedrin summoned..................147
  2. Botched trial at Caiaphas' house; Jesus
    confesses he is the Son of God 149
  3. Sanhedrin ask Pilate to execute Jesus;
    Pilate sends him to Herod Antipas..........150
  4. Herod Antipas returns him to Pilate...................152
  5. Pilate examines Jesus privately...................152
  6. Pilate seeks to release Jesus; Jews choose Barabbas........153
  7. Pilate orders Jesus scourged and released...................154
  8. Jesus is scourged...................155
  9. The wounds shown on the Shroud of Turin...................155
  10. History of the Shroud of Turin...................156

C. The Crowning with Thorns 163
  1. Jesus is crowned with thorns...................163
  2. The Sudarium of Oviedo...................164

    3. History of the Sudarium 165
    4. Jesus is struck with a rod .166
    5. "Behold the man"; "Ecce homo" 166
    6. Pilate again examines Jesus; "Where are you from?". 167
    7. "You are not Caesar's friend." 167
    8. Pilate condemns Jesus; his fear of Jewish
            connections in Rome 168
    9. Pilate as Everyman 170
    10. Pilate washes his hands 170

D. Jesus Takes Up His Cross 173
    1. The procession to Calvary. 173
    2. Nature of the cross and manner of its use. 174
    3. Jesus falls the first time 175
    4. Jesus meets his mother; her consent to his mission 176
    5. Simon of Cyrene carries the cross. 176
    6. Veronica cleans Jesus' face. 177
    7. Jesus falls the second time; he meets
            the women of Jerusalem. 177
    8. Jesus falls the third time; he is disrobed. 178
    9. Description of Golgotha and the tomb 178
    10. The titulus 180

E. The Crucifixion 183
    1. Manner of crucifixion. 183
    2. Those present at the crucifixion; "Father, forgive them". 185
    3. The two thieves. 187
    4. "Behold your mother" 188
    5. "I thirst"; Jesus' humanity. 188
    6. "My God, my God, why hast thou forsaken me?;
            Jesus' death 189
    7. Timing of crucifixion 190
    8. Pilate gives Jesus' body to Joseph of Arimathea;
            Glastonbury; King Arthur 192
    9. Deposition from the cross 197
    10. The entombment 200

IV. THE GLORIOUS MYSTERIES. 203

    A. The Resurrection. 205
        1. The temple guards at the tomb 205
        2. The women at the tomb; structure of the tomb 207

3. Jesus' prior appearance to Mary. 211
   4. Peter and John at the tomb .212
   5. The image on the Shroud 214
   6. Jesus appears to Mary Magdalene 216
   7. Jesus appears to two disciples on the road to Emmaus;
         his teaching 220
   8. Jesus appears to Peter; the primacy
         of Peter and his successors 223
   9. Jesus appears to the disciples 225
  10. The bribing of the guards 227

B. The Ascension 231
   1. Jesus again appears to disciples; "My Lord and my God" 231
   2. Travel to Galilee 233
   3. Jesus appears to the disciples on the beach 235
   4. "Do you love me?"; "Tend my sheep" 236
   5. Jesus appears to the 500 238
   6. Jesus appears to James the Greater 240
   7. Return to Jerusalem 240
   8. Jesus teaches the disciples in Jerusalem 240
   9. The Ascension 244
  10. Appearance of two angels 247

C. Pentecost: The Descent of the Holy Spirit 249
   1. Disciples 249
   2. Prayers of the disciples 249
   3. Peter tends the sheep; selection of Matthias 250
   4. Pentecost arrives; who was present 251
   5. "A sound . . . like the rush of a mighty wind" 251
   6. "Tongues as of fire" 251
   7. Speaking in tongues 252
   8. Peter's first sermon 253
   9. Conversion of 3,000; "Repent, and be baptized" 254
  10. "They devoted themselves to the apostles' teaching
         and fellowship, to the breaking of bread,
         and the prayers"; sola scriptura 255

D. The Assumption of the Blessed Virgin Mary 261
   1. The Immaculate Conception 261
   2. Mary as Ever-Virgin 263

3. Mary went to live with John 264
   4. John and Mary move to Ephesus; Mary
         as a gospel source 266
   5. The Neronian persecution; John moves
         Mary to the country .269
   6. Mary returns to Jerusalem 270
   7. Mary visits the disciples and the holy places;
         affirmation of Luke 271
   8. The Eastern tradition: the Dormition
         of the Virgin Mary 273
   9. Munificentissimus Deus:
         The Bodily Assumption of the Virgin Mary. 273
   10. Mary as the Ark of the Incarnation 274

 E. The Coronation of the Blessed Virgin Mary 277
   1. The proto-evangelium of Genesis 277
   2. Mary, the pre-eminent believer 278
   3. Mary, the Mother of God. 279
   4. Mary, the pre-eminent disciple 282
   5. Mary, the co-operatrix of salvation 283
   6. Mary, the Mother of the Church 284
   7. Mary, the model of Christian chastity. 288
   8. Mary, the Intercessor 292
   9. Mary and the dragon 294
   10. Coronation of the Virgin Mary 295

SELECTED BIBILIOGRAPHY. 297

PREFACE

These meditations are the fruit of a lawyer's efforts to understand the evidence regarding the events from which the Mysteries of the Rosary arise. I have sought to know what happened insofar as it is now possible to do so. As primary evidence, I have considered the Scriptures, assuming that they do not contradict themselves in any way and may, and must, be reconciled where necessary. I have considered some patristic writings and the "Tradition" of the Catholic Church as part of the Church's definitive teachings. I have referred to pertinent archeology, astronomy, art, history, and modern science as applied to the Shroud of Turin, the Sudarium of Oviedo, the *titulus*, and the Eucharistic miracles of Lanciano and Bolsena. I have read a number of modern writers; I agree or disagree with some of their conclusions. It has been my effort and intent not to stray from the teachings of the Magisterium.

The Scriptures are so brief as frequently to be almost cryptic. From the evidence I have sought to infer the most probable facts, as any lawyer may do. An inference is not as strong as direct evidence of the fact inferred, so there is always the possibility of error; one is dealing with probabilities. I have also done what the rules of evidence prohibit. Namely, I have drawn inferences from inferences (or "piled inference on inference"). From a probability, one infers another probability. Obviously, this is not as reliable as the original inference, but it is what we all do every day because we can then construct a factual picture that is normally reliable, though not perfect.

Nevertheless, I recognize the risks of doing so and have sought to take them into account in these meditations. As Blessed John Henry Cardinal Newman wrote, where inferences, or probabilities, converge or support each other, the risk of error is diminished. Indeed, a number of mutually supporting probabilities may rise to the level of a virtual certainty. None of what follows is dogmatic, at least insofar as it originates with me.

A friend asked me, why would one want to know such details of the events. A good question. Knowing the details will not get you into Heaven. My reasons are twofold: (1) Scripture frequently is open to interpretation. It is ambiguous, as witness the existence of a multitude of Christian ecclesial entities in the United States, most of them with some particular difference of interpretation that called that denomination into existence. I am reminded of a Texas Supreme Court decision that held by a vote of five to four that a will was unambiguous. In law, when a text is ambiguous, evidence of the extrinsic circumstances is admissible to assist in the interpretation. These meditations largely deal with the extrinsic circumstances. (2) The witness of each Gospel varies from the witness of the others. That is a good sign. Every lawyer who has spent much time in the courthouse knows that, when the witnesses all agree on every detail, the testimony has been "cooked." Different witnesses to the same event or transaction see different things, remember different things, and consider different things to be important. The testimony of each witness may be truthful, but their testimonies need to be correlated. These meditations involve a lot of correlation, particularly regarding the events of Holy Week and the post-Resurrection appearances.

I am a lawyer, not a theologian or philosopher, though I have read a little from both fields of study. Nor am I a student of ancient languages. I have read different translations of some passages and have imposed upon a friend who was a scholar to give me his translation in some instances. The scripture quotations are usually from the Revised Standard Version, 2nd Catholic Edition. Due to my own esthetic preferences, I occasionally use Coverdale's "Great Bible," used in the Book of Common Prayer, especially for the canticles, or the Authorized (King James) Version. With rare exception, I have made no attempt at exegesis between the New and Old Testaments. That is a different kind of work, appropriate to biblical scholars and theologians, for which I claim no qualification.

I accept the tradition of the Catholic Church for 1,800 years that the books of the New Testament were written by the named authors, all within the forty years following the death of Jesus and prior to the destruction of Jerusalem in AD 70, the Gospels being written in the order listed. I rely particularly on John A. T. Robinson's *Redating the New Testament* (1976), which basically supports the traditional authorship and dating. If the Gospels, particularly, and other books of the New Testament were written during the lifetime of many, or even most, of the participants and witnesses, the likelihood of their accuracy is greatly enhanced. (*See* Paul's use of this argument: **"Then he appeared to more than five hundred brethren at one time, most of whom are still alive, though some have fallen asleep"** (1 Cor 15:6).

This position is contrary to current doctrine in many seminaries today. I have no desire to wade into the voluminous controversies regarding the authorship and dating of the New Testament, but a word of explanation seems required because my acceptance of tradition is so out of step. Beginning about 1840 among Protestant theologians at Tuebingen University in Germany, the new biblical criticism dated most of the New Testament up to and beyond AD 150, including the *Gospel of John* at AD 160–170, and denied the authorship by the named authors for almost all of it. By 1897, Adolf von Harnack dated the synoptic Gospels (*Matthew, Mark,* and *Luke*) from AD 65–93, with *John* at AD 80–110 and *the Epistles of Jude, James* and *2 Peter* at AD 100–175. By 1950, a middle course steered by W. G. Kuemmel between his more radical German brethren and the more conservative English writers, dated *Mark* at AD 70, *Luke* at AD 70–90, *Matthew* at AD 80–100, and *John* at AD 90–100. Many writers went far beyond these dates, and most of them contended that most books of the New Testament were pseudonymous. A recent book by Richard Bauckham, *Jesus and the Eyewitnesses* (2006), assumes the Markan priority (that is, *Mark* was written first) and posits the writing of the Gospels to be in the 80s or thereabouts. His work is considered a great triumph by the "conservatives" because he purports to tie all the Gospels to writers who had personally met someone who saw Jesus or had talked to someone who had, thereby lending greater weight to the authenticity of their work. He denies that John, son of Zebedee, was the author of *John*. As of today, the books written on the subject are in academic jargon almost unintelligible to an educated reader, and they largely consist of quoting other academicians, either in support or in argument. Robinson's book (1976) is refreshingly straightforward and clear.

"Indeed what one looks for in vain in much recent scholarship is any serious wrestling with the external or internal evidence for the dating of individual books, . . . rather than an *a priori* pattern of theological development into which they are then made to fit. . . . (T)he chronology of the New Testament documents has scarcely been subjected to fresh examination. No one since Harnack (1897) has really gone back to look at it for its own sake or to examine the presuppositions on which the current consensus rests. It is only when one pauses to do this that one realizes how thin is the foundation for some of the textbook answers and how circular the arguments for many of the relative datings" (Robinson, pages 8–9). He then lays out his evidence for 350 pages and concludes that all the books of the New Testament were written between AD 40 and AD 68 and the Gospels between AD 40 and AD 65. He points out in his conclusion: "If one is dealing with a gap, say, of thirty years . . . , there is a good deal of built-in control in the form of living memory—whereas if the distance is doubled, the controls are much less than half as strong. Without access to public records, when parents or grandparents die, folklore takes over. And what applies to the Gospel stories applies also to the history researched by the author of *Acts*" (Ibid, page 355). Which is exactly the point St. Paul had made. Acceptance of the traditional datings before AD 70 also makes the reading of the texts much clearer.

What follows are meditations, not a history. Consequently, it does not flow in a straight line but rather sometimes meanders. Please bear with me; I do usually arrive at a point.

These are meditations, not a narrative, so the author will speak in the first person singular.

Those who know me know that I am a lamb of the Lord's own flock, but one for whom he went in search, leaving the ninety-nine behind. It is only through His grace that I have come this far.

What follows is structured as a Rosary meditation. It presupposes making the sign of the cross and the recitation, at the commencement, of the Apostles' Creed on the crucifix, an "Our Father," three "Hail Marys," and a "Glory Be to the Father" on the chain before the fifth bead. Then the Fatima Prayer, still on the chain, the announcement of the Mystery (the Roman numerals and the capital letters in the contents), and an "Our Father" on the succeeding single bead. Then the reading of the meditation (the Arabic numerals in the text), followed by a "Hail Mary" on each bead of the following decade of ten beads, followed by a "Glory Be to the Father" and the Fatima Prayer on the chain after the last bead of the decade. Repeat for the next four single beads and four decades. After the last decade, say a "Glory Be to the Father" and the Fatima Prayer. At the end, recite "Hail, Holy Queen" on the medal. For those not accustomed to the Rosary (virtually all Protestants and many Catholics), forms of each prayer follow. If you don't "do" the Rosary, try it for a while, preferably while reading these meditations. It's an acquired taste, so don't be put off if it doesn't appeal to you right away.

The sign of the cross: In the name of the Father, and of the Son, and of the Holy Spirit. Amen.

The Apostles' Creed: I believe in God, the Father Almighty, Maker of heaven and earth; and in Jesus Christ his only Son our Lord, who was conceived by the Holy Spirit, born of the Virgin Mary, suffered under Pontius Pilate, was crucified, dead, and buried. He descended into hell. The third day he rose again from the dead. He ascended into heaven and is seated at the right hand of God the Father Almighty. He will come again to judge the living and the dead. I believe in the Holy Spirit, the holy Catholic Church, the communion of saints, the forgiveness of sins, the resurrection of the body, and the life everlasting. Amen.

Our Father: Our Father, who art in heaven; hallowed be thy Name. Thy kingdom come; thy will be done on earth as it is in heaven. Give us this day our daily bread; and forgive us our trespasses as we forgive those who trespass against us, and lead us not into temptation, but deliver us from evil. Amen.

Hail Mary: Hail Mary, full of grace; the Lord is with thee. Blessed art thou among women, and blessed is the fruit of thy womb, Jesus. Holy Mary, Mother of God, pray for us sinners, now and at the hour of our death. Amen.

Glory Be to the Father: Glory be to the Father, and to the Son, and to the Holy Spirit, as it was in the beginning, is now and ever shall be, world without end. Amen.

Fatima Prayer: O my Jesus, forgive us our sins, save us from the fires of hell and lead all souls to heaven, especially those in most need of thy mercy. Amen.

Hail, Holy Queen: Hail, Holy Queen, Mother of Mercy, our life, our sweetness and our hope. To thee do we cry, poor banished children of Eve. To thee do we send up our sighs, mourning and weeping in this vale of tears. Turn, then, most gracious Advocate, thine eyes of mercy toward us, and after this, our exile, show unto us the blessed fruit of thy womb, Jesus. O clement, O loving, O sweet Virgin Mary! Pray for us, O holy Mother of God, that we may be made worthy of the promises of Christ.

THE JOYFUL
MYSTERIES

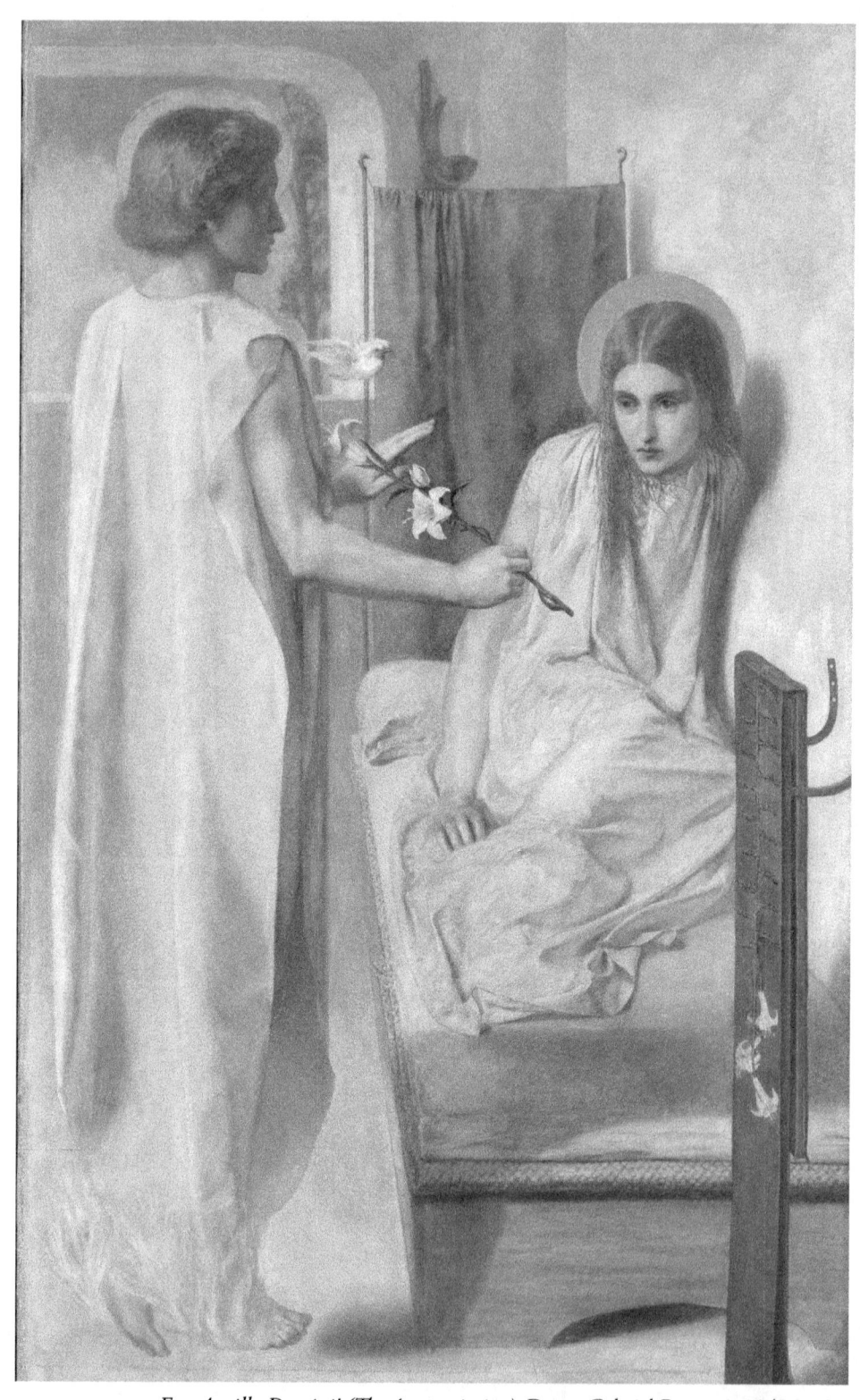
Ecce Ancilla Domini! (The Annunciation), Dante Gabriel Rossetti, 1849-1850, Tate Gallery, London

THE ANNUNCIATION

✦

(If you skipped the Preface, please go back and read it now. Do not read further until you have done so.)

1. "**In the sixth month** (of Elizabeth's pregnancy) **the angel Gabriel was sent by God to a city of Galilee, named Nazareth, to a virgin betrothed to a man whose name was Joseph of the house of David; and the virgin's name was Mary**" (Lk 1:26–27).

Mary was a young Jewish woman who lived in Nazareth. Upon reaching puberty, she was betrothed. In all probability, she was thirteen years old. St. John Paul II named 1987 as a Marian Year, in preparation for a Jubilee Year at the second millennium, in the belief that Mary was thirteen years old at the time of the Annunciation.

Mary's mother was Anne, who was approximately fifty years old. Anne's "kinswoman" was Elizabeth, the wife of Zechariah. Elizabeth was "a daughter of Aaron"—that is, her father was descended in the male line from Aaron. He was therefore a Levite of the legitimate priestly tribe, though many priests in his day were political appointees, not of the Levitical line. Neither Mary nor Anne is described as a daughter of Aaron, because only women whose fathers were Levites were so called. Therefore, Anne was related to Elizabeth through her mother, since her father was not a Levite. Anne's mother and Elizabeth were probably sisters. Elizabeth was approximately sixty years old, years past menopause and notoriously "barren."

Mary's father was Joachim. Scripture and Tradition say that Jesus was descended from King David, in fact, and not only through Mary's husband, juridically the "father" of Jesus (Rom 1:3; Ignatius, *Epistle to Ephesians*). According to the *Proto-evangelium of James,* Joachim was not a Levite. Since Anne was of the Levitical line, through her mother, probably, Joachim was the "son of David." Mary was the long-desired child of the "old age" of Anne and Joachim; her birth was late but not miraculous. There is no indication that Mary had any siblings.

Mary was literate at least in Hebrew, the language of Scripture and liturgy, and probably in Aramaic, the spoken language of the Jewish people. Since the reign of Queen Alexandra Salome (76–67 BC) basic education was compulsory for all Jewish children, girls as well as boys.

❖ ❖ ❖

2. Where did the Annunciation take place? It could not have been in a public place, since the conversation between Mary and an angel was confidential, intimate, and potentially dangerous. It therefore took place in privacy at Anne's and Mary's home in Nazareth. Joachim apparently had died previously.

There have been at least five churches in Nazareth over a grotto that tradition points out as the place of the Annunciation. The house itself had been converted into a house church, probably as early as the first century, by relatives of Jesus, traditionally descendants of Jesus' "brother," Jude. In the third century, the house was demolished and a church, having the architectural attributes of a synagogue, was built. Though built like a synagogue, it was a church. The village's Jewish synagogue was a different building altogether. Graffiti show devotion to Jesus and Mary. Archeological work prior to building the current basilica disclosed stones in a cistern covered over by the later Byzantine church, bearing inscriptions "Hail Mary" and "This is the holy place of Mary." They necessarily were from either the third-century or first-century structure. Some experts have identified them as second century, necessarily inscribed on a portion of the original house, connecting the site to the Annunciation at a very early date indeed.

The grotto was behind and at a lower level than the house. Steps led from the grotto to the courtyard, since the stored goods and materials would not have been carried through the house. The third-century synagogue-style church incorporated the steps and the grotto, as did the Byzantine church, which replaced it about AD 427, and as have subsequent churches on the site.

The community which used the site for almost four hundred years was Jewish Christian. The only first-century structures remaining on the site are the steps, the grotto in which the Annunciation is said to have taken place, and a smaller grotto connected to it.

Did the Annunciation take place in the grotto itself? Probably not. Not much is identifiable of the first-century grotto under the church, but it is typical of numerous other grottos in Nazareth. The grottos were used for storage and for agricultural use, such as a wine press. Silos and cisterns were dug into them, and many were connected with corridors. None of them show signs of being used as habitations. The grotto under the church itself had three large silos dug into its floor. The grotto was about 18' by 19' but, filled with the tools, materials, grain, and oil stored in it, it would have been a dark, dirty, and uninviting place for such an encounter. The history of the site is such that, in all reasonable probability, the Annunciation occurred on these premises. Following destruction of the original house, it was reasonable to identify the grotto as the place of the Annunciation, since it and the steps were the only surviving portions of the house of Anne and Mary. The standard small house of the period had two rooms, one semi-public for cooking and eating and the other private for sleeping. Very poor houses had no courtyard or shared a courtyard with other houses; Joachim's and Anne's probably had its own courtyard, since there is no indication that they were at the bottom of the scale financially. The courtyard was walled off from the street, with entrances to the street, to the grotto, and into the house, and served as an outdoor kitchen, living room, and workshop.

What size was the house? The excavations in Nazareth do not tell us. However, Mary appeared in a dream to a Saxon lady, Richeldis, in 1061 at Walsingham, County Norfolk, in East Anglia, England, and told her to build a chapel the size of the house of the Incarnation and to dedicate it to the Incarnation. The dimensions were about 23' by 12'. The size and shape are replicated in the Lady Chapel of Our Lady of Walsingham Church in Houston. The dimensions would conform well to a small house in a Galilean village.

Mary was particularly devout. We can well picture her withdrawing to the private room of the house to pray.

❖ ❖ ❖

3. "And he (the angel) came to her, and said, 'Hail, full of grace, the Lord is with you!' But she was greatly troubled at the saying, and considered in her mind what sort of greeting this might be" (Lk 1:28–29).

What did the angel look like? Contrary to many artistic renderings, he did not have wings. He had the form of a man. The prophet Daniel described him as "the man Gabriel" (Dn 9:21). The angels of the Ascension were "two men in white robes" (Acts 1:10). At the tomb after Jesus' resurrection, Mary Magdalene saw "two angels in white" (Jn 20:12). These angels were more precisely described: "His appearance was like lightning, and his raiment white as snow" (Mt 28:3). The "appearance like lightning" was similar to Jesus' appearance at his transfiguration, when "his face shone like the sun, and his garments became white as light" (Mt 17:2). The angel had a supernatural ability to appear and disappear, similar to Jesus' sudden appearances to his apostles after his resurrection (e.g., Jn 20:19). Mary saw a figure in the form of a man who took form from thin air in the privacy of her home. His features were supernaturally radiant, and his white robes were supernaturally white. She instantly recognized that it was an angel, rather than a man, who had invaded her bedroom.

The angel's greeting was unique. "Hail, full of grace." Mary knew of no person in the Scriptures who had been so addressed. She had reason to be troubled by the angel's appearance and the form of his greeting and to wonder what it meant for her.

The Greek word translated as "full of grace" has a connotation of holiness, of something connected with God. Protestant translations usually mistranslate it, such as "Hail, O favored one," in an effort to downplay Mary. Some recent Catholic translations have similarly mistranslated it, thoughtlessly in keeping with the general cultural, and Arian-like, attack on Jesus' divinity.

※ ※ ※

4. "And the angel said to her, 'Do not be afraid, Mary, for you have found favor with God. And behold, you will

conceive in your womb and bear a son, and you shall call his name Jesus. He will be great, and will be called the Son of the Most High; and the Lord God will give to him the throne of his father David, and he will reign over the house of Jacob forever; and of his kingdom there will be no end'" (Lk 1:30–33).

Mary knew that much was demanded of persons in Scripture who had "found favor with God." What was demanded of her was to bear a child described as destined to become the Messiah. Having recognized the figure before her as an angel sent by God, Mary believed the angel's message.

---

5. **"And Mary said to the angel, 'How shall this be, since I know not a man?'"** (Lk 1:34). Mary's question was not an expression of disbelief. It was a reasonable question. It was faith seeking understanding. Mary was a virgin who was perfectly aware of how babies were made. Mary understood the angel's message as calling upon her to conceive the child at this very time, rather than a conception which would take place naturally at some time in the future after she and Joseph had their formal wedding and began living together.

---

6. **"And the angel said to her, 'The Holy Spirit will come upon you, and the power of the Most High will overshadow you; therefore the child to be born will be called holy, the Son of God. And behold, your kinswoman Elizabeth in her old age has also conceived a son; and this is the sixth month with her who was called barren. For with God nothing will be impossible'"** (Lk 1:35–37). Mary understood that the conception was to be miraculous, brought about by the action of God upon her body. As a devout Jew, she understood that the child would be the long-awaited Messiah. It would be years before Mary understood the child's description as "holy, the Son of God."

❖ ❖ ❖

7. "And Mary said, 'Behold the handmaid of the Lord; be it unto me according to thy word'" (Lk 1:38).

Mary well understood the danger in the angel's message. She was called by God to conceive a son before she had sexual relations with Joseph. There was no way of knowing what Joseph's reaction would be to finding his wife pregnant with a child not his own. Death by stoning was a possibility. Even if Joseph just walked away, the child would be illegitimate. Mary's risk of being a single mother was underscored by being told that "*You* shall call his name Jesus." The naming of a child was done by the father, and the angel's statement implied the absence of a father. Jewish society was not forgiving of such behavior. Both she and her son could be thrust to the margins of society, to the status of day labor, or even worse.

❖ ❖ ❖

8. "And the angel departed from her" (Lk 1:38).

Mary was alone in the privacy of her bedroom. After the angel disappeared, the Holy Spirit "came upon" Mary, and she was "overshadowed" by the power of God.

Marriage is a "good" approved by the Church. Likewise, conjugal relations within marriage are a "good," approved by the Church. When the Holy Spirit "came upon" Mary, and she conceived Jesus in her womb, she experienced the perfect union.

Overcome by the experience, she was confirmed in her belief in the angel and his message. She knew that her encounter was not an illusion, teenage feminine hysteria, or any of the other grounds for explaining away what had happened to her. She knew that she was suddenly pregnant with Israel's Messiah.

The conclusions of the above paragraph, while not unique, are also not common; they result from a convergence of inferences that support each other. The first fact is Mary's absolute assurance of her pregnancy in a situation in which one normally could not be sure of the result, particularly in the case of a woman so young; from that one must infer that something unusual had taken place so to convince her. The second fact is the impregnation of Mary by the Holy Spirit; from that one may infer that God acted upon Mary's body in a material way, rather than waving a wand and saying, "Now you are pregnant." The third fact is the goodness of conjugal relations within the marriage bond, from which we may infer that the consummation of marriage of the world's only perfect woman with God, however it was done, must have given rise to the perfect union. The convergence of these three facts and their inferences gives rise to the conclusion that Mary's conviction arose from an extraordinary ecstasy, which left her absolutely certain of her encounter with the angel and the resultant pregnancy.

❖ ❖ ❖

9. Mary also knew, or came to know, that the author of her pregnancy, the father of her child, was God, acting as the Holy Spirit. She had become, in some fashion, the wife of God. While the angel had spoken to Mary of the Holy Spirit, a devout Jew, strongly monotheistic, would have had no idea at that time of the Trinity and would have simply considered that a unitary God had acted upon her, perhaps through an agent called the Holy Spirit; the actor, in Mary's mind, was simply God. Furthermore, because God does not commit fornication or adultery, their union necessarily occurred within a marriage bond of some sort between God and Mary. She knew that she could not become the wife of Joseph in the ordinary sense.

The foregoing, again, is not a unique thought, nor is it widely accepted. This is another example of convergence of probabilities. The Magisterium from a very early date has taught that Mary is "ever-virgin." When was the decision made that Mary and Joseph would not enjoy normal conjugal relations after their marriage? Some writers think that Mary had resolved on a life of virginity before her betrothal to Joseph. I find no evidence of such a decision, and virginity would have been contrary to the belief of a devout Jew, whose duty was to propagate and replenish the earth. There is no indication that Joseph voluntarily came up with the idea after he believed that the child that Mary was carrying was conceived by God. Indeed, for Joseph to have suggested that there be no conjugal relations would have been an improper denial of such relations to his lawful wife. If the idea did not originate with Joseph, in fairness to him, it had to be part of the package of information given to him with news of his wife's pregnancy. When Joseph consented to bring Mary into his home, he had to have known that he was agreeing to a platonic marriage. Since the idea had to originate with Mary, the only remaining question is that of timing. It is possible that Mary realized immediately after her conception that she was the bride of God and therefore could not be Joseph's wife in the normal sense, or she may have worked this out in her mind during the period before she returned to Nazareth from Ain Karem. The precise timing is not important; the important thing is that she had reached this conclusion, and it was presented to Joseph as part of the package. I will not lengthen these meditations by tracking the inferences in subsequent passages, but I hope these examples will allow the reader to do so.

10. When Anne returned home, Mary told her in detail what had happened. Anne was taken aback. She knew Mary as a devout, virtuous, obedient daughter; for Mary to have had an affair would have been out of character. Furthermore, in a small village like Nazareth, it would have been difficult for Mary to have done so without Anne at least having become suspicious. Nevertheless, Mary was obviously convinced that she was pregnant even though the normal results of such a pregnancy would be catastrophic for Mary and the baby. Further, Mary's confession of pregnancy, if illicit, was contrary to the normal course of quietly hoping that pregnancy had not resulted.

Mary slept in the same room, and probably in the same bed, as Anne. Anne clearly was aware of the timing of Mary's periods. While the timing was right for conception to have occurred, both Anne and Mary were well aware that, even if Mary had had a sexual encounter that day, pregnancy frequently did not result. Yet, Mary was convinced that she was pregnant. Anne, a practical country woman, knew that she would not be the first mother to be fooled by her daughter, if Mary had become pregnant by a man other than Joseph. Anne was full of doubt. Why was Mary so convinced of her pregnancy when she had had a normal period two weeks earlier and there had not been time for any indication of pregnancy to appear? If Mary were pregnant, who was the father?

Anne decided that there were two tests of Mary's story. If Mary was not pregnant, Anne would know in two weeks when Mary's next period began. If Mary missed her next period, the angel had told Mary that Anne's barren Aunt Elizabeth was five to six months pregnant with a son. They could go to Elizabeth and learn if it was true. Anne, full of doubt, decided to wait.

Visitation, Pietro Perugino, Accademia Gallery, Florence

THE VISITATION

❖

1. Two weeks passed, and Mary missed her period. Anne was then convinced that Mary's story was true. There was no other reasonable explanation for Mary's conviction of her pregnancy at a time no one could have known for certain. Anne therefore believed Mary's witness and became the second disciple.

"In those days Mary arose and went with haste into the hill country, to a city of Judah, and she entered the house of Zechariah and greeted Elizabeth" (Lk 1:39–40).

Scripture does not mention Anne, nor that Anne accompanied Mary to see Elizabeth. But there was no way that Mary, at age thirteen, could have made the trip by herself. Elizabeth and Zechariah lived at Ain Karem, about five miles north of Jerusalem. The direct route from Nazareth to Jerusalem, ninety miles to the south, led through Samaria. Due to religious and ethnic animosities between Jews and Samaritans, Jews from Galilee usually avoided Samaria by going east, crossing the Jordan River near Scythopolis (Bethsean), going down the east side of the Jordan and re-crossing it at Jericho, thence west through the desert climbing up to Jerusalem. Travel by Jews through Samaria could be dangerous as well as unpleasant, and two Jewish women would not have attempted it.

It was Anne who made the arrangements and provided the finances for a trip of about 140 miles, taking about eight days each way since they did not travel on the Sabbath. Anne began planning the journey during the two-week wait for Mary's period, so that they could go "in haste" if Mary was pregnant. Anne probably tentatively arranged to purchase a donkey on which they could load their travel gear and take turns riding. Anne had to tell Joseph and the neighbors that Elizabeth needed help, so they were going to her. Probably no one asked how Anne knew; if someone did, she evaded the question.

❖ ❖ ❖

2. When Elizabeth saw Mary and Anne at her door, she instantly knew why they were there. To see why this was so, we must go back in time about six months.

"In the days of Herod, king of Judea, there was a priest named Zechariah, of the division of Abijah; and he had a wife of the daughters of Aaron, and her name was Elizabeth. And they were both righteous before God, walking in all the commandments and ordinances of the Lord blamelessly. But they had no child, because Elizabeth was barren and both were advanced in years. Now while he was serving as priest before God when his division was on duty, according to the custom of the priesthood, it fell to him by lot to enter the temple of the Lord and burn incense" (Lk 1:5–9).

Zechariah was a member of one of the twenty-four divisions of priests, each of which served two one-week tours of temple duty during the year. In addition, all divisions served during the weeks of Passover, Pentecost, Atonement, and Tabernacles. A large number of men served in each division. They performed a myriad of duties required for the daily operation of the temple. Sleeping quarters and refectories were provided for them within the temple complex while they were on duty.

Within the Holy House, the liturgical heart of the temple, were three rooms. The first was a vestibule. The second was the sanctuary, which contained the menorah, the table for the shew bread, and the altar of incense at which incense was burned daily. The inner room was the Holy of Holies, which the high priest entered alone once a year on the Day of Atonement (Yom Kippur). Three priests were involved in the daily offering at the altar of incense. The three priests would enter the room together. Two of them would spread the coals and prepare the altar. They would withdraw, and the third priest, by himself, would burn the incense, make the offering, and recite the prayers. The first two priests were selected by lot. From the pool of priests who had thus served and seen the altar of incense once previously, a priest was selected by lot to burn the incense. He could do so only once during his lifetime. Many priests never saw the altar of incense, and to be selected by lot to make the offering was the high point of a priest's vocation. On this occasion, Zechariah had been selected by lot to make the offering.

"And the whole multitude of the people were praying outside at the hour of incense. And there appeared to him an angel of the Lord standing on the right side of the altar of incense. And Zechariah was troubled when he saw him, and fear fell upon him. But the angel said to him, 'Do not be afraid, Zechariah, for your prayer is heard, and your wife Elizabeth will bear you a son, and you shall call his name John. And you will have joy and gladness, and many will rejoice at his birth; for he will be great before the Lord, and he shall drink no wine nor strong drink, and he will be filled with the Holy Spirit, even from his mother's womb. And he will turn many of the sons of

Israel to the Lord their God, and he will go before him in the spirit and power of Elijah, to turn the hearts of the fathers to the children, and the disobedient to the wisdom of the just, to make for the Lord a people prepared.' And Zechariah said to the angel, 'How shall I know this? For I am an old man, and my wife is advanced in years'" (Lk 1:10–18).

The angel appeared after the incense had been offered and after Zechariah had completed his prayers. Zechariah's question, unlike Mary's, sprang from disbelief. Despite the circumstances, the angel's unexplainable appearance, and the prophecy, Zechariah asked for additional proof. "How shall I know this?"

Instead of explaining how Elizabeth could conceive a son at her advanced age, **"the angel answered him, 'I am Gabriel, who stands in the presence of God; and I was sent to speak to you, and to bring you this good news.'"** (Lk 1:19)

As a priest well-acquainted with the Scriptures, Zechariah then grasped the import of the angel's appearance and prophecy. During the Babylonian captivity, the prophet Daniel had visions of the desolation of Israel. Gabriel first appeared to Daniel to explain the duration of the exile. Later, when Daniel was praying for Jerusalem, Gabriel appeared to him again to prophesy the coming of the Messiah (Dn 8:1–9:27). The reappearance of Gabriel foretold the imminent coming of the Messiah, and his prophecy clearly foretold the baby's role as the Messiah's forerunner. Furthermore, when Gabriel said that Zechariah's prayer had been answered, the prayer to which Gabriel referred was Zechariah's prayer for the coming of the Messiah. Zechariah had not been praying for a child; he and his wife were long past the time for such a prayer. Gabriel had told him that the prayer for the Messiah was to be answered by Elizabeth's bearing a son.

"'And behold, you will be silent and unable to speak until the day that these things come to pass, because you did not

believe my words, which will be fulfilled in their time.' And the people were waiting for Zechariah, and they wondered at his delay in the temple. And when he came out, he could not speak to them, and they perceived that he had seen a vision in the temple; and he made signs to them and remained mute"** (Lk 1:20–22).

Zechariah remained in the Holy House for an unusually long period of time. The encounter with Gabriel did not take so long, but he needed time to absorb what he had been told, to adjust to being speechless, and to decide what he would, and would not, tell the others. The announcement of the Messiah's imminent arrival, along with his own role and that of his wife and child, was a dangerous secret. Herod the Great, especially in his old age, was a cruel and brutal despot. He had slain large numbers of his subjects on trivial causes and killed his own wife and sons when convinced that they were a threat to him. The future Messiah, the inheritor of David's throne, would be at risk from Herod. Zechariah therefore gave no explanation for his delay, nor why he had been struck dumb.

"And when his time of service was ended he went to his home. After these days his wife Elizabeth conceived, and for five months she hid herself, saying, 'Thus the Lord has done to me in the days he looked upon me, to take away my reproach among men'" (Lk 1:23–25).

Zechariah told Elizabeth all that had happened, writing it down for her to read. From the time of her conception, confirming Gabriel's prophecy, they prayed to have the Messiah's identity disclosed to them. Zechariah and, through him, Elizabeth, knew from Scripture that the Messiah was to be born of a virgin of the house of David in the village of Bethlehem, six miles south of Jerusalem. One day, Mary and Anne appeared unannounced at their door.

3. Mary was the one who greeted Elizabeth. Ordinarily, Anne would have spoken for them, being both her mother and the older woman, but Anne deferred to Mary as the mother of the Messiah. Elizabeth noticed Anne's deference. The presence of the visitors so far from home, not in connection with any festival in Jerusalem, could signify only one thing to Elizabeth. Mary was a virgin of the house of David and was pregnant with the Messiah. She obviously had been told by God that Elizabeth was pregnant with the Messiah's forerunner. Elizabeth's prayers to know the Messiah's identity had been answered, and she instantly believed that the Messiah would be born of Mary.

"And when Elizabeth heard the greeting of Mary, the child leaped in her womb . . . " (Lk 1:41). The infant John supernaturally recognized the presence of Jesus. As Gabriel had foretold, "He will be filled with the Holy Spirit, even from his mother's womb." John's reaction confirmed Elizabeth in her belief.

4. Anne saw Elizabeth's pregnancy and was confirmed in her belief in Mary's story that she was the mother of the Messiah, miraculously begotten of God.

5. **"Elizabeth was filled with the Holy Spirit and she exclaimed with a loud cry, 'Blessed are you among women, and blessed is the fruit of your womb! And why is this granted me, that the mother of my Lord should come to me? For behold,**

when the voice of your greeting came to my ears, the child in my womb leaped for joy. And blessed is she who believed that there would be a fulfillment of what was spoken to her from the Lord'" (Lk 1: 41–45).

Elizabeth's belief was the fruit of her perceptiveness, her prayers, and a supernatural insight. Elizabeth divined that, unlike Zechariah, Mary had believed what God told her.

❖ ❖ ❖

6. "And Mary said, 'My soul doth magnify the Lord, and my spirit hath rejoiced in God my Savior. For he hath regarded the lowliness of his handmaiden. For behold, from henceforth all generations shall call me blessed. For he that is mighty hath magnified me, and holy is his name. And his mercy is on them that fear him throughout all generations. He hath showed strength with his arm; he hath scattered the proud in the imagination of their hearts. He hath put down the mighty from their seat, and hath exalted the humble and meek. He hath filled the hungry with good things; and the rich he hath sent empty away. He remembering his mercy hath holpen his servant Israel; as he promised to our forefathers, Abraham and his seed, forever'" (Lk 1:46–55).

Many scholars suggest that Mary's *Magnificat* is based largely on the Song of Hannah (1 Sm 2:1–10). Perhaps. Doubtlessly, Mary was familiar with it. Nevertheless, her *Magnificat* is gentler. The first section rejoices in what God has done for Mary. The second section rejoices in what God has done for Israel, assisting the poor, the humble, and the meek against those who wrongfully use their strength to oppress them.

Mary's reference to herself as the "handmaid" of the Lord is surely derived from Psalm 86:16: **"[G]ive thy strength to thy**

servant, and save the son of thy handmaid." And from Psalm 116:16: **"O Lord, I am thy servant; I am thy servant, the son of thy handmaid."** If Mary is the Lord's handmaid, her son will be the Lord's servant, the Messiah. Mary knew the Psalter very well.

"From henceforth all generations shall call me blessed." Hence, one of Mary's titles: "the Blessed Virgin Mary." Yet many Christians repudiate, and even recoil, from this title. How can it be denied in the face of explicit Scripture?

❖ ❖ ❖

7. During the next three months, Mary and Zechariah told each other what they had experienced. Zechariah communicated in writing. The angel who spoke to Mary had not told her his name, but Zechariah could identify him as Gabriel from Mary's description. They discussed the Scriptures identifying the Messiah. Mary was the virgin of the house of David, but how was the baby to be born in Bethlehem? We can be certain that Elizabeth and Zechariah knew that Mary was carrying the Messiah and that Mary and Anne knew that Elizabeth was carrying his forerunner, who would go before the Messiah "in the spirit and power of Elijah."

❖ ❖ ❖

8. Mary and Anne helped Elizabeth through the last months of what, at her age, must have been a difficult pregnancy.

"And Mary remained with her for about three months, and returned to her home. Now the time came for Elizabeth to be delivered, and she gave birth to a son" (Lk 1:56–57). The Gospel is not a chronology. Luke finishes his story about Mary's stay at Elizabeth's before starting up with John's birth and circumcision and the Song of Zechariah.

"And her neighbors and kinsfolk heard that the Lord had shown great mercy to her, and they rejoiced with her. And on the eighth day they came to circumcise the child; and they would have named him Zechariah after his father, but his mother said 'Not so; he is to be called John.' And they said to her, 'None of your kindred is called by this name.' And they made signs to his father, inquiring what he would have him called. And he asked for a writing tablet, and wrote, 'His name is John.' And they all marveled. And immediately his mouth was opened and his tongue loosed, and he spoke, blessing God" (Lk 1: 58–64). Upon the naming of the child as "John," Gabriel's words to Zechariah, **"You shall call his name John,"** were fulfilled, and he was again able to speak.

❖ ❖ ❖

9. "And his father Zechariah was filled with the Holy Spirit, and prophesied, saying, 'Blessed be the Lord God of Israel; for he hath visited and redeemed his people; and hath raised up a mighty salvation for us, in the house of his servant David; as he spake by the mouth of his holy prophets, which have been since the world began; that we should be saved from our enemies, and from the hand of all that hate us. To perform the mercy promised to our forefathers, and to remember his holy covenant; to perform the oath which he sware to our forefather Abraham, that he would give us; that we being delivered out of the hand of our enemies might serve him without fear; in holiness and righteousness before him, all the days of our life. And thou, child, shalt be called the prophet of the Highest; for thou shalt go before the face of the Lord to prepare his ways; to give knowledge of salvation unto his people for the remission of their sins, through the tender mercy of our God;

whereby the day-spring from on high hath visited us; to give light to them that sit in darkness, and in the shadow of death, and to guide our feet into the way of peace'" (Lk 1:67–79).

The first section of Zechariah's song concerns the Lord's promises to Israel. Zechariah is ambiguous as to when the Lord has visited and redeemed his people and has raised up their salvation in the house of David. He makes a veiled reference to the conception of Jesus (meaning "the Lord saves" or "Salvation") in the womb of Mary of the house of David. A reference apparent to Mary, Anne, and Elizabeth, but veiled to the others present.

The second section of Zechariah's song deals with John, foretelling how he will prepare Israel for the coming of the Lord by instructing the people for the remission of their sins. He thereby prophesies John's role, bringing a baptism of repentance for the forgiveness of sin. He does not clearly link John's mission to the Messiah's coming. His ambiguities avoid placing John and his parents in peril from Herod.

❖   ❖   ❖

10. After John's circumcision and after seeing Zechariah released from being dumb, upon hearing his song of prophecy, Mary and Anne returned to Nazareth. All that Gabriel had told Mary about Elizabeth had come to pass. Mary was four months pregnant by the time they reached home.

The Nativity, John Singleton Copley, about 1776, Museum of Fine Arts, Boston

THE NATIVITY

1. Joseph was of the house of David. The genealogies given in Matthew and Luke vary greatly (Mt 1:1–16; Lk 3:23–38). Much learned ink has been spilled over the centuries, and I draw no conclusion other than Joseph's remote descent from King David. Since Joseph was considered the legal father of Jesus in determining Jesus' qualification to be the Messiah, that was all that counted. Since such genealogies normally recite descent only in the male line, it is significant that Matthew lists the wives of four ancestors. Two of the women, Tamar and "the wife of Uriah" (Bathsheba), had questions affecting their reputations. This likely is an oblique reference to Mary's irregularly timed conception of Jesus.

Joseph lived in Nazareth, working as a carpenter. A village carpenter's work included skilled cabinetwork, furniture, and house construction. Joseph was not rich, certainly not a "contractor," as some have described him. When it came time to make the offering at Mary's purification after Jesus' birth, the offering was two doves, a less costly offering allowed for those who could not afford a lamb and a dove. Neither was Joseph at the bottom of the economic ladder, among those who sought—and occasionally found—labor by the day.

Joseph is frequently portrayed as an old man at the time he married Mary. It is improbable that he was truly "aged," as some portray him, since he was still vigorous enough to travel to Jerusalem for Passover twelve years later. Such portrayals represent an effort to bolster Mary's continued virginity by creating a physical impediment, infirmity of age, to consummation of the marriage. We do not know his age, other than that he was no longer young. He took Mary to his own house, not his parents' house, as a young man would have done.

What family did Joseph have? He had at least one brother, Cleophas (also spelled Cleopas or Clopas). Clopas is a rare Semitic version of the Greek name, Cleophas. This may indicate that Joseph's family was Hellenized to some degree, while still being devout Jews. Cleophas was married to Mary, sometimes called the "sister" of the Virgin Mary, a term that can include kinswomen (Jn 19:25). **"And are not his brothers James and Joseph and Simon and Judas? And are not his sisters with us?"** (Mt 13:55–56). Cleophas' wife, Mary, was the widow of Alpheus, by whom she had two sons, the apostle James, son of Alpheus (Mt 10:3; Mk 3:18) and Joses (also spelled Joseph), who was sometimes referred to as Joseph Barsabbas (Acts 1:23). Their mother, Mary, is sometimes called the mother of James, Joses, and Salome (Mk 15:40). She probably was widowed early and married Cleophas when the two boys were very young. Salome likely was a child of the first marriage, being thus linked to James and Joses. Salome later married Zebedee; their children were the apostles James and John. Because John was old enough to be the youngest apostle, Salome most likely was the oldest of Mary's children by Alpheus.

There is much disagreement as to the biography of James, son of Alpheus. I will go with the conclusions of Pope Benedict XVI, a safe bet. James, the son of Alpheus and the stepson of Cleophas, was one of the twelve apostles, sometimes called James the Younger or James the Less (Jacobus Minor). When the apostles were dispersed from Jerusalem in AD 41–42, he became the leader of the church in Jerusalem. We know that James the apostle was James the "brother" (which includes cousin or even kinsman) of Jesus (Mt 13:55) because Paul wrote, **"Then after three years I went up to Jerusalem to visit Cephas, and remained with him fifteen days. But I saw none of the other apostles except James the Lord's brother."** (Gal 1:18–19) James, leader of the Jerusalem church, is also sometimes called James the Just. He is the author of the *Epistle of James*. Because he was head of the Jerusalem church for many years, and James the Greater, the son of Zebedee and brother of John, was martyred in August, AD 41, references to "James" in an appropriate context refer to him.

Cleophas and Mary had two sons, Simon (also Simeon) and Jude (also Judas). This Judas was not the apostle Jude. The apostle Judas or Jude (other than Judas Iscariot) was Judas, son of James (Lk 6:16; Acts 1:13). James was a common name, and neither of the apostles named James would have been old enough to be his father, since men married only when they could support a family. Jude, son of Cleophas and Mary, is traditionally believed to be the author of the *Epistle of Jude*. The author of the Epistle refers to himself as brother of "James," to be understood in its context as referring to the head of the Jerusalem church, James the Less, but he refers to himself as not being among the apostles (Jude 1, 17). Cleophas and Mary also had either one or two daughters, Mary of whom nothing is known, and possibly Salome. If Salome was not the daughter of Alpheus, she probably was the oldest child born to Cleophas and Mary, in order to have had sons as old as James and John.

"For even his brothers did not believe in him" (Jn 7:5). This statement was made regarding the state of affairs shortly before the second Passover of Jesus' ministry, about a year before his death. Since his "brother" James, son of Alpheus, was a disciple, how could this be? Furthermore, Joseph Barsabbas is described as having been a disciple from the beginning of Jesus' ministry (Acts 1:21–23). If John's Gospel does not intend to include stepcousins within the meaning of "brother," but rather only blood kin, then not only Joseph Barsabbas but also likely Salome's sons, James and John, were not included within the term "brother." If the other two blood "brothers," Simon and Jude, had not yet become disciples at that time, the statement would have been correct. It should be noted that they later came over, because his brothers were members of the band of disciples before Pentecost (Acts 1:14).

It has been claimed by some writers that some or all of the children of Cleophas and/or Mary, were really children of Joseph by a marriage prior to his marriage to the Virgin Mary or were children of Joseph and Mary. Other than relying upon a strictly limited and literal meaning of the word translated into English as "brother," there is little or no support for such a position. James is referred to by Paul as Jesus' brother, but his father was Alpheus and his mother was Mary, later married to Cleophas. "Brother" obviously is at least sometimes used to describe cousins, including a stepcousin in this instance, as well as siblings, and the position that Joseph and Mary had more children is not well-founded.

❖   ❖   ❖

2. It was Anne who told Joseph that Mary was pregnant. Just as Mary's marriage to Joseph would have been arranged by Anne, so Anne would have served as the go-between to break the news to Joseph. Anne told him the entire story, both as related by Mary and by Zechariah. Anne could assure Joseph that she personally knew that Mary knew of her pregnancy the day she saw Gabriel, and that all that Gabriel told Mary was true. Elizabeth had been delivered of a son. But Anne made Joseph's position even harder when she told him that Mary was married to the Lord; in a marriage between Joseph and Mary, he would have to forego conjugal relations.

This was a hard tale for Joseph to believe and a hard future for him to accept. We are accustomed to the "Christmas story" by long acquaintance with it. But the plain fact is that the story flies in the face of all our experience and common sense. The ordinary Jew did not know the details of the Messianic prophecies—that he would be born in Bethlehem to a virgin of the Davidic line. Witness Herod's need to consult his scholars to learn the place of the Messiah's birth. This was a subject for the rabbis and priests. Joseph likely asked the rabbi oblique questions to be sure of Anne's tale of what scripture foretold about the Messiah's origins. In addition to his doubt as to the child's paternity, the requirement of birth in Bethlehem cast further question on Anne's tale. He eventually decided **"to divorce her quietly. But as he considered this, behold, an angel of the Lord appeared to him in a dream, saying, 'Joseph, son of David, do not fear to take Mary your wife, for that which is conceived in her is of the Holy Spirit; she will bear a son, and you will call his name Jesus, for he will save his people from their sins. . . .' When Joseph woke, he did as the angel of the Lord commanded him; he took his wife, but knew her not until she had borne a son; and he called his name Jesus"** (Mt. 1:19–25).

Having heard from Anne the descriptions of an angel's appearance to Mary and to Zechariah, Joseph had no difficulty recognizing an angel in his dream. We do not know whether the angel was Gabriel or another. Likewise, having heard Anne's story of the communications of the angel to Mary and to Zechariah, and how one of them believed and the other did not, Joseph's heart had already been softened and his mind prepared to accept the truth. When he awoke, he believed the angel's message to him and therefore what Anne had told him.

In law, Joseph and Mary were already married upon their betrothal. Custom dictated a delay in consummation until proper quarters could be prepared for the bridal couple, and a long nuptial celebration was held at the time the bride moved in with her bridegroom. Joseph already had a home, so he simply moved Mary in with him. His home in Nazareth traditionally is believed to have been a site about one hundred yards north of Mary's house. Due to Mary's advanced pregnancy, no wedding feast was held. Luke refers to Mary on the road to Bethlehem as Joseph's "betrothed," a wife in law by betrothal rather than by wedding (Lk 2:5). While custom delayed consummation of a marriage from betrothal until wedding, a premature consummation was not unusual and was not sinful, because it was lawful. There nevertheless was some irregularity, as reflected in Matthew's going out of his way to include Tamar and Bathsheba in Joseph's genealogy (Mt 1:3, 6). Joseph was the father of Jesus under Jewish law. He was Jesus' father in the same way that he was Mary's husband—in his mind.

❖ ❖ ❖

3. Sometime after Mary moved in with Joseph, a Roman order for a census was received in Nazareth. Every man had to report to his tribal "home" for the census. As a member of the house of David, Joseph was required to travel to Bethlehem, the city of David. The missing piece in Scripture's description of the Messiah, that he would be born in Bethlehem of a virgin of the house of David, had been supplied. All those privy to the secret—Mary, Anne, Zechariah, Elizabeth, and Joseph—had wondered how Mary was carrying the Messiah although she lived in Nazareth. Suddenly the Scripture was fulfilled. They were overjoyed, especially Joseph, since his faith had thereby been confirmed.

Augustus and his early successors issued orders for a census of the Empire and its allies every fourteen years. In 8 BC, Augustus ordered a census of the Empire, including the quasi-independent "friends" ("*Amici*") such as the "king" of the nearby city-state of Apamea. There is disagreement as to whether Herod's kingdom was included in this census. About this time, Augustus demoted Herod from a "friend" to a "subject." I find it likely that Herod resisted the taking of a census in his territories because of his knowledge of the people's resistance to a census, and Augustus demoted him in punishment for this and, perhaps, other offenses. Such a controversy could have delayed the announcement of the census in Herod's territories by a year or more, until about the summer of 7 BC. The "enrollment" covered both people and property. We know that the census in Egypt was spread over a two-year period. The Romans, the best administrators of the ancient world, would have minimized the economic dislocation and burden on travel accommodations by staggering the periods of registration, or "enrollment," for different tribes. Each tribe would have been given a window of time during which its members must appear at the ancestral town. This would also diminish the burden on the military and civil establishments conducting the census, since a small number of officials would move from place to place for the duration of enrollment at each town. Only the heads of families were required to appear, since the Romans did not encumber the roads and travel facilities with women and young children. A likely period of enrollment in a given town would have been a lunar month.

4. Unlike most men, Joseph took Mary with him. The reason given out to others would have been his desire to be with Mary at her delivery and to present a potential son without a second trip to the temple, but Joseph and Mary knew the real reason. The Messiah was to be born in Bethlehem. It was definitely odd for Joseph to bring Mary with him. She could have been purified in Nazareth at the fortieth or eightieth day, depending on whether the child was a boy or a girl. Presentation could have waited until the next Passover trip to Jerusalem. Joseph, Mary, and the other men of Davidic descent in the neighborhood of Nazareth would have traveled together, taking the direct route to Jerusalem through Samaria since they traveled as a large group. Thence south six miles to Bethlehem.

Upon their arrival in Bethlehem, there was no room for them in the inn. The village was overflowing with members of the house of David. Bethlehem was a small village. It probably had one or two establishments that combined the functions of café, bar, and a few rooms for travelers. Some scholars have portrayed the inn as a caravanserai, a large facility for caravans. But Bethlehem was off the main caravan routes, and it seems unlikely in any event that caravans would have stopped two hours short of their destination, Jerusalem. Some scholars contend that a large sheepfold built 600 years earlier, the "khan" of Chamaan, had later been converted into a caravanserai and was still in business 600 years later. I find insufficient evidence to support this theory. It is more likely that the inn was a purely local establishment. Again, some scholars have suggested that Joseph would have been taken in by his "relatives" in Bethlehem, but for his being crosswise with them, perhaps over Mary's premature pregnancy. I find it unlikely that Joseph knew any "relatives" in Bethlehem; it had been almost a thousand years since David's reign, and most of the people then in Bethlehem would not have been related to David anyway.

Upon the arrival of Joseph and the others, all men, the innkeeper took compassion on Mary. Though his inn was full, he gave her and Joseph his own stable, built into a grotto, that would be dry and free from drafts. I find little support for the view that the innkeeper and residents of Bethlehem were cold and unfeeling to Mary's plight. The Romans and civil officers undoubtedly had commandeered the best quarters in town for their own use, and the village was overflowing with descendants of David. The innkeeper's act in housing them in his own stable was an act of charity, since it doubtlessly handicapped his own operation. Some scholars believe the grotto was a part of a house, rented by Joseph. I doubt that any such unrented property was available in Bethlehem that month due to the crowds descending on the village for the census.

The use of a cave for shelter gave Mary and Joseph far more privacy than would have been available in the inn. As recently as colonial Williamsburg, even important men were housed several to a room and even two or more to a bed. There would have been no privacy for Mary in the inn.

---

5. Upon arriving in Bethlehem, the group from Nazareth reported to the authorities to be enrolled as rapidly as possible. The rest returned home. Joseph and Mary stayed in order that the child would be born there in fulfillment of the prophecy.

There are two schools of thought as to whether Joseph enrolled his household before or after the birth of Jesus. The majority view is that the enrollment occurred after the Nativity, in order that Jesus would be enrolled as a human, as the first step toward his taking all humanity's sins upon himself. I find that argument to be theologically driven. It is more likely that, immediately after arrival, along with the rest of the group from Nazareth, Joseph enrolled his household before Jesus' birth, so that a newborn baby would not show on the record. Joseph and Mary were well aware of Herod's fear of any rival claim to his own, and the birth of the Messiah would be considered dangerous by Herod. If the Romans had no record of Jesus, he and his parents would be harder to identify and then find.

6. Joseph located the local midwife and arranged for her services after their arrival in Bethlehem. The delivery of babies was always a risky proposition and even more so in the case of a first birth to such a young woman. It was a skill in which women were particularly knowledgeable and in which men were far less experienced. Though the midwife is not mentioned in Luke's narrative, it is inconceivable that Joseph would not have sought out the best help available.

When Mary went into labor, Joseph called the midwife. The child was born after sundown, during the night, because the angels subsequently notified the shepherds that night that the savior was born "this day" (Lk 2:11). After the child's birth the midwife cleaned up and got Mary and the child settled before leaving, sometime during the middle of the night.

The baby's garments, the "swaddling cloths," were made by Mary and brought to Bethlehem in her luggage. We can visualize the pregnant young woman sewing her child's garments.

7. "And there were in the same country shepherds abiding in the field, keeping watch over their flock by night" (Lk 2:8). A flock of sheep were normally closed at night in a walled, partially roofed enclosure, a "sheepfold," guarded by a "gatekeeper" to protect them from predators and thieves (Jn 10:1–3). This could not be done during lambing season because the ewes needed privacy to lamb, and concentration would cause trampling and infection. The shepherds were staying with the sheep at night because it was lambing season and the ewes were not in their sheepfold.

Those having their first lamb, especially, could need assistance. The shepherds were there to "pull" lambs as well as to guard the flock from predators.

Some have argued that Jesus was born in the springtime, since spring is the normal season for lambing. That is true in most situations. However, Jewish law required that the Passover lamb must be a year old. Since Passover occurs in March and April and the rams would cover the ewes over a period of several weeks, lambing season in Judea was timed to produce lambs born in late December, January, and February, which would be a year old at the next year's Passover.

In view of Jesus' later comments regarding hireling shepherds, we may be confident that these shepherds were the owners of their flocks.

8. **"And, lo, the angel of the Lord came upon them, and the glory of the Lord shone round about them: and they were sore afraid. And the angel said unto them, 'Fear not: for, behold, I bring you good tidings of great joy, which shall be to all people. For unto you is born this day in the city of David a savior, which is Christ the Lord. And this shall be a sign unto you; ye shall find the babe wrapped in swaddling cloths, lying in a manger. . . .' And it came to pass, as the angels were gone away from them into heaven, the shepherds said one to another, 'Let us now go even unto Bethlehem and see this thing which is come to pass, which the Lord hath made known unto us'"** (Lk 2:9–15).

It was still dark when the angel appeared to the shepherds. Upon his departure the shepherds conferred and decided to go look for the child. The common artistic rendering of the scene, showing the shepherds bringing a lamb, is most likely correct. It would not have been inappropriate to visit so illustrious a person without taking a gift. As proprietors, they were free to make the child the gift of a lamb. A newborn lamb would have been too small a gift, so they gave a yearling lamb being held for that year's Passover. The Passover sacrifice, the Lamb of God.

❧   ❧   ❧

9. "And they came with haste, and found Mary, and Joseph, and the babe, lying in a manger. And when they had seen it, they made known abroad the saying which was told them concerning this child. And all they that heard it wondered at those things which were told them by the shepherds" (Lk 2:16–18).

The shepherds arrived at first light as the village began to stir. They made inquiry at the obvious place, the local café-bar-inn, and learned that there was a woman far advanced in pregnancy in the inn's stable and that activity had been heard from that direction during the night. The shepherds followed the directions to the stable and found the Holy Family. The shepherds addressed themselves to Joseph, as was, and is, done in a patriarchal culture. They told Joseph and Mary what they had seen and heard. They made obeisance to the newborn Messiah and presented their gift.

"But Mary kept all these things and pondered them in her heart" (Lk 2:19). The shepherds, however, went back to the inn and told those present "the saying which had been told them concerning this child"—namely, that he was the Messiah. In a small village, such gossip spread rapidly, although it was dangerous information.

In all probability, the Roman and civil officials had departed. The village had not yet been cleared of visitors, as Mary and Joseph were still lodged in the stable. Nevertheless, it is probable that the census officials had left, or they would have taken gossip of the Messiah's birth back to Jerusalem. Since Herod did not learn of this until later, we may conclude that the officials left before the Nativity.

10. Soon after, the enrollment having ended and the village cleared out, Joseph was able to move the Holy Family into a house (Mt 2:11). Some writers have argued from the killing of all boys two years of age and younger that Joseph planned to stay in Bethlehem because he moved his family into a house, and they then lived there for two years. I find this improbable. Joseph had his home, his business, and his family in Nazareth and its environs. More comfortable accommodations became available when the enrollment ended in Bethlehem, and Joseph simply improved his family's living conditions. They intended to stay forty days, so Mary could be purified and Jesus presented in the temple before they returned home. Joseph and Mary were well aware of the danger from Herod and would not have remained so near the court unnecessarily. I have seen no credible evidence of a prolonged stay in Bethlehem.

Jesus had been born in Bethlehem. The name "Bethlehem" means "the house of bread." Surely it was no accident that the bread of life, the Eucharistic bread, was born in the house of bread. **"And when eight days were accomplished for the circumcising of the child, his name was called Jesus, which was so named of the angel before he was conceived in the womb"** (Lk 2:21). Any rabbi could circumcise, so this was done in Bethlehem. There was no need to subject Mary to a trip to the temple so soon after her delivery.

Simeon and Anna in the Temple, Rembrandt Harmensz van Rijn, 1628, Hamburger Kunsthalle, Hamburg

THE PRESENTATION

⬦

1. "And when the time came for their purification according to the law of Moses, they brought him up to Jerusalem to present him to the Lord (as it is written in the law of the Lord, 'Every male that opens the womb shall be called holy to the Lord') and to offer a sacrifice according to what is said in the law of the Lord, 'a pair of turtle doves, or two young pigeons'" (Lk 2:22–24). Two separate rituals were involved.

If a woman gives birth to a son, she is ritually unclean for forty days (Lv 12:2–4). When the forty days are past, she shall bring the priest a lamb for a burnt offering and a young pigeon or a turtle dove for a sin offering, and the priest shall sacrifice them in atonement for her, and she will be ritually clean. But if she cannot afford a lamb, she may offer two young pigeons or two turtle doves (Lv 2:6–8).

"Consecrate to me all the firstborn; whatever is the first to open the womb among the people of Israel, both of man and of beast, is mine. . . . Every firstborn of man among your sons, you shall redeem" (Ex 13:2, 13). This was done in memory of the flight from Egypt, when all the firstborn of Egypt were killed. As a firstborn son, Jesus had to be "redeemed." At the time of Jesus' presentation and ritual redemption, the price paid to the priest was five silver shekels, a heavy obligation for a man who could not afford a lamb.

Many post-Enlightenment writers argue that "firstborn son" implies the birth of later sons. This does not follow. "Firstborn" refers back to the death of all firstborn children and livestock at the Passover and their consequent dedication to God under Jewish law. The firstborn son is also a word of art with defined obligations and rights under Jewish law.

❖ ❖ ❖

2. Joseph and Mary, carrying the infant Jesus, walked the six miles from Bethlehem to Jerusalem no earlier than the fortieth day after Jesus' birth. In the event of illness of any member of the Holy Family or of inclement winter weather, they may have waited longer than forty days. They approached the temple's south side. Between the two sets of gates leading into the temple were baths for ritual purification, where Mary bathed. Purification was done first; otherwise Mary could not have entered the temple.

They ascended a flight of steps 214' wide and entered the Court of Gentiles, the largest part of the temple complex. As the name indicates, Gentiles as well as Jews could enter this large court, colonnaded around. They purchased two young pigeons or turtle doves for the sacrifice for Mary's purification. They passed a five-foot-high balustrade, on which were posted signs warning Gentiles to come no further, on pain of death. They passed through a gate in the east side of the wall surrounding the inner courts and entered the Court of Women, to which Jewish women had access. Mary could not enter the Nicanor Gate into the Court of Israel. In the Court of Priests, separated from the Court of Israel by a low wall, was the altar upon which blood sacrifices were offered.

The Court of Priests surrounded the Holy House, containing a vestibule, the sanctuary, and the Holy of Holies. Mary stopped at the foot of the steps to the Nicanor Gate. She could go no farther.

❖ ❖ ❖

3. **"Now there was a man in Jerusalem, whose name was Simeon, and this man was righteous and devout, looking for the consolation of Israel, and the Holy Spirit was upon him. And it had been revealed to him by the Holy Spirit that he should not see death before he had seen the Lord's Christ"** (Lk 2:25–26). Simeon's prayers "for the consolation of Israel" were for the coming of the Messiah. The reference is to the second portion of Isaiah, forecasting the Messiah, beginning with the fortieth chapter: **"Comfort ye, comfort ye my people. . . ."** As Joseph and Mary, carrying the infant, came up to the steps to the Nicanor Gate, they were accosted by an old man. It was Simeon. Knowing that the Messiah was to be born of a virgin, he posted himself at the gate through which all firstborn sons must be brought to be presented for their redemption. He necessarily would have checked all babies being presented. One can hear the old man say, over and over, "What a fine baby! Where was he born?" Only a handful of times a year would he hear the answer, "In Bethlehem," because a village its size would produce about two to five firstborn sons a year. Only when he heard "Bethlehem" as the place of birth would Simeon pursue his examination. "Oh, really. Are you of the house of David?" A thousand years after David, it would be a rare occasion indeed that the answer would be affirmative. This time it was.

"And inspired by the Spirit he came into the temple; and when the parents brought in the child Jesus, to do for him according to the custom of the law, he took him up in his arms

and blessed God...." (Lk 2:27–28). We can hear Simeon say, after the response that Joseph was of the house of David, "May I see the child?" Taking the baby in his arms, Simeon looked down into the eyes of the Second Person of the Trinity, and, "inspired by the Spirit," he recognized Jesus as the Messiah.

There are writers who picture this as Simeon's "coming into the temple" and providentially bumping into the Holy Family. One should avoid piling miracle upon miracle. It seems more likely that, having had his vision as a result of his constancy in prayer for the Messiah, Simeon simply continued or, perhaps, increased his attendance at the temple, concentrating on the gate into the Court of Israel. He probably did this for years. His questions may not have been exactly as I have phrased them, but his questions had to be short, direct, and friendly.

"[Simeon] **said, 'Lord, now lettest thou thy servant depart in peace, according to thy word. For mine eyes have seen thy salvation, which thou hast prepared before the face of all people; to be a light to lighten the Gentiles, and to be the glory of thy people Israel'"** (Lk 2:28–32). Simeon not only recognized the Messiah; surprisingly, he prophesied that the Messiah would be for "all people; to be a light to lighten the Gentiles," and not just the liberator of Israel. Further, he prophesied the nature of Jesus' mission: "mine eyes have seen thy salvation...." Jesus' name said as much, "the Lord saves" or "Salvation."

Simeon **"said to Mary his mother, 'Behold, this child is set for the fall and rising of many in Israel, and for a sign that is spoken against (and a sword will pierce through your own soul also), that thoughts out of many hearts may be revealed'"** (Lk 2:34–35). Simeon thereby set forth the conflict that this child would generate within Israel and the ill treatment he would receive. It is clear from Mary and Joseph's behavior when Jesus stayed behind their caravan twelve years later, that they still had not comprehended Simeon's prophecy. Nor even did John the Baptist till near the end of his life. Simeon was the first to have interpreted the scriptures correctly.

      ❖   ❖   ❖

4. **"And there was a prophetess, Anna, the daughter of Phanuel, of the tribe of Asher; she was of a great age, having lived with her husband seven years from her virginity, and as a widow till she was eighty-four. She did not depart from the temple, worshiping with fasting and prayer night and day. And coming up at that very hour she gave thanks to God, and spoke of him to all who were looking for the redemption of Jerusalem."** (Lk 2:36–38) Anna obviously was familiar with Simeon and his mission, since they were both constantly at prayer in the temple. Simeon and Anna are sometimes held to represent the men and women of the true Israel, who thus welcomed the Messiah.

There is no indication that Simeon shared his knowledge with anyone but Mary, Joseph, and Anna, for he would have recognized the danger to the Holy Family. But Anna demonstrated the adage, "Two can keep counsel, if one is away." Joy overcoming prudence, she broadcast news of the Messiah's birth to many people, and it was only a matter of time until such a rumor would reach hostile ears. Providence hastened the pace of events, so that the infant Jesus would escape the dangers that encompassed him.

      ❖   ❖   ❖

5. Probably on the evening before the presentation of Jesus, three wise men, or magi—most likely astrologers—arrived in Jerusalem from the East, probably from Babylonia or Persia. The Jewish scriptures and religion had been known in Babylonia and

Persia for almost 600 years, since the destruction of Jerusalem and the Exile, the forced deportations of large portions of the populations of the Kingdom of Israel by the Assyrians and the Kingdom of Judea by the Babylonians. While some Jews returned to Judea at the end of the exile, many remained in the East. Portions of the Apocrypha (*e.g.*, *Tobit*) are set in the East. Just as devout Gentiles in the West were drawn to the high moral teachings of the Jewish religion, there is every reason to believe that some Gentiles in the East similarly knew it and were drawn to it. Such were the Magi. The tradition that the Magi came from Africa or elsewhere is probably in error, since they came from "the East," where they had seen his star.

"'Where is he who has been born king of the Jews? For we have seen his star in the East, and have come to worship him.' When Herod the king heard this, he was troubled, and all Jerusalem with him; and assembling all the chief priests and scribes of the people, he inquired of them where the Christ was to be born. They told him, 'In Bethlehem.' . . . Then Herod summoned the wise men secretly and ascertained from them what time the star appeared; and he sent them to Bethlehem, saying, 'Go and search diligently for the child, and when you have found him bring me word, that I too may come and worship him'" (Mt 2:2–8).

The wise men arrived in Jerusalem at the end of a day's travel, probably the long day from Jericho to Jerusalem, since they came from the East. On the next day they made inquiry at the temple, the logical place to seek information about ancient religious prophecies. Someone at the temple alerted Herod. Herod's palace adjoined the south side of the "Tower of David," on the west wall of the current walled city, about a ten- to fifteen-minute walk from the temple. Herod summoned the Magi and gathered a council to give him intelligence about the Messiah. This council was not the

Sanhedrin (in Jerusalem, the kingdom's supreme religious council or court), but rather was a group of the "chief priests and scribes" who were political appointees of Herod, and whose primary loyalty was to him. Upon being advised by his council, Herod called in the Magi and ingratiatingly gave them the information they requested, seeking to enlist them as unwitting spies in his own behalf. All these events took up the day, and the Magi spent a second night in Jerusalem. That night, they were warned in a dream not to return to Herod with the information requested. The Magi probably found that the dream confirmed what they had already suspected about Herod's request.

Early the next morning, the day after the presentation, the Magi made their short trip to Bethlehem. **"When they had heard the king they went their way; and lo, the star they had seen in the East went before them, till it came to rest over the place where the child was. When they saw the star, they rejoiced exceedingly with great joy; and going into the house they saw the child with Mary his mother, and they fell down and worshiped him. Then, opening their treasures, they offered him gifts, gold and frankincense and myrrh. And being warned in a dream not to return to Herod, they departed to their own country by a different way"** (Mt 2:9–12). The Magi had supernatural help from the star, but local inquiry at the cafe-bar-inn also unearthed the local gossip of the Messiah and helped lead them to the house where the Holy Family lodged. They introduced themselves, disclosed their mission, and presented their gifts. They worshiped the infant Jesus and visited at some length with Joseph and Mary, telling them also about their encounter with Herod the previous day.

Each of the Magi, being conversant with the Jewish scriptures, had interpreted them differently. One brought gold, as for a king. The others brought frankincense and myrrh, as for a god and for a sacrificial death. At least two, though not Jews themselves, had penetrated the mysteries of the Scriptures and interpreted them correctly. The next to do so would be Jesus himself. The Magus who gave the child gold for a king perhaps did so in the belief that the child would rule a Greater Israel; did he penetrate the sense in which Jesus acknowledged himself the king of a kingdom "not of this world?" (Jn 18:36).

※ ※ ※

6. Many theories have been advanced about the "star" of Bethlehem and the timing of Jesus' birth. The theory which appears most likely to me involves the triple conjunction of Jupiter and Saturn and the subsequent massing of Jupiter, Saturn, and Mars. In 7 BC there were three conjunctions of Jupiter and Saturn in the constellation Pisces, namely: on May 27, October 6, and December 1. Each time, over a period of weeks, the two planets appeared to draw together in the sky in a conjunction. On each conjunction the two planets arrived at a "stationary point," when they appeared no longer to move relative to the stars or "came to rest." Each time there was an "achronychal rising," when Jupiter and Saturn rose at sunset and were visible all night, this being the time at which they were brightest. After the "stationary point" the planets separated. Triple conjunctions of Jupiter and Saturn occur every 139 years, but the conjunction only occurs in the constellation Pisces every 854 years. None of these three conjunctions had the two planets appearing to draw so close together to appear as one star, though they did approach each other more closely than during the later "massing." There have been conjunctions of planets that appeared as one star, but the closest in time was either too early (Mars, Saturn, and Venus in 12 BC) or too late, after Herod's death in March–April 4 BC (Jupiter and Venus in 3 BC).

The triple conjunction was followed by a "massing" of Jupiter, Saturn, and Mars in Pisces in mid- to late-February 6 BC. Such massings of these planets occur only once every 805 years and in Pisces only once in recorded history, the February 6 BC event. The planets appeared to draw together ("mass") slowly over a period of weeks, but their separation was very rapid. One of the early modern astronomers, Johannes Kepler, calculated the massing of planets in February 6 BC to be the star of Bethlehem.

In Babylonian astrology, Jupiter represents the highest god of the universe, and Saturn represents the Hebrews. Pisces is the constellation associated with Syria and Palestine. Mars introduces a sinister astrological note, consistent with a prophecy of conflict and sacrificial death. The astrologers "in the East" would have calculated, or "seen," the conjunctions and subsequent massing of planets before they occurred and timed their arrival in Jerusalem for the actual event, which had not been foreseen by the local people. In fact, a Babylonian almanac forecasting the astronomical events for the year 7–6 BC has been found and shows the triple conjunctions and subsequent massing, each in the month in which it occurred.

Some writers argue that the second or third conjunction was the "Star." The conjunctions of Jupiter and Saturn have the benefit of appearing, disappearing, and reappearing, perhaps as described in *Luke*. An October or even a December 1 date would not place the birth in lambing season, requiring the shepherds to be with their flocks at night. Some argue that a nova or comet in the constellation Capricorn is the "Star," but it lacks any astrological connection to the Hebrews as well as being past the lambing season.

Arguments in favor of some other astronomical event all are too many years before 7 BC or assume Jesus' birth after the death of Herod in March–April 4 BC. Some writers argue that Herod can be shown to have died in 1 BC, instead of in 4 BC, so astronomical events subsequent to 4 BC can be considered. I find that uncontroverted, clear evidence that at least two of Herod's sons, Archelaus and Herod Antipas, began their reigns in 4 BC makes such an argument untenable.

Still other writers argue that Joseph and the family stayed in Bethlehem for ten months to two years after Jesus' birth, and the Magi arrived long after Jesus' birth but before Herod's death, either in 4 BC or in 1 BC. I have seen no evidence to explain why Joseph would have remained in Bethlehem, far from his family, property, and business but in close proximity to a court and its numerous agents who would destroy the child if his presence became known. Nor have I seen any explanation as to why the Magi would have delayed their journey to a date long after the date astrologically forecast for the important birth.

The timing of the Magi's arrival was providential. Note that Matthew does not say that Jesus was born "under the star." If the Magi had appeared at Herod's court at the time of Jesus' birth, we can hardly imagine Herod's waiting forty days or more, till after Mary's purification, to make his preemptive strike on the babies of Bethlehem. Since the massing was in mid- to late-February, Jesus' birth was at least forty days earlier in early January 6 BC or late December 7 BC. The sudden movement of the three massed planets away from each other on a night in mid- to late-February was the climax of the series of three conjunctions, followed by the massing. It seems likely that the "break" of the massed planets, the climax of this heavenly show, satisfies the description "the star they had seen in the East went before them, till it came to rest over the place where the child was." The break likely occurred the night after the Magi's interview with Herod, the night before they found the Holy Family in Bethlehem. It appears that the date on which

Jesus' birth is celebrated by the Church has more to do with fact and less to do with Saturnalia (the Roman celebration of the winter solstice) than many writers have assumed, though the Roman celebration of Saturnalia was certainly a convenient, or providential, circumstance, making the Christian celebration less apparent to outsiders.

◆ ◆ ◆

7. The Magi told Joseph and Mary that Herod had told them to return to him and disclose the Messiah's location, and that they had been warned in a dream not to do so. Since they were going to disobey Herod, they needed to put distance between themselves and Herod's wrath before Herod realized that they were not going to return. They concluded their visit with the Holy Family and started home by a different route, probably leaving no later than noon on the day after the presentation.

Who was the witness to Joseph's dream of the angel who told him, **"Do not fear to take Mary your wife, for that which is in her is of the Holy Spirit"**? Who was the witness of the Magi's story and their meeting with the Holy Family? The only possible witness of the first was Joseph; both he and Mary were witnesses of the Magi, but Joseph most likely is the one who told the tale. Because all of Cleophas' children became disciples, Joseph at some time told his brother, Cleophas, who passed on the story within his family after Jesus began his mission. Cleophas also told it to the apostles and other disciples after Jesus' death. It found its way into Matthew's Gospel, which was known in the early Church, probably from the AD mid-40s, and tells the Church who Jesus was, the miraculously conceived Son of God. Much later, Luke answered the Church's need to know how this was done, which was Mary's story.

THE JOYFUL MYSTERIES

8. Joseph was concerned by the gossip in Bethlehem since the shepherds' visit, by Anna's public proclamation of the Messiah's birth and presentation, and by Herod's knowledge of the wise men's mission. Soon after falling asleep, **"an angel of the Lord appeared to Joseph in a dream and said, 'Rise, take the child and his mother, and flee to Egypt, and remain there till I tell you; for Herod is about to search for the child, to destroy him.' And he rose and took the child and his mother by night, and departed to Egypt, and remained there until the death of Herod"** (Mt 2:13–14).

Joseph's concerns were definitively confirmed by the dream. He instantly arose and prepared to depart. Undoubtedly, he had been required to pay for their accommodations in advance, so no one had to be notified. They left in the middle of the night, taking a minor road that led from Bethlehem toward the coast and "the Way of the Sea" to Egypt. By daylight they were far out of sight from Bethlehem, and when the town awakened, no one knew when or whither they had gone. The Holy Family had to flee from Herod's jurisdiction. They could not risk a return to Nazareth, since it was part of Herod's kingdom, and someone in Bethlehem might remember that they had come with the Nazarene caravan.

9. By Herod's reckoning, the Magi should have gone to Bethlehem, located the Messiah, and returned to Jerusalem that night. He expected to see them the following morning.

The day that the Magi had left for Bethlehem, Herod probably received a report of gossip that a baby boy presented in the temple the day before was the Messiah. Such a report to Herod came on the heels of the Magi's question, based on the birth of the Messiah. The combination of these two events aroused Herod's deepest suspicion and fear.

When the Magi failed to report the next morning, Herod knew that he had been gulled. **"Then Herod, when he saw that he had been tricked by the wise men, was in a furious rage, and he sent and killed all the male children in Bethlehem and in all that region who were two years old or under, according to the time which he had ascertained from the wise men"** (Mt 2:16).

Herod's order would have been given by mid-morning, and his soldiers arrived in Bethlehem by noon or soon after. The Magi and the Holy Family had left the day and the night before, respectively. The massacre of the Holy Innocents involved the killing of about ten children of no political importance and escaped contemporaneous mention by Josephus or other writers who recorded some of Herod's numerous politically more important crimes.

Why did Herod order the killing of boys as old as two years? The Magi themselves were uncertain as to the time relationship between the massing in the sky and the date of birth of "the king of the Jews." They probably had expected the massing of the planets to coincide with his birth. Herod's questioning of the Magi had undoubtedly elicited the information that the Magi had ascertained the triple conjunction and massing, using their astrological knowledge, long before they began their journey. They probably told Herod that they had calculated the planetary movements two years before their actual appearance. In case the time of discovery of the movements indicated the time of birth, Herod decided it was better to kill too many rather than not kill enough, and thereby miss the Messiah.

10. We do not know in what part of Egypt the Holy Family spent their exile. Joseph's skill as a carpenter was a portable trade, and he could make a living at it anywhere there was work. The gifts of the Magi provided the capital to finance the travel and reestablishment of the family. Doubtless, Cleophas protected Joseph's property in Nazareth.

"But when Herod died, behold, an angel of the Lord appeared in a dream to Joseph in Egypt, saying, 'Rise, take the child and his mother, and go to the land of Israel, for those who sought the child's life are dead.' And he rose and took the child and his mother, and went to the land of Israel. But when he heard that Archelaus reigned over Judea in place of his father Herod, he was afraid to go there, and being warned in a dream, he withdrew to the district of Galilee. And he went and dwelt in a city called Nazareth...." (Mt 2:19–23).

About six months after Herod's death in March–April 4 BC, Augustus decided to divide Herod's kingdom into three shares, awarded to three of Herod's surviving sons. The major share, composed of Judea, Samaria, and Idumea (south of Judea), was given to Archelaus. Galilee and Perea (east of the Jordan) were given to Herod Antipas. The remaining territories north and east of the Jordan were given to Philip. The southwestern coastal enclave of Ascalon, Phoenicia, and the Decapolis, lying east and west of the Jordan between Galilee and Perea, were ruled by Rome directly as part of Syria. Augustus' division of the kingdom would not have been known in Israel until sometime during the winter of 4–3 BC. In AD 6 Augustus deposed Archelaus and put his territories also under direct Roman rule.

Under the prompting of Joseph's dream, the Holy Family left Egypt after receiving news of Herod's death and before learning of the division of the kingdom. News of Herod's death would have arrived in Egypt about the first of May, already into the heat of summer.

If Joseph led his family toward Palestine during the fall, they could have arrived after news of the division and the allotments to Herod's three sons. As the Holy Family returned along the Way of the Sea to Israel, when they arrived in Ascalon, peaceful under Roman rule, they learned that large areas of Israel had erupted in civil war and brigandage. This period of turmoil went on for up to two years following Herod's death. By that time Archelaus' brutality was obvious to all. The safest way through Archelaus' kingdom was the well-traveled highway through Caesarea, thence into Phoenicia. Again prompted by a dream, Joseph waited in a safe place, probably Tyre in southern Phoenicia. The territory around the capital of Galilee, Sepphoris, would have been pacified sooner than the remoter areas. It is likely that the reference in *Revelation* to the woman fleeing into the wilderness for three and a half years is to the period of Mary and Joseph's exile (Rv 12:6). The earliest date for the Holy Family's safe return to Nazareth was in late summer or fall of 3 BC, when Jesus was three and a half years old, a date that probably not coincidentally is the same as the three and a half years in *Revelation*.

Some writers argue that, because Joseph was afraid to go to Judea due to Archelaus, Joseph had intended to settle in Judea, perhaps even in Bethlehem. Joseph knew the danger of a claim to be the Messiah. It is doubtful that he would deliberately dwell near the temple and the court. Besides, he and Mary had property and family in Nazareth and its environs. It is probable that the reference to Archelaus was an abbreviated reference to the generally troubled and dangerous conditions in Israel. The time of arrival was too early to know that Archelaus would be more brutal than his brothers. That became apparent only with time, culminating in his removal by Augustus in AD 6. It seems more likely that Joseph decided to wait in Roman territory in Phoenicia, due to its proximity to Galilee, where they were safe but close enough to obtain accurate information regarding the regaining of governmental control over brigandage and the end of the civil war, the establishment of peace.

Christ among the Doctors, Bernardino Luini, probably about 1515-1530, National Gallery, London

FINDING THE CHILD JESUS IN THE TEMPLE

◆

1. Nazareth was four miles southeast of Sepphoris, which was the largest city in Galilee. Sepphoris was the predominantly Gentile capital of Galilee until AD 18, when Herod Antipas built a new city, Tiberias, and moved his capital to it. During Jesus' entire youth, Herod Antipas conducted a succession of major building programs at Sepphoris, including palaces, theaters, and baths. It was the market center for the area and undoubtedly was the market at which Joseph, and later Jesus, purchased tools, materials, and supplies. Joseph may have benefitted, directly or indirectly, from the continuous construction an hour and a half's walk away. There is a tradition that Sepphoris was the home of Anne's family. The verbal picture often encountered that Nazareth was an isolated village is false.

Jesus' basic education was at the synagogue, where the local rabbi taught children to read and write Hebrew, so they could read the Scriptures, and also Aramaic, the language of daily life. Since books were expensive, the children memorized large portions of scripture. Jesus memorized the entire Old Testament. In doing so, he may have been assisted by his uniquely high intelligence. On the other hand, since there are many ordinary mortals who have had the gift of a photographic memory, it would be reasonable to conclude that Jesus also had a photographic memory.

Jesus also learned to speak, read, and write Greek, though it may or may not have been taught at the synagogue. Greek was the lingua franca of the Eastern Mediterranean, the language of commerce and of intellectual life. If a tax collector like Matthew Levi, a physician like Luke, a Pharisee like Paul, Jesus' kinsmen James and Jude, and even fishermen like Peter and John could write in Greek, why would anyone think that Jesus could not? Had he been unable to speak, read, and write in Greek, he would have been an ignoramus bumpkin, to whom no one would have paid attention. When the Greeks asked to speak with Jesus, we may be sure that they did not plan to converse in Aramaic (Jn 12:20–21). Contact with Roman officials and soldiers, who used Latin, would not have been as common, but there is no reason to think that Jesus did not learn Latin, the language of authority, also. His interrogations by Pilate were probably in Latin, rather than in Greek.

To Americans, who generally know no foreign language, Jesus' ability to speak, read, and write in Aramaic, Hebrew, Greek, and Latin may seem unusual. But anyone who has traveled in the Eastern Mediterranean, even today, knows that ordinary businessmen and merchants have a working knowledge of six or seven languages, or even more.

Joseph taught Jesus his own trade of carpentry, as fathers were expected to do. What set Jesus apart from others was the high degree in which he was devout and, not as readily observable, that he was without sin.

As Jesus studied the Scriptures while growing up, he noticed that the religious faith and obligations taught by the Scriptures varied from the faith and obligations taught by the rabbis and practiced by those who had the reputation of being devout Jews. One such distinction which he expressly noted and later denounced was the use of *corban*, a pledge for later temple use, to avoid the financial obligation to support one's parents (Mk 7:9–13).

---

2. Joseph, Mary, and Jesus went to Jerusalem for Passover every year (Lk 2:41). They traveled in caravan with a large group of family and friends from Nazareth, probably through Samaria due to the size of the group. Every year the Holy Family saw Elizabeth, Zechariah, and John, who only had to travel five miles from Ain Karem. The two sets of parents visited privately and compared notes on the events of the preceding year. They could not tell the two boys what they knew about them until they had reached an age of discretion, due both to the danger of their secret and to avoid a child's making an indiscreet childish reference to what he had been told. Due to the growing age of Zechariah and Elizabeth, and possibly of Joseph as well, one Passover the parents agreed that they would tell the boys all that they knew, sometime before the next year's Passover. In all probability, this decision was reached at the Passover when the boys were eleven years old.

---

3. Sometime during that following year, Mary and Joseph told Jesus what they knew about him and about John. One can hear Jesus ask them if John was also being told. This new knowledge placed Jesus' prayers and studies in a new perspective.

4. The Holy Family traveled with the annual Nazareth caravan to Passover. John and Jesus had both turned twelve that year and were to be catechized and confirmed (the predecessor of the bar mitzvah). When the two families met, the boys spoke privately about the new information regarding themselves and what it all meant. Each boy also had the opportunity to hear the other boy's parents' story himself, firsthand.

When the boys were catechized by the priests, Zechariah was allowed to observe and participate in the catechizing of his own son and of his wife's great, great-nephew. The priests were "amazed at his (Jesus') understanding and his answers" (Lk 2:47). Both boys passed their examinations with flying colors and were confirmed.

5. One effect of Jesus' confirmation was that it changed his status from a child to a man. He was therefore accountable, first, to his own conscience. It is apparent from what followed, that in Jesus' prayers, the Father then told him to take this opportunity to learn what the leading teachers in Israel taught about Judaic practices, rather than his being limited to what he could learn in Nazareth and Sepphoris.

6. When the Nazareth caravan left in the pale light of dawn, Jesus stayed behind. He did not intend to deceive Mary and Joseph, even by his silence. Rather, his entire focus was on learning the current teachings of Judaism. Jesus simply allowed Mary to assume that he was traveling with the men and Joseph to assume that he was traveling with the women and children, as had been his prior practice. Mary and Joseph did not learn otherwise until the end of a long day's journey (Lk 22:44). There is a tradition that Joseph and Mary discovered Jesus' absence at the caravanserai at Bireh, about twenty miles north of Jerusalem. Their assumption that Jesus was in the caravan is evidence of their confidence in his maturity and responsibility. But Jesus had exercised his new responsibility as a man to obey his Father's direction.

❖   ❖   ❖

7. After the Nazareth caravan had left, Jesus went into the temple and joined the groups listening to the leading teachers of the day, who taught in the porticos of the Court of Gentiles. Though Jesus was only twelve, he was welcomed into the circles of students and disciples. He was known to be kin to Zechariah, and word of his deep understanding of Scripture had spread quickly in scholarly circles. Each rabbi viewed him as a potential disciple.

Jesus respectfully questioned the different rabbis. He did not instruct or argue with them; he was there to learn. Those who heard his questions were likewise amazed (Lk 2:46–47). The Sunday School pictures of the child Jesus teaching a rapt group of rabbis are unrealistic.

❖   ❖   ❖

8. The temple compound included sleeping quarters and dining facilities, especially for the divisions of numerous priests serving in the temple. One of the rabbis arranged for Jesus to be admitted to these accommodations. He was not sleeping and eating in unsafe surroundings.

The Joyful Mysteries

Jesus attended on the rabbis for two full days, the first being the day that Mary and Joseph traveled north and the second being the day they traveled back to Jerusalem.

✣ ✣ ✣

9. By the time Mary and Joseph arrived in Jerusalem upon their return, the gates to the temple were closed. They frantically sought Jesus in the city. The next morning ("the third day") they found him in the temple in one of the groups of students and disciples gathered around a teacher (Lk 2:46). They had been in great fear for Jesus, knowing his importance not only to themselves, but also to others.

✣ ✣ ✣

10. "[H]is mother said to him, 'Son, why have you treated us so? Behold, your father and I have been looking for you anxiously.' And he said to them, 'How is it that you sought me? Did you not know that I must be in my Father's house?' And they did not understand the sayings which he spoke to them" (Lk 2:48–50).

Since Mary had told Jesus of his miraculous conception and that the angel had said that he was the Son of God, Jesus was genuinely surprised by Mary's and Joseph's anxiety and their failure to realize that he would be safe in the temple. Jesus had realized, through his prayer life and knowledge of Scripture, the significance of what he had been told—that God was his Father in fact, and that he was more than the Messiah. Mary and Joseph were still focused on his being a miraculously provided Messiah.

In two days in the temple, Jesus had learned that the different schools of thought in Judaism taught conflicting views of the

Scriptures, and that none of them interpreted the Scriptures in the manner that he did.

Jesus returned to Nazareth with Mary and Joseph and was obedient to them as their child. He increased in his depth of understanding of the Scriptures and what they foretold for him, but that took time, study, and prayer.

THE LUMINOUS MYSTERIES

Baptism of Christ in the Jordan River, Giotto di Bondone, 1305, Scrovegni Chapel, Padua

THE BAPTISM

❖

1. John was born about six months before Jesus, in June 7 BC. We do not know John's age when Zechariah and Elizabeth died. He was twelve when he was confirmed. In all likelihood the Lord gave them enough years to allow John to grow to full maturity. He went into the wilderness as a hermit, perhaps after their deaths freed him from family responsibilities. From that time he ceased going to the temple festivals and no longer saw Jesus each Passover.

❖ ❖ ❖

2. No rabbi was considered to have studied enough to teach until he was at least thirty (Nm 4:3). John came out of the wilderness and began preaching in the fifteenth year of Tiberius' reign (Lk 3:1). Scholars differ as to which calendar to use. I find the Syro-Macedonian calendar is most likely. It was used by the Seleucid successors of Alexander the Great in Syria and Palestine. Luke, a Greek, wrote for Theophilus, a Greek, and a mostly Eastern Greek-speaking church. Accordingly, John's ministry began in or after October, AD 27. His ministry was short but intense, because many recognized him as the first prophet in centuries. Jesus' ministry included three Passovers—those of AD 30, 29, and 28—so Jesus' ministry began in late AD 27 or very early AD 28. Jesus was then thirty-two or thirty-three years old.

❖ ❖ ❖

3. John preached "a baptism of repentance for the forgiveness of sins." He specifically denied that he was the Messiah or Elijah come again or the prophet foretold by Moses. Rather, he identified himself as the voice crying in the wilderness announcing the coming of the Comforter of Israel, the Messiah, as foretold in Isaiah 40. He said, "the one to come will baptize with the Holy Spirit."

❖ ❖ ❖

4. When Jesus approached John, John said, **"Behold the Lamb of God, who takes away the sin of the world.... For this I came baptizing...."** (Jn 1:29–31). John's idea of Jesus as Messiah was deeper than the general populace's, a man on a white horse to free them from Rome and restore the Davidic kingdom. He at least partially understood the sacrificial aspect of the Messiah's ministry.

❖ ❖ ❖

5. John objected to baptizing Jesus, whom he knew to be free of sin, and asked Jesus to baptize him instead (Mt 3:14). Jesus said, no, John should do so, **"for thus it is fitting for us to fulfill all righteousness"** (Mt 3:15). John is the end of the Old Covenant and the greatest of the prophets. Though Jesus was not in need of repentance, his baptism fulfills and closes the Old Testament era and opens the new era. **"All the prophets and the law prophesied until John; and if you are willing to accept it, he is Elijah who is to come"** (Mt. 11:13–14; Lk 16:16).

⁂

6. How was Jesus baptized? He was not fully disrobed, as shown in the Arian Baptistry in Ravenna which sought to emphasize Jesus' lack of divinity; that was unthinkable to a devout Jew. He stood in the Jordan River to be baptized. There is a division of Christian opinion as to the method. Most Catholics think that John poured water over Jesus' head but did not fully immerse him. This is shown in the recent statuary group at the Jordan River. The Constantinian Baptistery pool at St. John Lateran in Rome is not now deep enough for immersion; it may have been deeper originally, but, if so, was it so used? The pool under the Cathedral in Milan, in which St. Ambrose baptized St Augustine, is not deep enough for immersion. The baptistery pool at St. John's Basilica in Ephesus has a sealed-off area in which the priest remained while baptizing those who waded by him, perhaps waist deep, in a long, narrow lane, certainly not suitable for immersion. A baptismal site east of the Jordan had many individual cups, which may indicate a pouring of water over the head. Yet Matthew describes Jesus as going "up immediately from the water," which some Christians believe indicates immersion. Sprinkling apparently came later, as the Church expanded into colder climes.

⁂

7. After John baptized Jesus and Jesus was praying, Jesus **"saw the Spirit of God descending like a dove and alighting on**

him" (Jn 1:32; Mk 1:10; Lk 3:22; Mt 3:16). John bore witness that he also saw the Spirit descend as a dove from heaven and remain on Jesus. The Lord had foretold to John that, **"He on whom you see the Spirit descend and remain, this is He who baptizes with the Holy Spirit"** (Jn 1:32–33). This event confirmed for John what he had been told, and believed, about Jesus.

※　※　※

8. **"And when he came up out of the water, immediately he saw the heavens opened and the Spirit descending upon him like a dove; and a voice came from heaven, 'Thou art my beloved Son; with thee I am well pleased'"** (Mk 1:10–11; Lk 3:22; Mt 3:16–17). The evidence of the Spirit's descent and of the Father's approbation confirmed Jesus in his interpretation of scripture and prayer, that the time to commence his own ministry had arrived.

※　※　※

9. John bore witness to those present at Jesus' baptism, that Jesus was "the Son of God." The next day John again described Jesus to others as "the Lamb of God," thereby encouraging his own disciples to follow Jesus (Jn 1:34–35).

※　※　※

10. While John had a better understanding of Jesus' role than most Jews, his understanding was incomplete, and he knew it. When Jesus came to be baptized, John called him the Lamb of God but added, **"I myself did not know him, but for this I came baptizing with water, that he might be revealed to Israel"** (Jn

1:31). Again, after John saw the Spirit descend on Jesus as a dove, John said: **"I myself did not know him. . . . I have seen and borne witness that this is the Son of God"** (Jn 1:32-34). In both instances the word translated as "know" carries the connotation of perception or understanding. John obviously had known his cousin Jesus all his life, but, even though John had some insight into Jesus the Messiah's sacrificial mission, he did not understand why Jesus was going about his mission in the manner being pursued. While John was later imprisoned by Herod Antipas, he received reports of Jesus' activities and still was puzzled by Jesus' method of ministry. He sent a question to Jesus, **"Are you He who is to come, or shall we look for another?"** Jesus responded, tell John **"the blind receive their sight and the lame walk, lepers are cleansed and the deaf hear, and the dead are raised up, and the poor have good news preached to them"** (Mt 11:2–5). Jesus' reference to the signs foretold by Isaiah and an even greater sign not foretold, the raising of the dead, was the answer and satisfaction John had sought and finally understood. He knew with certainty before his execution that he had accomplished his own mission.

The Marriage at Cana (detail), Luca Giordano, Museo Nazionale di Capodimonte, Naples

THE WEDDING AT CANA

◈

1. The wedding was at Cana, a village five miles northeast of Nazareth. A Jewish wedding was a celebration lasting as long as a week. Mary was invited. Jesus "also" was invited (Jn 2:2). Whose wedding was it? We do not know, a family member or a friend. The host, probably the father of the bridegroom, was a man of substance and religious standing. His house contained six twenty- to thirty-gallon stone jars to hold water for purification (Jn 2:6). The expense of the jars and of housing set aside for them was significant. What was the householder's connection with "the Jewish rites of purification"? Presumably, this refers to such rites as the purification after childbirth of women who did not travel to the temple or the purification of one who was defiled by touching the dead (Nm 19:13, 18–21). In all probability he was the local rabbi. What connection was he to Mary and to Jesus?

◈   ◈   ◈

2. Jesus was there, and his disciples were included because of him. Andrew, Peter, James, John, and Philip had been called, so at least these five were there and perhaps more. Nathanael Bartholomew himself was from Cana (Jn 21:2). He may or may not have been a disciple prior to the wedding. It seems likely that Nathanael and Simon the Zealot, also called Simon the Cananaean, were present and that the miracle contributed to their decision to follow Jesus (Mt 10:4). The host, who invited not only Jesus but also his disciples, undoubtedly was familiar with Jesus' new ministry. While he approved of what he had seen or heard, he may or may not have been a disciple himself. It is possible that he was the father of Nathanael or Simon. The wedding party was large, since the addition of Jesus' disciples made no difference in the arrangements. The guests came from a broad area, and whatever happened at the wedding would be talked about throughout much of Galilee.

3. At a wedding in a household of substance, servants would be present and would do the most menial work. As in any age, the women guests and especially the matrons would help the hostess with cooking and serving. Mary was one of the matron guests. She became aware that the party was running out of wine, either by observing it herself or by someone bringing it to her attention as a person particularly close to the hosts, when one would not want to embarrass the hosts by mentioning it to them directly. The problem was worse than just a shortfall of alcohol for the party. It would humiliate the hosts. Mary approached Jesus and told him, **"They have no wine"** (Jn 2:3). Mary knew who Jesus was and knew he could do something to solve it.

4. Jesus said, **"O woman, what have you to do with me?"** (Jn 2:4). Some writers say "woman" was condescending. But it is the same word used at the cross: **"Woman, behold your son"** (Jn 19:26). The term was not condescending, but a term of respect and affection. The term was applied to Eve, the woman. "What have you to do with me?" is idiomatic. It conveys respect and deference, an acknowledgment that whatever is about to be requested will be done. It occurs several times in scripture; for example, the Gadarene possessed by demons: **"What have you to do with me Jesus, son of the Most High God? I beseech you, do not torment me"** (Lk 8:26–28).

5. Jesus responded to Mary, **"My hour has not yet come"** (Jn 2:4). Jesus had been baptized and proclaimed by John to be the Messiah and the Lamb of God, and he had gathered a few disciples, but he had performed no miracles, or "signs." But it was Mary who determined that now was the time, place, and event for his first miracle.

6. Mary saw Jesus' acquiescence in her request. She had anticipated his acquiescence by rounding up servants and bringing them with her when she sought out Jesus (Jn 2:5). Servants were not at each guest's elbow. For whatever reason, whether as a kinswoman to the host or otherwise, Mary obviously was recognized by the servants as having authority. She told the servants, **"Do whatever he tells you"** (Jn 2:5). She knew he could prevent his hosts' humiliation and believed he would do so, though she may not have known how.

Let us reflect. What was the personality of Mary? We are too accustomed to the saccharin sweet pictures of her. It is easy to see her as devout. She was extremely intelligent, knowing the scriptures unusually well at thirteen years of age. At the commencement of Jesus' ministry, she was about forty-six or forty-seven years old. She was the one primarily invited to the wedding at Cana; Jesus was invited "also." The host's servants regarded her as a person of authority and took their instructions from Mary. They obeyed Jesus because Mary told them to do so. Later, she was the matronly head of the group of women disciples who traveled with Jesus and whose presence made it possible for them to do so. She was a central figure during the Crucifixion and at Pentecost. Jesus gave Mary to John as his mother and her protector. But John was also given to Mary as her son. John was probably seventeen or eighteen when he began following Jesus as a disciple, so he was about twenty or twenty-one years old at the time of the Crucifixion. Mary was given to John as his mother, but also as his advisor and as confidants one to the other. As we go through this meditation on the Rosary, we will encounter Mary many times in different settings. As we do so, let us meditate at greater length on what Mary was like, a remarkable woman in every good sense.

---

7. Jesus told the servants to fill six stone jars with water, and they filled them to the brim. Each jar held four to six five-gallon buckets of water. Depending on the manner of washing in purification, one jar may have been sufficient for one person, or six jars would have totally immersed one person. The jars had stone lids which, unlike brass or ceramics, could not be ritually contaminated. The lids kept the jars clean. Servants filled one jar at a time and covered it. The house had its own well nearby in its own courtyard, not relying on the village well. Servants filled all six jars without any indication of any change in the water (Jn 2:6–7).

8. Jesus told the servants, **"Draw some out and take it to the steward of the feast"** (Jn 2:8). When the servants drew out a ewer, they saw it was wine instead of water (Jn 2:9). They took it to the steward, the equivalent of the best man, and waited for his reaction.

9. The steward tasted the wine and told the bridegroom, **"You have kept the good wine till now"** (Jn 2:10). The bridegroom asked what he meant. The bridegroom tasted the wine and asked where it came from. The steward asked the servants. They related what had happened. It became the talk of the party. Did Jesus leave to avoid being questioned? If he stayed, how did he answer questions? We do not know. He probably left to avoid distracting from the proper center of attention, the bridal pair, and to avoid being questioned.

10. The effect of Mary's intercession was, **"His disciples believed in him"** (Jn. 2:11). The disciples had accepted Jesus' call, because John said Jesus was the Lamb of God and because they liked Jesus' teaching. This first miracle confirmed their belief that Jesus was the Messiah. It was an effect of grace. Jesus not only provided wine to forestall its running out. He also provided a super-abundance of it. A minimum of 120 gallons, if served up in the standard bottle of .7 liters, would amount to at least 725 bottles of wine.

The Raising of Lazarus, Duccio di Buoninsegna, 1310-1311, Kimbell Art Museum, Fort Worth, Texas

THE PROCLAMATION OF THE GOSPEL

1. Jesus drew many disciples, men and women, who accepted his teaching and, in some instances, traveled with him. Being a disciple was not necessarily a full-time undertaking, since Andrew, a disciple of John the Baptist, also spent time at his occupation of fishing. The disciples were such a large group that, from among them, Jesus at one time selected seventy and sent them out two by two to preach and heal in his name (Lk 10:1–12, 16–20). A tradition says that one of the seventy was Jesus' cousin, Simon, who became Bishop of Jerusalem after the martyrdom of James, son of Alpheus. In Jewish tradition, seventy was deemed to be the number of nations in the world.

From these numerous disciples, Jesus selected and called twelve to be his "apostles" or "envoys" (Lk 6:13). The twelve apostles represented the twelve tribes of Israel (Mt 19:28). In calling twelve apostles as his inner circle, Jesus set himself apart from all other rabbis, who limited themselves to five, thereby underscoring the significance of Jesus' action as reconstituting a new covenant Israel to replace the old covenant Israel. Unlike most of Jesus' disciples, the apostles were constantly with Jesus.

Scholars do not agree on whether to begin the list of the bishops of a particular diocese with the name of a founding apostle. From their consecration at the Last Supper, the apostles had the attributes of a bishop but were more than bishops, due to their intimate and prolonged contact with Jesus and the prestige arising from his calling them out before the Ascension. Unlike bishops, their particular mission was evangelization generally, not confined to a single geographic area. I have chosen to refer to an apostle functioning as head of a local church, such as James the Younger in Jerusalem or Paul in Ephesus, as the leader or head of that church, rather than its bishop.

After John had baptized Jesus in the Jordan River, John pointed Jesus out to two of his own disciples and said, **"Behold the Lamb of God!"** The two disciples, Andrew and another unnamed disciple, followed Jesus. Since John never refers to himself by name in his Gospel, it is likely that John was the unnamed disciple of John the Baptist who accompanied Andrew. They asked Jesus where he was staying. Jesus replied, **"Come and see."** They did so and stayed with him that day. Andrew subsequently told his brother, Simon Peter, **"We have found the Messiah (which means Christ),"** and Andrew brought Simon to Jesus (Jn 1:35–42). We must infer that, having found the man at least one of them regarded as the Messiah, these three spent a considerable time with Jesus.

On a later occasion, Jesus had returned to the Sea of Galilee to preach. **"While the people pressed upon him to hear the word of God, he was standing by the Lake of Gennesaret** [Sea of Tiberias or Sea of Galilee]**. And he saw two boats by the lake; but the fishermen were gone out of them and were washing their nets. Getting into one of the boats, which was Simon's, he asked him to put out a little from the land. And he sat down and taught the people from the boat. And when he had ceased speaking, he said to Simon, 'Put out into the deep and let down** your nets for a catch.' And Simon answered, 'Master, we toiled all night and took nothing! But at your word I will let down the nets.' And when they had done this, they enclosed a great shoal of fish; and as their nets were breaking, they beckoned to their partners in the other boat to come and help them. And they came and filled both the boats, so that they began to sink. But when Simon Peter saw it, he fell down at Jesus' knees, saying, 'Depart from me, for I am a sinful man, O Lord.' For he was astonished, and all that were with him, at the catch of fish which they had taken; and so also were James and John, sons of Zebedee, who were partners with Simon. And Jesus said to Simon, 'Do not be afraid; henceforth you will be catching men.' And when they had brought their boats to land, they left everything and followed him" (Lk 5:1–11).

Matthew and Mark telescope these events into accounts which, while essentially the same, are much less detailed. "**And passing along by the Sea of Galilee, he saw Simon and Andrew the brother of Simon casting a net in the sea; for they were fishermen. And Jesus said to them, 'Follow me and I will make you fishers of men.' And immediately they left their nets and followed him. And going on a little farther, he saw James the son of Zebedee and John his brother, who were in their boat mending the nets. And immediately he called them; and they left their father Zebedee in the boat with the hired servants, and followed him**" (Mk 1:16–20; Mt 4:18–22).

It seems a disservice to the faith to interpret the calling of these disciples, or the others, as a spirit-filled moment in which Jesus fixes a man with some sort of semi-hypnotic stare, tells him simply, "Follow me," and the man walks away from his family and occupation. Such an event does not conform to what we experience, and we must wonder why we do not have such faith. But that is not how Jesus called his disciples.

We have the most information about the calling of Simon Peter. Simon was so devout that he went to see and hear John the Baptist. Presumably, Simon had been baptized by him; he may or may not have gone further and become a disciple of John, like his brother Andrew. In any event, he was actively seeking God. Andrew told him that he and another disciple had found and spent time with the Messiah, the man John had pointed out to them as the Lamb of God. Simon returned with Andrew to meet Jesus and spent some time with him. At some later time, Jesus returned to the Sea of Galilee, where he found Simon and Andrew and their partners, James and John, winding up a night of unsuccessful fishing. In order to avoid the press of the crowd, Jesus called on his acquaintance, Simon, to use his boat as a waterborne rostrum. We may infer that Jesus had seen and taught Simon in between their meeting on the Jordan and this encounter on the Sea of Galilee, from Simon's addressing Jesus as "Master." When Jesus finished teaching, he freed himself from the crowd by asking Simon to put out to sea, so the crowd dispersed. Simon took his boat back out onto the lake and let down the nets he had already partially or wholly cleaned, and he was astonished at the enormous draft of fish in the net. Andrew motioned for their partners to join them, who thereupon ceased their cleanup and put out to join the others and were likewise astonished. Only after this event demonstrating his power did Jesus call the two sets of brothers to follow him, and they did.

This series of events is more in accord with the way things work than some peremptory "Follow me," followed by instantaneous obedience. Indeed, we normally see a series of events and increasing openness to God as leading up to conversion. The great draft of fish was the conversion moment or conversion experience, following extensive prior contacts, which led the four fishermen to accept Jesus' call. Some Christians have such a particular conversion event which prompts them to accept Christ, and some do not. It apparently is an aid but is not essential.

It seems to me that it is not helpful to emphasize the instant of the call and acceptance, since it can even discourage the would-be believer who is struggling with his unbelief and wonders why something special does not happen to him. Rather, it seems more helpful to emphasize that conversion and acceptance is the end product of many encounters and many decisions to act or to refrain from acting, which occur over a period of time leading to conversion and thereafter, which one struggles through till death.

The fifth disciple was Philip. Jesus was in Galilee when he called Philip, briefly described as a "Follow me" event (Jn 1:43–44). The inner circle of disciples was Peter, James, and John. The next in closeness to Jesus included Andrew and Philip. When Jesus fed the 5,000, he asked Philip how they could feed such a multitude, and Philip returned a common-sense answer regarding the cost. It was Philip whom Jesus tested. It was Andrew who pointed out what was available, the boy with five loaves and two fish (Jn 6:2–9). On a later occasion, when some Greeks wanted to speak with Jesus, they asked Philip; Philip went to Andrew, and the two of them went to Jesus. Philip clearly was recognized by outsiders as a person particularly close to Jesus (Jn 12:20–22).

Philip introduced Nathanael to Jesus. **"Philip found Nathanael, and said to him, 'We have found him of whom Moses in the law and also the prophets wrote, Jesus of Nazareth, the son of Joseph.' Nathanael said to him, 'Can anything good come out of Nazareth?' Philip said to him, 'Come and see.' Jesus saw Nathanael coming to him, and said of him, 'Behold, an Israelite indeed, in whom is no guile!' Nathanael said to him, 'How do you know me?' Jesus answered him, 'Before Philip called you, when you were under the fig tree, I saw you.' Nathanael answered him, 'Rabbi, you are the Son of God. You** are the King of Israel!' Jesus answered him, 'Because I said to you, I saw you under the fig tree, do you believe? You shall see greater things than these.' And he said to him, 'Truly, truly, I say to you, you will see heaven opened, and the angels of God ascending and descending upon the Son of Man'" (Jn 1:45–51).

When Jesus went to the wedding at Cana "with his disciples" (Jn 2:2), he was accompanied by at least the first five of these six disciples. Nathanael was from Cana (Jn 21:2). Simon the Zealot was also from Cana (Mt 10:4; Mk 3:18; Lk 6:15; Acts 1:13). While it is difficult to determine chronology from the Gospels, it appears that Nathanael may already have been a disciple when Jesus performed his first miracle. It seems likely that Simon the Zealot, or the Cananaean, was a guest at the wedding and was drawn to Jesus by the miracle, as a result of which, "his disciples believed in him" (Jn 2:11). We have no information on the prior connections between Mary and Jesus on the one hand and the bridegroom, his family, and the other wedding guests on the other, but it seems likely that there were preexisting relations among a number of these.

Jesus' call to Matthew the tax collector is also described briefly as a "Follow me" event (Mk 2:13–14; 3:18; Lk 5:27–28; 6:15; Mt 10:3; Acts 1:13). While the tax collector disciple is named "Levi," or "Levi the son of Alpheus," in the descriptions of his call in *Mark* and *Luke*, the same Gospels name him as "Matthew" in their lists of apostles, and Matthew's Gospel names him as "Matthew the tax collector." Levi and Matthew are clearly the same man. Another disciple is named as "James the son of Alpheus" (Mt 10:3; Mk 3:18; Lk 6:15). Mark calls Levi "the son of Alpheus." Since Levi-Matthew is not included in the list of Jesus' "brothers," they were sons of two different men named Alpheus.

The lists of apostles agree on ten of the twelve, namely: the brothers Simon Peter and Andrew; James and John, sons of Zebedee; Philip; Thomas; Matthew-Levi; James, the son of Alpheus; Simon the Zealot, or the Cananaean; and Judas Iscariot (Mt 10:2–4; Mk 3:13–19; Lk 6:12–16; Acts 1:13–14). All list Bartholomew as an apostle, but tradition treats him as being the same person as the disciple Nathanael, who is sometimes referred to as Nathanael Bartholomew. *Matthew* and *Mark* include Thaddeus on their lists (Mt 10:3; Mk 3:18). *Luke* and *Acts* do not list a Thaddeus, but rather list Judas, or Jude, the son of James (Lk 6:16; Acts 1:13). Tradition holds these two to be the same man, referred to as Jude Thaddeus.

Peter, Andrew, and Philip were from Bethsaida, at the north end of the Sea of Galilee east of the Jordan River, in the tetrarchy of Philip, a son of Herod the Great (Jn 1:43–44). Peter had moved across the Jordan to Capernaum on its west side, since his house was there at the time Jesus healed Simon's mother-in-law (Mt 8:14–15). Capernaum was in the tetrarchy of Herod Antipas, a son of Herod the Great, who had married Herodias, the wife of Philip, and who executed John the Baptist.

It is notable that Andrew, Peter, James, and John were partners. Zebedee, father of James and John, did not travel with Jesus, though his wife Salome did. Zebedee's obvious contribution was to manage the fishing partnership, using hired workers, some of whom were already on the payroll when James and John left to follow Jesus (Mk 1:20). In other words, Zebedee managed the partnership in order that its revenues would help support Jesus' ministry and provide for the families of the married partners, of whom Peter was married and perhaps Andrew and James.

2. Jesus taught us how to pray. **"Pray then like this: Our Father who art in heaven, hallowed be thy name. Thy kingdom**

come. Thy will be done, on earth as it is in heaven. Give us this day our daily bread; and forgive us our trespasses, as we forgive those who trespass against us; and lead us not into temptation, but deliver us from evil" (Mt 6:9–13).

Prayer, before all else, is to glorify God. We begin by acknowledging his holiness, "hallowed be thy name." We pray for the coming of his kingdom, the return of Jesus Christ. We pray that his will shall be done by ourselves and by the world at large, a condition which will occur upon the Second Coming.

We pray for our "daily bread," the necessities of life, which Jesus has assured us will be provided to us if we first seek the kingdom of God (Mt. 6:33; Lk 12:31). In a different sense, we pray for the daily gift of Jesus himself in the bread of daily communion. We seek God's forgiveness, acknowledging that it is conditioned upon our own forgiveness of those who have "trespassed" against us. "Trespass" has a much broader meaning than "debts." A trespass is any wrongful action against the person, land, or movable goods of another, giving rise to a civil cause of action. "Debts" is a weak substitute for a word of such breadth.

"Lead us not into temptation." The translation has been criticized on the basis that it presumes that God might lead us into temptation and be the agent of our spiritual injury. What nonsense! The prayer is that we not allow ourselves to be led into temptation by ourselves or by others. Such a prayer is one to avoid "occasions of sin."

"Deliver us from evil." We pray that God will protect and deliver us from every form of evil, physical and spiritual, to our persons, our property, and our relationships.

Luke's version of the Lord's Prayer contains five of these seven petitions, folding "Thy will be done on earth as it is in heaven" into "Thy kingdom come," and "Deliver us from evil" into "Lead us not into temptation" (Lk 11:2–4). These combinations of the two petitions into one arguably are of the same prayers, but the shades of meaning are better differentiated in the seven petitions in Matthew and for that reason have been more generally in use.

The doxology at the end of the prayer is in general use among Protestants. Catholics use both versions with and without the doxology in the liturgy but most commonly pray the shorter form without the doxology. Curiously, the Revised Standard Version, a Protestant work, omits the doxology, claiming it to be a later addition. Many Protestants continue to pray the doxology, which their bible no longer includes.

❖   ❖   ❖

3. Jesus taught us how to think. We incur penalties, whether criminal or civil, based on our actions, our conduct. This is as it should be. Laws that seek to read the human heart almost invariably do so in determining motivation that may categorize conduct, such as whether an act is done with willful disregard of the rights of others, which may convert negligence into gross negligence. Where law judges human thought, not expressed in conduct, we begin to deal with George Orwell's "thought crime" and tyranny of the worst sort.

Jesus, however, insists that our thought processes go beyond determining our course of conduct. Though the law should not judge our thoughts, unexpressed in conduct, God does. He recognizes that our thoughts can help or injure our spiritual health, even if we do not allow them to influence our conduct, though they may certainly lead to harmful conduct, as well.

"You have heard that it was said to the men of old, 'You shall not kill; and whoever kills shall be liable to judgment.' But I say to you that every one who is angry with his brother shall be liable to judgment; whoever insults his brother shall

be liable to the council, and whoever says, 'You fool!' shall be liable to the hell of fire" (Mt 5:21–22). Jesus equates anger, a root cause of murder, with murder itself, even where the anger does not boil over into words or other conduct.

"You have heard that it was said, 'You shall not commit adultery.' But I say to you that every one who looks at a woman lustfully has already committed adultery with her in his heart" (Mt 5:27). Jesus equates lust, unexpressed in word or deed, with adultery.

"You have heard that it was said, 'An eye for an eye and a tooth for a tooth.' But I say to you, do not resist one who is evil. But if any one strikes you on the right cheek, turn to him the other also; and if any one would sue you and take your coat, let him have your cloak as well; and if any one forces you to go one mile, go with him two miles" (Mt 5:38–41). Here Jesus demands that, rather than seeking justice for our reasonable grievances, we should submit to abuse and take on more of it voluntarily. Thoughts are obliged to mature into a new form of conduct. A hard saying indeed; who can listen to it?

"You have heard that it was said, 'You shall love your neighbor and hate your enemy.' But I say to you, love your enemies and pray for those who persecute you, so that you may be sons of your father who is in heaven; for he makes his sun rise on the evil and on the good, and sends rain on the just and on the unjust. For if you love those who love you, what reward have you? Do not even the tax collectors do the same?" (Mt 5:43–46). Jesus demands such a reformation of our "normal" thoughts, that we not only do good to those who abuse us, as in *Matthew* 5:38–41, but that we even learn to love them. What a radical transformation in our thought processes! Yet, history is replete with instances in which the souls of the unjust have been turned and saved by the meekness of their victims, who gave love where only hatred was expected.

Such a reformation of our thinking is a tall order, and each example above posed by Jesus becomes progressively more difficult. Let no man consider himself good or worthy of heaven, because few indeed would meet the requirements declared by Jesus. It is God's mercy on which we must rely.

❖   ❖   ❖

4. Jesus taught us how to live. "**And he opened his mouth, and taught them, saying, 'Blessed are the poor in spirit: for theirs is the kingdom of heaven. Blessed are they that mourn: for they shall be comforted. Blessed are the meek: for they shall inherit the earth. Blessed are they which do hunger and thirst after righteousness: for they shall be filled. Blessed are the merciful: for they shall obtain mercy. Blessed are the pure in heart: for they shall see God. Blessed are the peacemakers: for they shall be called the children of God. Blessed are they which are persecuted for righteousness' sake: for theirs is the kingdom of heaven'**" (Mt 5:2–10). Luke gives an abbreviated version (Lk 6:20–23). Jesus is the man who perfectly fulfilled the life described in these beatitudes. The beatitudes describe the perfect life from the standpoint of character attributes.

Jesus also described it from the standpoint of conduct. "'**Master, which is the great commandment in the law?' Jesus said unto him, 'Thou shalt love the Lord thy God with all thy heart, and with all thy soul, and with all thy mind. This is the first and great commandment. And the second is like unto it. Thou shalt love thy neighbor as thyself. On these two commandments hang all the law and the prophets'**" (Mt 22:36–40; Mk 12:28–31).

Both of these passages require interpretation in their application to a given situation. But no interpretation is required in order to apply Jesus' teaching regarding our duty to the less fortunate: "[T]he Son of Man . . . will separate them one from another as a shepherd separates the sheep from the goats, and he will place the sheep at his right hand, but the goats at the left. Then the king will say to those at his right hand, 'Come, O blessed of the Father, inherit the kingdom prepared for you from the foundation of the world; for I was hungry and you gave me food, I was thirsty and you gave me drink, I was a stranger and you welcomed me, I was naked and you clothed me, I was sick and you visited me.' . . . Then they** [those at his left hand] **also will answer, 'Lord, when did we see thee hungry or thirsty or a stranger or naked or sick or in prison, and did not minister to thee?' Then he will answer them, 'Truly, I say to you, as you did it not to one of the least of these, you did it not to me.' And they will go away into eternal punishment, but the righteous into eternal life"** (Mt 25:31–46).

Jesus summarized our obligation to our fellow man in one word: service. **"'You know that the rulers of the Gentiles lord it over them, and their great men exercise authority over them.**

It shall not be so among you; but whoever would be great among you must be your servant, and whoever would be first among you must be your slave; even as the Son of Man came not to be served but to serve, and to give his life as a ransom for many'" (Mt 20:25–28; Mk 10:42–45). It is no accident that one of the titles of the Pope is "Servant of the servants of God."

✠ ✠ ✠

5. Jesus taught us how to forgive. Since the Lord's Prayer underscores our forgiveness by God as being conditional on our forgiveness of others, this is an important skill. **"For if you forgive men their trespasses, your heavenly Father also will forgive**

you, but if you do not forgive men their trespasses, neither will your Father forgive your trespasses"** (Mt 6:14–15).

How often should we forgive a person who harms or offends us? **"Then Peter came up and said to him, 'How often shall my brother sin against me, and I forgive him? As many as seven times?' Jesus said to him, 'I do not say to you seven times, but seventy times seven'"** (Mt 18:21–22). By this answer Jesus did not mean that we should keep a running tally on those obnoxious to us until we have counted 490 offenses, so we may then retaliate. Rather, he meant that there should be no limit to the number of offenses which we should forgive.

Are any offenses so minor that they need not be forgiven? In a parable, Jesus describes the king's servant who was unable to repay 10,000 talents he owed to the king. Rather than selling him and his family into slavery, the king forgave the debt. But the servant squeezed a fellow servant for 100 denarii, a comparatively trifling sum, and put him in prison for his nonpayment. The king, being notified of this, put his servant in jail until the 10,000 talents should be paid. **"So also my heavenly Father will do to every one of you, if you do not forgive your brother from your heart"** (Mt 18:23–35). No offense is so trifling or so great that it is not included in the requirement that we forgive, if we desire forgiveness of our own sins.

❖ ❖ ❖

6. Jesus taught us our duty to the state. **"'Tell us** [the Pharisees and Herodians], **then, what you think. Is it lawful to pay taxes to Caesar, or not?' But Jesus, aware of their malice, said, 'Why put me to the test, you hypocrites? Show me the money for the tax.' And they brought him a coin. And Jesus said to them, 'Whose likeness and inscription is this?' They**

said, 'Caesar's.' Then he said to them, 'Render therefore to Caesar the things that are Caesar's and to God the things that are God's'"** (Mt 22:17–22; Mk 12:13–17; Lk 20:21–26). The Christian undoubtedly owes his support to a legitimate government, to pay his taxes, to defend it, and to obey its just laws. The tension arises in the ambiguity of determining when the state exceeds its bounds and encroaches on that which is owed to God. This tension has frequently placed the Western, or Catholic, Church in conflict with the state, most strikingly in the medieval conflict between Pope and Holy Roman Emperor, and most recently in such matters as abortion and, still more recently, where clerical opposition to homosexuality has resulted in prosecution of pastors in Sweden and Canada for "hate crimes." The Orthodox churches have inherited the Byzantine and Russian tradition of Caesaropapism, control of the church by the state, and conflicts between church and state have been less frequent, or even rare.

❖ ❖ ❖

7. Jesus had the gift of healing, not with the mission of healing all the world's ailments but rather to lend credibility to his teaching. In the great majority of his healings, he was assisted by the patient's faith that Jesus' action would be efficacious, or in some cases, by the faith of those who solicited Jesus' intervention where the patient was unable to make the request.

In the first category, Jesus healed the following: (1) A leper. **"Lord, if you will, you can make me clean"** (Mt 8:5–13; Lk 5:12–14). (2) The paralytic let down through the roof, so Jesus saw their faith (Mk 2:1–12; Mt 9:2–7; Lk 5:18–26). (3) The woman with a flow of blood for twelve years. **"If I only touch his garment, I shall be made well"** (Mt 9:20–22; Mk 5:25–34; Lk 8:42–48). (4) Two blind men. **"'Do you believe that I am able to** do this?' They said to him, 'Yes, Lord'" (Mt 9:27–31). (5) The Canaanite woman's daughter. **"Yes, Lord, yet even the dogs eat the crumbs that fall from their master's table"** (Mt 17:14–21; Mk 7:25–30). (6) Bartimaeus, a blind man. **"Have mercy on me, Son of David"** (Mt 20:29–34; Mk 10:46–52; Lk 18:35–43). (7) Ten lepers. **"Jesus, Master, have mercy on us."** (But only the Samaritan leper returned to thank Jesus [Lk 17:11–19]).

Where people solicited Jesus, in faith, for healing on behalf of those not able to petition for themselves, Jesus healed: (1) The paralyzed servant of a centurion. **"Lord, I am not worthy to have you come under my roof, but only say the word, and my servant shall be healed"** (Mt 8:5–13; Mk 1:29–31; Lk 4:38–39). (2) Peter's mother-in-law (Mt 8:14–15; Mk 1:29–31). Peter's house, having served as a house church, has been excavated under a fifth century church in Capernaum. (3) A deaf man with a speech impediment (Mk 7:32–37). (4) A blind man (Mk 8:22–26). (5) After the transfiguration, the boy with a demon. **"Lord, have mercy on my son"** (Mt 17:14–24; Mk 9:14–29). (6) The official's son. **"'Go; your son will live.' The man believed the word that Jesus spoke to him and went his way"** (Jn 4:46–53).

In these first two categories, the healings are conditioned upon the faith of the patient or of the person interceding for the patient. In the third category of healings, the healing is initiated by Jesus for the glorification of God, without any petition by or on behalf of the patient. (1) A dumb demoniac (Mt 9:32–33). (2) A man with a withered hand in the synagogue (Mt 12: 9–13; Mk 3:1–5; Lk 6: 6–11). (3) A blind and dumb demoniac (Mt 12:22–24). (4) Malchus' ear (Jn 18:10–11; Lk 22:49–51). (5) An unclean spirit in the synagogue (Mk 1:21–27). (6) Demons cast out into swine (Mk 5:1–19). (7) A woman in the synagogue bent over for 18 years (Lk 13:10–13). (8) A man with dropsy healed on the sabbath (Lk 14:1–5).

It is true that faith is an aid to divine healing. The faith may exist on the part of the patient or on the part of those interceding for the patient. The hazard is that those by or for whom healing prayers are offered may consider that the failure to obtain healing is due to their own lack of faith, a dangerously depressing reaction. That is not so. Judea and Galilee were full of patients Jesus did not heal. The issue is muddled by the healing of those who really did not seek it, in order to glorify God. It is clear that the Lord selects the cases in which he will grant healing, for reasons known only to Him. While we should pray for healing for ourselves and for others, and while such prayers may increase the odds in our favor, experience shows that the percentage of physical healings is low. Nevertheless, the percentage of spiritual healings is an unknown figure but one which anecdotal evidence indicates is significantly higher than that for physical healings.

✦ ✦ ✦

8. On three occasions, Jesus raised the dead, the ultimate form of physical healing. The first time he did so at Nain, a village eight miles south of Nazareth on the border of Samaria. **"[H]e went to a city called Nain, and his disciples and a great crowd went with him. As he drew near to the gate of the city, behold, a man who had died was being carried out, the only son of his mother, and she was a widow; and a large crowd from the city was with her. And when the Lord saw her, he had compassion on her and said to her, 'Do not weep.' And he came and touched the bier, and the bearers stood still. And he said, 'Young man, I say to you, arise.' And the dead man sat up and began to speak. And he gave him to his mother"** (Lk 7:11–17).

The second time was at Capernaum. **"And there came a man named Jairus, who was a ruler of the synagogue; and falling** at Jesus' feet, he besought him to come to his house, for he had an only daughter, about twelve years of age, and she was dying.... (A) man from the ruler's house came and said, 'Your daughter is dead; do not trouble the teacher any more.' But Jesus on hearing this answered him, 'Do not fear; only believe, and she will be well.' And when he came to the house, he permitted no one to enter with him, except Peter and John and James, and the father and mother of the child. And all were weeping and bewailing her; but he said, 'Do not weep; for she is not dead but sleeping.' And they laughed at him, knowing that she was dead. But taking her by the hand he called, saying, 'Child, arise.' And her spirit returned, and she sat up at once; and he directed that something should be given her to eat. And her parents were amazed" (Lk 8:41–42, 49–56; Mt 9:18–19, 23–26; Mk 5:22–24, 35–42).

On the first of these resurrections, Jesus stepped forward as a volunteer. The circumstance—the death of a widow's only son—stirred his pity. In the days before pensions and welfare, the widow was totally bereft. Jesus halted the funeral procession and restored the son to life. This was done in the presence of two crowds, one of his disciples and those who had come to see and hear him, and one of strangers in the funeral procession. The impact on the two crowds must have been great.

On the second occasion, Jesus was solicited to heal the only daughter of Jairus, a ruler of the synagogue of Capernaum. Since Capernaum was Jesus' city, his headquarters during his ministry, and Jesus had taught in its synagogue, Jairus obviously knew Jesus and was well aware of his healing power. That is why he sought Jesus out, to heal his daughter who was still alive. As they were on the way to Jairus' house, they learned that she had died. By the time they reached the house, the professional mourners (the flute players, Mt 9:23), family, and neighbors had commenced the ritualized wailing; in an age before undertakers and hospitals, people were familiar with death, and there is no reason to doubt that she had died. Yet Jesus announced to the father, "only believe, and she will be well." The crowd mocked him. Jesus raised the child from death in the presence of five witnesses—Peter, James and John, and her two parents.

The third resurrection was at Bethany, just outside Jerusalem on the eve of Jesus' last Passover, with enormous crowds in the area. A messenger was sent to Jesus by Mary and Martha that their brother Lazarus was sick, asking him to come. Jesus tarried to allow Lazarus to die. Martha met and reproached Jesus for not coming sooner. When Jesus reassured her that Lazarus would rise again, she answered that she knew he would rise **"'in the resurrection at the last day.' Jesus said to her, 'I am the resurrection and the life; he who believes in me, though he die, yet shall he live, and whoever lives and believes in me shall never die. Do you believe this?' She said to him, 'Yes, Lord; I believe that you are the Christ, the Son of God, he who is coming into the world.' . . . Jesus said, 'Take away the stone.' Martha, the sister of the dead man, said to him, 'Lord, by this time there will be an odor, for he has been dead four days.' . . . (H)e cried with a loud voice, 'Lazarus, come out.' The dead man came out, his hands and feet bound with bandages, and his face wrapped with a cloth. Jesus said to them, 'Unbind him, and let him go'"** (Jn 11:1–44).

All three accounts are clear, that Jesus brought the dead back to life in the presence of more than a legally sufficient number of witnesses, even in the presence of crowds. In none of these cases did anyone expect or request him to do so. It was obvious to the participants that healing was something a great prophet might do, but to raise the dead was a thing entirely apart. It obviously smacks of the divine, though Elijah had done it once before. In a sense, Jesus' resurrection of others was a foretaste of his resurrection and our own.

9. Jesus exercised dominion over the natural world. In addition to being able to correct deficiencies in the material world by healing the sick, he had the ability to make nature behave in a manner contrary to itself, submitting to his will.

The first example was the change of water into wine at the wedding at Cana. He changed water into wine, the blood of the grape, just as he would later change his own blood into wine.

In similar manner, Jesus could alter the molecular structure of food in order to multiply it and make it more accessible to the many. On two occasions, he multiplied food brought and existing in reality before him into some multiple of the same food. Unlike Cana, where water turned into wine, the loaves and fishes were multiplied into more of the same thing.

On the first occasion, Jesus multiplied five loaves and two fish to feed 5,000 men plus their wives and children (Mt 14:14–21; Mk 6:37–44; Lk 9:11–17; Jn 6:2–14). On a subsequent occasion, Jesus fed 4,000 men with seven loaves and "some" fishes (Mt 15:32–38; Mk 8:1–10). On both of these occasions, consider the effect on the crowd. On the first occasion, the crowd accepted the "sign" that Jesus was the prophet foretold by Moses and sought to make him king. But worldly power was not Jesus' mission, and he evaded them (Jn 6:1–15). On both occasions, the multiplication of the loaves was a type of Jesus' ability to multiply his own body in the Eucharist to feed the multitudes of believers.

On three other occasions Jesus caused the natural order to reconfigure itself. He caused a draft of fish as a sign to Peter and his partners that, in addition to what had gone before, caused them to follow him (Lk 5:3–9). On another occasion, the resurrected Jesus caused a draft of fish as a sign of his identity to the apostles

(Jn 21:4–8). He either called or ordered the fish to move into a position to be caught on these two occasions. But John did not consider these "miracles," since the first occurred before the wedding at Cana, and John said that the wedding at Cana was the first "miracle." In the same category was the occasion on which Jesus had Peter catch a fish in whose mouth was a shekel to pay the poll tax for Peter and himself (Mt 17:24–27).

With a word he could kill living beings. With a curse, Jesus withered the non-productive fig tree (Mt 21:18–22; Mk 11:12–14, 20–21).

Just as Jesus could command the fish's movements and kill the fig tree, he could control the actions and effects of the sea and wind. As Jesus and some disciples crossed the Sea of Galilee, Jesus slept while a great storm arose. **"And they went and woke him, saying, 'Save us, Lord; we are perishing.' And he said to them, 'Why are you afraid, O men of little faith?' Then he rose and rebuked the winds and the sea; and there was a great calm. And the men marveled, saying, 'What sort of man is this, that even winds and sea obey him'"** (Mt 8:23–27; Mk 4:35–41)? The answer is in Psalm 65. God is the one **"who dost still the roaring of the seas, the roaring of their waves. . . . "** (Ps 65:7). Jesus, by his action, had proclaimed his identity to those who would see and hear.

After feeding the 5,000, Jesus sought to be alone and told the apostles to cross the lake to go home. They were held back by a strong wind. Jesus set out to cross the lake on foot. The apostles saw him walking on the water, which frightened them more than the contrary wind. Peter sought to walk across the water to Jesus, but he looked down and was frightened and began to sink until Jesus pulled him out. Jesus joined them in the boat **"and immediately the boat was at the land to which they were going"** (Jn 6:16–21; Mt 14:22–33; Mk 6:47–52).

10. Jesus declared himself to be God. If Jesus unambiguously claimed to be God, then G. K. Chesterton's comment is controlling, namely: if he was not God, then he cannot have been a good man or a great philosopher, if he made such a claim falsely. In such case, he was either a charlatan or a madman. The latter possibility includes the contingency that he was honestly mistaken. The extravagant nature of the claim precludes a good faith mistake by anyone but a madman.

Did Jesus unambiguously claim to be God? It is true that in the early stages of his ministry, he avoided making such an extreme claim prematurely, which might thereby interfere with the acceptance of his Gospel. Disciples were taught the truth gradually. Who would attend a carpenter who began by claiming to be God? Most frequently, Jesus claimed to be the Messiah, or the Christ, or to be the "Son of Man" or a "Son of God." A man bearing these titles and characteristics was expected by devout Jews. One might question whether Jesus was the man awaited without doubting its possibility, however remote. Because of their monotheism, no Jew was prepared for God to appear as a divine man. Hence, Jesus' claim to be Messiah and Son of Man became acceptable to some, while being in no way inconsistent with his claim to divinity. While those who heard him sometimes understood these claims to include a claim of divinity, they were not in themselves blasphemous, at least the claim to be the Messiah was not. So, some ambiguity allowed Jesus to maneuver in the early stages.

In order to avoid an untimely precipitation of his "hour," Jesus even played on the ambiguity of this claim to be "Son of Man" or the "Son of God." When the Jews would have stoned him, they said, **"'It is not for a good work that we stone you but for blasphemy because you, being a man, make yourself God.'**

Jesus answered them, 'Is it not written in your law, "I said, you are gods"? If he called them gods to whom the word of God came (and scripture cannot be broken), do you say of him whom the Father consecrated and sent into the world, 'You are blaspheming' because I said, 'I am the Son of God?' If I am not doing the works of my Father, then do not believe me; but if I do them, even though you do not believe me, believe the works, that you may know and understand that the Father is in me and I am in the Father.' Again they tried to arrest him, but he escaped from their hands" (Jn 10:33–39). Without denying his divinity, Jesus clouded the issue to postpone his "hour."

Nevertheless, at the same period of time (between the first and second Passovers of his ministry), Jesus culled his disciples by uncompromisingly driving home the necessity that they must eat his flesh and drink his blood (Jn 6:28–69). He also declared his divine origin. **"'For I have come down from heaven, not to do my own will, but the will of him who sent me; . . . '"** (Jn 6:38). During the feast of Tabernacles between the second and the last Passovers of his ministry, he made a similar but somewhat more definite statement. **"I proceeded and came forth from God; I came not of my own accord, but he sent me"** (Jn 8:42). When the Jews objected, he made his teaching more explicit. **"'Your father Abraham rejoiced that he was to see my day; he saw it and was glad.' The Jews then said to him, 'You are not yet fifty years old, and have you seen Abraham?' Jesus said to them 'Truly, truly, I say to you, before Abraham was, I am.' So they took up stones to throw at him; but Jesus hid himself and went out of the temple"** (Jn 8:56–59). The Jews correctly understood that Jesus had identified himself with God, Yahweh, "He is," the third person singular. "I am," *ehyeh,* is the first person singular of the same statement. God told Moses that his name is "I am," so Moses, referring to God's statement, told the Hebrews that his name is Yahweh, "He is" (Ex 3:14). Jesus, referring to himself, said "I am."

At the Feast of Dedication during the winter before his Passion, Jesus took his teaching a step farther, no longer relying on an implication. **"So the Jews gathered round him and said to him, 'How long will you keep us is suspense? If you are the Christ, tell us plainly.' 'I and the Father are one'"** (Jn 10:22–30). When the Jews prepared to stone him, he used the play on words discussed previously, citing scripture that said "You are gods," to escape.

During the Last Supper, **"Philip said to him, 'Lord, show us the Father, and we shall be satisfied.' Jesus said to him, 'Have I been with you so long, and yet you do not know me, Philip? He who has seen me has seen the Father. . . . '"** (Jn 14:8–9).

Later that evening in the garden of Gethsemane, those who came to arrest Jesus sought to identify him. **"'Whom do you seek?' They answered him, 'Jesus of Nazareth.' Jesus said to them, 'I am he.' . . . When he said to them, 'I am he,' they drew back and fell to the ground"** (Jn 18:4–6). Again, Jesus had identified himself as Yahweh. In Aramaic, "I am" and "I am he" are the same. The others so understood it and reacted accordingly.

During his trial before Caiaphas, the high priest, Jesus unambiguously claimed to be divine. Matthew describes the scene in the idiom probably used. After Caiaphas failed to obtain witnesses whose testimony agreed, being therefore on the verge of having his prosecution of Jesus fail, Caiaphas turned to Jesus and demanded, **"'I adjure you by the living God, tell us if you are the Christ, the Son of God.' Jesus said to him, 'You have said so. But I tell you, hereafter you will see the Son of Man seated at the right hand of Power, and coming on the clouds of heaven.' Then the high priest tore his robes and said, 'He has uttered blasphemy. Why do we still need witnesses?'"** (Mt 26:63–65; Lk 22:70–71). In his question to Jesus, Caiaphas asked a multifarious question, as to whether Jesus made two distinct claims: first, to be the Christ and second, to be the Son of God.

Jesus replied in the idiom of the day, **"You have said so,"** or "You got it" in our parlance. Jesus expanded on his affirmative answers to both questions in such a way as to be sure that no one missed the point. **"You will see the Son of Man seated at the right hand of Power, and coming on the clouds of heaven."** Caiaphas correctly construed the answer as blasphemous, if it was not true. Interestingly, Jesus passed the opportunity to let Caiaphas' prosecution fail for lack of evidence, setting Jesus free. His "hour" had come, and the full sacrifice was to be made, not to be frustrated by Caiaphas' ineptness.

Mark tells the same story about Jesus' response to Caiaphas, except that he restates the answer in proper Greek rather than a Greek restatement of Jewish idiom. **"Again the high priest asked him, 'Are you the Christ, the Son of the Blessed?' And Jesus said, 'I am; and you will see the Son of Man seated at the right hand of Power, and coming with the clouds of heaven'"** (Mk 14:61–62).

Even the apostles were slow to understand the full import of Jesus' declarations of his identity. They recognized Jesus as the Messiah or even as an unidentified "someone" more than the Messiah. Thomas was the first to comprehend who Jesus was and to put it into words during Jesus' second post-resurrection appearance to the apostles in the upper room. **"Thomas answered him, 'My Lord and my God'"** (Jn 20:28). Thomas had drawn the correct conclusion when he first heard of Jesus' resurrection. Only God could do that. Thomas initially recoiled from his conclusion in the face of Jewish dedication to a monotheistic God, but once he accepted the fact of resurrection, he also accepted the conclusion as to Jesus' divinity.

Transfiguration, Girolamo Savoldo, Uffizi Gallery Museum, Florence.

THE TRANSFIGURATION

❖

1. Jesus led Peter, James, and John up a high mountain apart (Mt 17:1). The mountain was either Mt. Hermon or Mt. Tabor, the two "high" mountains in the area of Galilee. The geographic location mentioned in the text immediately before the Transfiguration was Caesarea Phillipi, forty miles north of the Sea of Galilee, and closer to Mt. Hermon (Mt 16:13). However, the subsequent geographic location mentioned in the text is that they passed through Galilee to Capernaum (Mk 9:30–33). This would apply to Mt. Tabor, the more likely location. Origen, writing in the early third century, says that there was a very old tradition that the site was on Mt. Tabor, and churches have been built on it, as the political situation has allowed, since the fourth century. Though some writers argue in favor of Mt. Hermon, there is little to support their claim, other than the mention of Caesarea Phillipi in the text.

❖ ❖ ❖

2. Jesus selected Peter, James, and John, the inner circle of disciples. The same disciples went apart with him when he raised Jairus' daughter and at Gethsemane (Mt 26:37).

3. The timing of the transfiguration is important. Beginning shortly before the Transfiguration, Jesus began to teach his disciples that he must go to Jerusalem and be killed, to be raised on the third day (Mt 16:21). Soon after the Transfiguration, Jesus "set his face to go to Jerusalem" and began moving toward it (Lk 9:51). It was the confirmation of his interpretation of scripture that encouraged him to do so.

4. On the mountaintop Jesus prayed (Lk 9:28). He went aside from the three disciples to do so, as he did at Gethsemane, which was his practice. The disciples fell asleep and awakened to an astonishing tableau (Lk 9:32).

5. Jesus was transfigured before them. His clothes were dazzling white or white as light, as no fuller on earth could bleach them (Lk 9:29; Mt 17:2; Mk 9:3). The appearance of his face was altered, shining "like the sun" (Lk 9:29; Mt 17:2). Jesus thus appeared before them for the first time in his divinity, an appearance obviously difficult to describe.

6. Jesus was speaking with two other figures, identifiable in some fashion as Moses and Elijah, since Peter named them without being so told by Jesus (Mt 17:3–4; Lk 9:32). Moses possibly was recognizable by the rays from his face, portrayed as horns by Michelangelo, which necessitated Moses' veiling his face in the presence of others. Perhaps Elijah was recognizable by carrying a scroll of *The Books of the Kings*, describing his acts, which is how he is commonly pictured.

***

7. Why did Moses and Elijah appear to Jesus in his divinity? Jesus had studied the scriptures for more than twenty-five years. He had prayed fervently to his Father to learn what the scriptures told him of himself and to determine what course his ministry should take. His conclusion, as he taught his disciples before the Transfiguration, was truly terrifying. He was to suffer crucifixion. But many men had been crucified. Far worse, he was to take upon himself the sin of the world. Moses and Elijah **"appeared in glory and spoke of his departure, which he was to accomplish at Jerusalem"** (Lk 9:30–31). The Father granted him the opportunity to confer with Moses and Elijah to confirm his own conclusions regarding the interpretation of the law and the prophets. They "spoke of his departure . . . at Jerusalem." In other words they talked with Jesus about his coming passion, crucifixion, and resurrection, all as had been foretold in the scriptures. Jesus was thereby strengthened for the ordeal that lay ahead.

***

8. As Moses and Elijah were parting from Jesus, Peter sought to encourage them to stay by proposing to build booths or tabernacles for the three of them. *Matthew* and *Mark* say the Transfiguration happened "after six days." Some scholars conclude that this was the sixth day of the Feast of Tabernacles, during which such booths or tabernacles were erected, so Peter's suggestion was not entirely outlandish (Mk 9:5–6; Mt 17:4). This argument would appear to conflict with the detailed description of Jesus' actions at the same Feast of Tabernacles in Jerusalem (Jn 7:1–39). As has been frequently pointed out, the faith was not to be advanced by staying on the mountaintop but rather by descending to the confusions of the world.

❖   ❖   ❖

9. A bright cloud overshadowed the disciples as Peter spoke and hid Jesus and the others from them. A voice came out of the cloud, saying, **"This is my beloved Son, with whom I am well pleased; listen to him"** (Mt 17:5; Lk 9:34–35). The disciples fell on their faces in growing fear and awe (Mt 17:6; Mk 9:6; Lk 9:34). Then the cloud lifted, and the disciples were alone with Jesus in his normal appearance.

❖   ❖   ❖

10. As they came down the mountain, Jesus told the disciples to tell no one what they had seen, until he had risen from the grave. Why keep the Transfiguration secret until the Resurrection? The disciples did not accept Jesus' teaching that he was to be killed in Jerusalem; as late as the Last Supper, they were quarreling among themselves regarding who should have which office in the new government. Even the three disciples who saw the Transfiguration did not realize its import.

As they began their ascent from Jericho to Jerusalem in the days before Palm Sunday, thinking that Jesus would soon form the government of a new Davidic kingdom, James and John, accompanied and egged on by their mother, Salome, asked Jesus to give them the two highest ministerial portfolios in his imminent government, elbowing their way ahead of Peter (Mt 20:20–21). Salome was Jesus' first cousin or stepcousin. If there was to be a new kingdom, Jesus' family would form part of the dynasty, and they might reasonably anticipate that they should have precedence over a non-kinsman like Peter. When Jesus asked if they could drink the cup he was to drink, both claimed that they could. Jesus denied their request on the ground that the appointments were not his to give, but **"those for whom it is to be prepared"** (Mk 10:35–40).

When their petition became known to the other disciples, it caused dissension, and Jesus indirectly rebuked James and John by teaching the disciples that whoever wanted to be first must be the servant of the others. This incident could not have pleased Jesus. While he included James among the three that accompanied him at Gethsemane, James is not as prominent in scripture afterward. As the older of the two brothers, he was the one primarily responsible, and Jesus so treated him. John, on the other hand, redeemed himself during Jesus' lifetime by his subsequent courage during Jesus' Passion and by his deference to Peter. But James' repentance and Jesus' forgiveness is indicated by Jesus' appearance to him in a private epiphany after the Resurrection (1 Cor 15:7).

Why did Jesus have three disciples witness the Transfiguration? When Thomas declared his recognition that Jesus was not only Messiah but also God, there were three witnesses to Jesus' divinity. Jewish law required consistent testimony of two or more witnesses in many situations; for example, blasphemy (Mk 14:56–59) and adultery (Sus 19–21, 52-59; Dn 13:19-21, 52–59). Jesus knew that he was going to be betrayed. **"Even my bosom friend in whom I trusted, who ate of my bread, has lifted his heel against me"** (Ps 41:8–9). It may well be that Jesus took three witnesses because he had not yet identified his betrayer and he was protecting himself against the possibility that one of the three closest to him would betray him.

Last Supper, Pietro Annigoni, 1984.
Refectory of the Friary of the Basilica of Saint Anthony, Padua

INSTITUTION OF THE EUCHARIST

1. Jesus knew from scripture that he would be betrayed (Ps 41:8–9). He deemed it critically important that the betrayal should not interfere with his plans for the Last Supper. He used a classic of intelligence work. He prearranged with the owner of the house at which the Last Supper would be held that a man would meet some disciples and lead them to the house to prepare the Passover dinner. He would be identified by the disciples as a man carrying a jar of water, an unusual sight since that was woman's work. Jesus waited until the last minute and then sent Peter and John to meet the man (Mt 26:17–19; Mk 14:12–16; Lk 22:7–13). They were the most trusted disciples, so there was no way the betrayer could ascertain the location and pass the information to the temple, interfering with Jesus' plans.

It is likely that Jesus had not yet identified his betrayer when he secretly made these arrangements for the Passover meal. He may have had a question about James, in view of his attempted "coup" against Peter just days previously, so he sent only Peter and John. He believed that he would be betrayed before the Passover holidays, so he gave directions for the preparation of this meal at least a day in advance. Preparation for the Passover meal included cleaning the leaven out of the house and preparing bitter herbs and other ingredients. Peter and John presumably killed and prepared the lamb. When all was ready, Jesus then led all disciples to the house, and his betrayer could not absent himself to betray them.

❖ ❖ ❖

2. Present in the upper room of the house to celebrate the Passover meal were Jesus and the twelve apostles. The householder, the householder's family, the servants, and the women disciples who accompanied and served Jesus and his entourage were present in the house but ate elsewhere when not serving Jesus and the twelve. In all likelihood, the house belonged to the mother of John Mark, the author of the *Gospel of Mark*. The mother was named Mary. Her husband was probably dead, since the house was referred to as "the house of Mary" (Acts 12:12). A young man accompanied Jesus and the disciples to Gethsemane, though he was not present at the Last Supper, so he was a member of the household. John Mark is traditionally believed to be the unidentified young man (age twelve or older) who escaped at Gethsemane by slipping out of his linen cloak and running off naked (Mk 14:51–52).

❖ ❖ ❖

3. What was the date of the Last Supper? Leviticus says, **"In the first month, on the 14th day of the month in the evening, is the Lord's Passover. And on the 15th day of the same month is the Feast of Unleavened Bread; seven days you shall eat unleavened bread"** (Lv 23:5–6). On the Passover itself, one also eats unleavened bread (Ex 12:8). **"Now on the first day of Unleavened Bread, the disciples came to Jesus, saying, 'Where will you have**

us prepare for you to eat the Passover'" (Mt 26:17)? **"And on the first day of Unleavened Bread, when they sacrificed the Passover lamb, his disciples said to him, 'Where will you have us go and prepare for you to eat the Passover'"** (Mk 14:12)? **"Now the feast of Unleavened Bread drew near, which is called the Passover. . . . Then came the day of Unleavened Bread on which the Passover lamb had to be sacrificed"** (Lk 22:1, 7). **"I have earnestly desired to eat this Passover with you before I suffer"** (Lk 22:15). "Now before the feast of the Passover [emphasis supplied]**, when Jesus knew that his hour had come to depart out of this world to the Father, having loved his own who were in the world, he loved them to the end"** (Jn 13:1). **"Now it** [the day of crucifixion] **was the** Day of Preparation for the Passover [emphasis supplied]**; it was about the sixth hour** [when Pilate condemned Jesus]" (Jn 19:14).

Some writers interpret John to say that Jesus was crucified and died at the hour the Passover lamb was sacrificed in the temple, rather than on the day after the Passover meal. It had been a long time since Moses and the writing of Leviticus. It is clear that, regardless of technical distinctions between the feasts of Passover and Unleavened Bread, the feasts were conflated in common parlance, Passover itself being a day of unleavened bread also. As Luke says, "the feast of Unleavened Bread . . . which is called the Passover. . . . " Furthermore, while the Jewish liturgical day starts at sundown, the common parlance of the first century AD sounds more like the day begins at sunup. Thus, Matthew, Mark, and Luke all described the daylight hours preceding the Last Supper as the first day of Unleavened Bread, though the Passover itself was the first day of Unleavened Bread, and it would have begun liturgically at the *preceding* sundown. The synoptic Gospels seem clear that the Last Supper was the Passover meal.

All four Gospels and the entire Christian tradition agree that Jesus was crucified on a Friday. The question is whether that Friday morning and afternoon was the day of Passover, running from Thursday sundown till Friday sundown, or the Day of Preparation for a Passover which began at Friday sundown. The Passover lamb was to be ritually sacrificed at 3:00 in the afternoon before the Passover meal. All Gospels relate the busy activities of the priests, the Sanhedrin, the temple guards, and the courts, all of which would have been prohibited on the Passover, which was treated for most purposes as a sabbath. It is also clear from all the Gospels that the priests wanted to conclude the arrest, trial, execution, and clearing away of the bodies before the Passover began, so they individually and the feast itself would not be ritually defiled. For example, that is why the Jews would not enter a Gentile's dwelling and had Pilate come out to them, **"so that they might not be defiled, but might eat the Passover"** (Jn 18:28).

If Passover began at sundown on Thursday, then at sundown Friday began the 15th day of the month Nissan. The 15th Nissan did not commence on a Friday in any year between AD 28–33, the period during which almost all scholars agree the Crucifixion occurred. John is in all reasonable probability correct. Passover began at sundown Friday, and the Last Supper was eaten on the day before, the Day of Preparation.

Then why did Jesus hold the Last Supper a day early and why did he and the disciples treat it as if it had been the Passover meal? Jesus obviously had sources of information (intelligence, if you will) as well as divine powers and assistance. He had become aware, or had concluded, that the temple hierarchy would arrest and execute him before the feast; otherwise, they would have to wait a week for the Feast of Unleavened Bread to end, and they feared an insurrection during that delay. Indeed, the disciples themselves anticipated such an imminent insurrection and argued about who among themselves would benefit the most from it.

Jesus therefore held the Passover a day early and celebrated it with the full ritual of Passover. **"I have earnestly desired to eat this Passover with you before I suffer"** (Lk 22:15). Since Jesus celebrated the meal as the Passover meal, the Gospel writers and the Church have done so. Just as Jesus was Lord of the sabbath, so also was he Lord of the Passover and could change its timing, as the circumstances necessitated.

Some scholars have theorized that Jesus was following a calendar used by the Essenes, a Jewish sect, under which the Passover began on Tuesday evening that year, so that the Passover meal was on Tuesday, allowing two extra days for the various interrogations and trials before crucifixion on Friday. I think that this theory most notably does not account for the delay in execution until Passover eve, when death had to be hastened, and the risk of insurrection during the two days that Jesus was being held prisoner. All the Gospel accounts give the impression of breathless speed in getting the job done in fear of intervention by Jesus' followers, the haste of a lynch mob. The Gospels have the ring of authenticity, and the theory that the proceedings dragged over a period of an extra two days has no support in scripture.

When Jesus had the householder prepare for Passover a day early, she must have been somewhat mystified. It was also unusual for Peter and John to kill the Passover lamb; that was normally done in the temple by a priest. All these unusual preparations were done in secret to safeguard the Last Supper.

Did Jesus have a source of information within the temple bureaucracy? Why not? Two members of the Sanhedrin itself are named in the Gospels as becoming Christians. If at least two members of the Sanhedrin secretly sympathized with Jesus, there undoubtedly were members of the temple bureaucracy, down to the menial workers, who also secretly sympathized, though they could not do so openly without losing their positions. If the source was still alive, he could not be named in the Gospels, just as Peter was not named as having drawn sword at Gethsemane, except in the one gospel written after he was dead.

※ ※ ※

4. When Jesus took the bread during supper, he gave thanks (hence, "Eucharist" or "Thanksgiving") and then broke it, declaring, **"This is my body"** (Mt 26:26; Mk 14:22; Lk 22:19; Jn 13:2; 1 Cor 11:24). Judas took this first communion, to his everlasting damnation. Luke makes clear that the bread, at least, was eaten before Jesus announced that he would be betrayed and before Judas left (Lk 22:19-22). The presence of Judas at the Last Supper should protect us from surprise when some Church leaders fail Jesus and the Church in our own day.

※ ※ ※

5. The disciples thought this Passover week would witness Jesus' seizure of power, restoration of the kingdom of Israel, and their own elevation to power. A dispute arose among the apostles as to which would be the greatest (Lk 22:24). Jesus both rebuked and instructed them by washing their feet. Jesus washed Judas' feet, as well as Peter's and the others' (Jn 13:3–19).

"He who has bathed does not need to wash, except for his feet. . . . " (Jn 13:10). What does that tell us about how to prepare for supper with Jesus? The disciples had bathed before the Passover meal with Jesus. They did not show up in their work clothes. If one is to have supper with the Lord, one should dress for the occasion.

Institution of the Eucharist

❖ ❖ ❖

6. At the Last Supper, Jesus placed Judas Iscariot in a place of honor, next to himself, and placed John at his other side (Jn 13:10–11, 18–19; Lk 22:21). If Jesus had known with certainty at the commencement of the meal that his betrayer was Judas, why would he have done so? What Judas had failed to learn and believe over three years' ministry, Jesus surely would not expect to teach Judas during dinner. It is more likely that he placed Judas next to himself in order to test him, and to test his own suspicion that the betrayer was Judas.

Judas had gone to the temple a day or two before the Last Supper and agreed with "the chief priests" to deliver Jesus to them (Mt 26:14; Mk 14:10). In doing so, he necessarily was passed up the line to the "chief priests," being seen and identified by a number of temple functionaries. One of these, who secretly sympathized with Jesus, recognized Judas as a disciple. In all likelihood, that temple employee contacted one of Jesus' disciples outside of Jesus' presence and told him. The temple employee did not tell Jesus directly out of fear of being seen talking to Jesus in private, with repercussions to himself. The disciple to whom this was told was neither Peter nor John, since neither of them knew at the dinner who the betrayer was (Jn 13:21–25). Jesus was then told by this disciple that Judas had been in the temple in a private audience with "the chief priests." Jesus thus had information identifying his betrayer, but such information needed further proof. Jesus therefore placed Judas next to himself in order to test the accuracy of his intelligence and the purpose of Judas' meeting with the chief priests. During the course of the evening Jesus ascertained that Satan had "entered into" Judas, whether from Judas' coldness toward him, or otherwise (Jn 13:27). Jesus had held Judas at the dinner long enough that he would not be able to inform on its location in time to disrupt it. Then Jesus sent Judas on his way. **"What you are going to do, do quickly"** (Jn 13:27). Judas left, becoming the first person to leave communion early.

Could Jesus have learned the betrayer's identity through a divine revelation instead of through a human agent? Of course. But the Lord normally works his will through human agents; God does not normally and unnecessarily work as the *deus ex machina*.

❖ ❖ ❖

7. Jesus taught the disciples during dinner. Where he was going, they could not follow, but the Father would send the Holy Spirit in Jesus' name, and Jesus would join with the Father in sending the Holy Spirit, who would further teach the disciples and **"bring to your remembrance all that I have taught you.... [I]f I do not go away, the Counselor [the Paraclete] will not come to you; but if I go, I will send him to you"** (Jn 13:36; 14:25–26; 16:7). Hence the *filioque* ("and the Son") clause in the Apostle's Creed that the Holy Spirit proceeds from the Father and the Son. He concluded with the "high priestly prayer," praying for the disciples and **"all who believe in me** through their word [emphasis supplied]...."** (Jn 17:20). Jesus had administered the first communion of his body and blood to the apostles, though none of them connected the eucharist to his words quoted in *John 6* at the time. He also consecrated them as the first priests and as apostles to the New Israel, his Church. Belief is in the person of Christ Jesus, which comes through belief "through the word" of the successors of the apostles, the bishops, and their priests, not through the worship of an infallible, but ambiguous, book.

❖ ❖ ❖

8. "'This is my body which is given for you. Do this in remembrance of me.' And likewise the cup after supper, saying, 'This cup which is poured out for you is the new covenant

in my blood'" (Lk 22:19–20; 1 Cor 11:23–26). The Church's liturgy has always consecrated the bread, then the wine.

On an earlier occasion, the disciples had asked Jesus, **"'Then what sign do you do that we may see, and believe you? Our fathers ate the manna in the wilderness, as it is written, 'gave them bread from heaven to eat.' Jesus then said to them, 'Truly, truly, I say to you, it was not Moses who gave you the bread from heaven; my Father gives you the true bread from heaven. For the bread of God is that which comes down from heaven, and gives life to the world'"** (Jn 6:30–33). It is God, not Moses, who sent the bread from heaven.

The disciples ask for such bread. **"They said to him, 'Lord, give us this bread always.' Jesus said to them, 'I am the bread of life; he who comes to me shall not hunger, and he who believes in me shall never thirst'"** (Jn 6:34–35). Jesus ambiguously suggests that in some way he is, or can provide, the bread from heaven.

The disciples question how this can be, since they think they know that Jesus did not come down from heaven. **"The Jews then murmured at him, because he said, 'I am the bread which came down from heaven.' Is not this Jesus, the son of Joseph, whose father and mother we know? How does he now say, 'I have come down from heaven'?"** (Jn 6:41–42).

"I am the bread of life. Your fathers ate the manna in the wilderness, and they died. This is the bread which comes down from heaven, that a man may eat of it and not die. I am the living bread which came down from heaven; if any one eats of this bread, he will live forever; and the bread which I shall give for the life of the world is my flesh" (Jn 6:48–51).

❖ ❖ ❖

Jesus claims that in some fashion he himself is the bread from heaven, and in some fashion one can eat of his flesh.

The disciples are skeptical and puzzled. "**The Jews then disputed among themselves, saying, 'How can this man give us his flesh to eat?' So Jesus said to them, 'Truly, truly, I say to you, unless you eat the flesh of the Son of Man and drink his blood, you shall have no life in you; he who eats my flesh and drinks my blood has eternal life, and I will raise him up on the last day. For my flesh is food indeed, and my blood is drink indeed. He who eats my flesh and drinks my blood abides in me, and I in him. As the living Father sent me, and I live because of the Father, so he who eats me will live because of me. This is the bread which came down from heaven, not such as the fathers ate and died; he who eats this bread will live forever'"** (Jn 6: 52–58).

Jesus removes all ambiguity from his teaching and is crystal clear as to what he demands the disciples accept.

The disciples are horrified. "**This he said in the synagogue, as he taught at Capernaum. Many of his disciples, when they heard it, said, 'This is a hard saying; who can listen to it?' . . . After this many of his disciples drew back and no longer went about with him. Jesus said to the twelve, 'Do you also wish to go away?' Simon Peter answered him, 'Lord, to whom shall we go? You have the words of eternal life; and we have believed, and come to know, that you are the Holy One of God'"** (Jn 6:59–60, 66–69).

Transubstantiation. Jesus taught it, here insistently and explicitly, as do many other passages of the New Testament. As did the Fathers. St. Ignatius, in his *Letter to the Church at Smyrna*, written in AD 107 as he was on his way to Rome to be executed: "**They [the heterodox] abstain from the eucharist and from prayer, because they do not confess that the eucharist is the flesh of our Savior Jesus Christ.**" And this from St. Justin Martyr's *First Apology*, written before his martyrdom about AD 150. "**For we do not receive these as common bread and common drink; but**

just as Jesus Christ our Savior, having been made flesh by the word of God, had both flesh and blood for our salvation, so likewise have we learned that the food over which thanks has been given by the prayer of the word which comes from him and by which our blood and flesh are nourished through a change, is the flesh and blood of the same incarnate Jesus." The quotations from the Fathers could be multiplied, but not here.

The usual Protestant response, even among those who claim to read the Bible as the literal and/or inerrant word of God, is to pass this off as Jesus' speaking metaphorically, as where he elsewhere calls himself a door or a vine. But in the long passage quoted from *John 6*, every time the Jews and most disciples murmur, Jesus grinds the lesson in ever more explicitly, finally being brutally graphic as to what he meant. What Jew did not hear him with horror? They would not even eat the blood of a sheep, but this rabbi was insisting that they drink his blood! The whole passage reeks of cannibalism, an accusation frequently made against the early Church. When most of his disciples were leaving him, Jesus did not call them back and say, "Now, now, I was only speaking metaphorically, symbolically." No. He let them go. The twelve apostles were in shock. Simon Peter could only speak for them in saying, "Lord, to whom shall we go? You have the words of eternal life. . . . " Jesus meant exactly what he said, but no man could imagine how he would do it. Jesus explained the manner of doing so at the Last Supper, but no apostle grasped it until after the Resurrection.

On the very day before Jesus' exchange with his disciples which caused most of them to leave him, he had given them a demonstration of his power. He had fed more than 5,000 people with five loaves of bread and two fish (Jn 6:1-14). He thereby exhibited his miraculous power to multiply the subjects of the miracle to whatever number he chose. Just as, in the Mass, the substance of his body, contained in the Hosts, can be multiplied into as many Hosts as are consecrated. On the night following the feeding of the 5,000, Jesus again demonstrated his control over the normal operations of nature. He walked on the Sea of Galilee three or four miles to the boat, and then the boat immediately arrived at its destination (Jn 6:16-21). At the wedding in Cana, he had changed one substance—water—into another—wine. These miracles, two occurring within twenty-four hours preceding his dialogue with the disciples, showed them that he could perform the miracle of feeding them his body and blood. The timing of these miracles was no coincidence. At the Last Supper, Jesus showed the disciples how they and their successors would duplicate this miracle, as it is done thousands of times every day, all over the world, every time the sacrifice of the Mass is offered.

Transubstantiation. It has stuck in the craw of a long line of successors to the disciples who "drew back and no longer went about with him." When believers have in good faith doubted the dogma and prayed for assistance to overcome their unbelief, the Lord has answered the prayers of at least two such doubters in spectacular fashion.

During the eighth century the iconoclast Byzantine emperors persecuted the Catholics. A monastery of refugee Basilian (Greek rite) monks was established as St. Legontian at Lanciano, Italy, a few miles from the Adriatic coast. The name of the monk is lost in the mists of time, but the story is that he constantly prayed to overcome his doubt as to whether the consecrated bread and wine are truly the body and blood of Christ. One day, as he was celebrating Mass, as he spoke the words of consecration, the elements visibly became flesh and blood. The congregation responded to his outcry and was likewise overcome. The host and five globules into which the blood congealed have been preserved for more than 1,200 years and are on exhibition behind the altar of St.

Francis' Church, built over the earlier St. Legontian. One may walk entirely around the relics and examine them closely.

In 1970 the relics were examined, with permission of the ecclesiastical authorities, by two professors on the medical faculties of the Universities of Arezzo and Siena, Italy. This examination predated testing of the blood on the Shroud of Turin (see below). The professors found that the five globules are dried blood. The Host is a cross-section of a human heart. The blood type of both is AB, later found to be the blood type on the Shroud of Turin and on the Sudarium of Oviedo (see below). The section of the heart is a vertical one, containing tissue from both an auricular (upper) and a ventricular (lower) chamber, so that the entire heart is represented by the section. The section is an "even and continuous slice." Since the first anatomic dissections on a human body were done in the fourteenth century, it is impossible that anyone could have created such a section in the eighth century, and only a handful of trained people could have done so after the fourteenth century. In all probability the relics are what they purport to be—a miraculous gift of the body and blood of Christ, in order that, like Thomas, we may "not be faithless, but believing."

The second miraculous event is thoroughly documented. A German priest, Peter of Prague, was experiencing doubt about transubstantiation. He made a pilgrimage to Rome in 1263, praying that it would resolve his doubt. Unsuccessful, he started home on the road north, Via Cassia, stopping at Bolsena about seventy-five miles from Rome. He celebrated his daily Mass at Santa Cristina before an eighth century altar, praying for faith. As he consecrated the Host, it bled profusely, and he wrapped it in the corporal (a linen cloth on which the consecrated elements are placed). The congregation crowded around him and saw the Host bleeding. It bled on the corporal, the purificators, and onto the marble altar steps and floor. Pope Urban IV and his court were at

Orvieto, twenty-five miles to the east. Peter of Prague, the clergy of Santa Cristina, and the witnesses went to Orvieto to notify the Pope of this extraordinary event. He sent the Bishop of Orvieto and two theologians, Thomas Aquinas and Bonaventure, to Bolsena to take the depositions of all the witnesses and to ascertain the facts. Upon examination of the depositions, the decision was made to transfer the relics to Orvieto, the diocesan seat. The Pope and a great procession came out to meet and receive the relics and take them to the cathedral. On September 8, 1264, Urban IV proclaimed the Feast of Corpus Christi to celebrate the institution of the Eucharist and the gift of Christ's body and blood, which are touched on but submerged in the many other events of Holy Week and Holy Thursday. The Pope asked Thomas Aquinas and Bonaventure to submit to him their proposals for a liturgy for the new feast. Thomas worked faster. When Bonaventure saw Thomas' proposal, he tore up his own and asked the Pope to use Thomas'. Thomas composed some of the Church's greatest hymns as a portion of the Corpus Christi liturgy, including *Pange lingua* and *Adoro te devote*.

The relics are kept and, in part, exhibited at Orvieto Cathedral and Santa Cristina. The corporal is on view above the altar of the Chapel of the Corporal in Orvieto. There are numerous blood stains of varying sizes scattered upon the linen. The remains of the Host and the purificators are kept in a reliquary and are not on view. Unlike the miracle at Lanciano, the Host did not change its accidents; it remained bread, now just crumbs, but it miraculously bled. The wine was unaffected. At Santa Cristina in Bolsena, four pieces of marble are on view above a chapel altar. Though the stone is impermeable, it nevertheless was permanently stained with the blood that fell upon it.

Of the artistic renditions of the miracle at Bolsena, Raphael's fresco in the Raphael Rooms in the Vatican is not only the best known, but it is also truly sublime in capturing the expression of Peter of Prague. The first time I saw it, I considered it to be Counter-Reformation propaganda. But it was painted by Raphael in 1512, five years before Luther nailed his theses to the door in Wittenberg, Germany.

What are we to make of Christ's consecration of the bread and wine that Thursday night? What the Christian Church, except for the Reformation and its progeny, has always taught is that the bread and wine become in fact the body and blood of Jesus. How they do so is a mystery.

Thomas Aquinas, relying on the distinctions formulated in Greek philosophy, took the description one step further into the mystery. He contended that the elements, the bread and wine, remain unchanged as to their "accidents," their physical characteristics. Put under a microscope, they are still bread and wine. However, upon the pronouncement of Christ's words by a validly ordained priest, acting as the agent of his bishop, a successor to the apostles, the unseen substance of the elements is radically and miraculously transformed. They become in fact the body and blood of Christ, with the effects on us that Jesus described in *John 6*. I am aware that some argue from modern physics that the Thomist explanation is scientifically incorrect and that one must rely simply on the mystery, which is where the Church was before Aquinas. Until science comes up with some explanation that can replace the one step forward into the mystery taken by Aquinas, I submit that the Thomist explanation is an improvement toward understanding the mystery.

John the Baptist identified Jesus as the "Lamb of God," the sacrificial lamb. Jesus' death at the hour of the sacrifice clearly identifies the sacrificial lamb as the Passover lamb. To be efficacious, the Passover lamb was not merely adored; it had to be eaten. Jesus likewise must not just be worshiped; he also must be eaten.

In his mercy the Lord has granted the miracles at Lanciano and Bolsena in order to fortify our own faith and belief in the occurrence of the miracles on our altars, in our presence, which, absent faith, are literally incredible.

※ ※ ※

9. Jesus and the eleven remaining apostles sang a closing hymn, "The Great Hallel," Psalms 115–118; "The Little Hallel," Psalms 113–114 having been sung before the meal (Mt 26:30). Psalm 115 is *Non nobis Domine* (Not to us, O Lord), which was sung centuries later by Henry V after Agincourt. Luke, having described the first three cups, does not mention the fourth, taken with the Great Hallel.

Some scholars argue that Jesus altered the Passover liturgy by omitting the fourth cup, or that the fourth cup was his sacrifice on Calvary. Some others argue that the vinegar (sour wine) given to Jesus, hanging on the cross, on a stalk of hyssop was the fourth cup, thereby completing the Passover meal on Calvary. I incline to the last theory. Jesus deliberately omitted the fourth cup of the Passover ritual, because he supernaturally foresaw, as part of the preview of his crucifixion, the offering to him of sour wine on a hyssop stalk as the fourth cup of the Passover ritual. I believe that his prayer at Gethsemane that "this cup" might pass from him without his having to drink it, refers literally to the sour wine he tasted at the Crucifixion being the fourth cup, rather than metaphorically referring to the entire ordeal at Calvary as being a "cup."

※ ※ ※

10. Jesus and the apostles, followed by John Mark, left the upper room of the house on Mount Zion. They descended the hill along a street broken by many steps which one may walk today in Jesus' path, to a city gate. They went out the gate and walked to the left, toward the head of Brook Kidron, and around to the brook's far side, where there was an olive grove and an olive press at the base of the Mount of Olives.

THE SORROWFUL
MYSTERIES

Seizure of Christ, Anthony van Dyck, 1620–1621, Museo del Prado, Madrid

THE AGONY IN THE GARDEN

1. Jesus and the eleven apostles went into an olive grove at the base of the Mount of Olives, followed by John Mark. In the olive grove was a grotto, the site of an oil press, called Gethsemane (the grotto and its press, not the grove). The grotto is irregular in shape, but generally 54' x 30' and up to 11' high. It was well-suited as accommodation for Jesus and his apostles to sleep and use as their base close to the city. The owner obviously was a disciple.

Jesus called aside Peter, James, and John. It is likely that Jesus and the three apostles went outside the grotto into the olive grove, leaving the other apostles to sleep in the grotto. Jesus told them that his soul was sorrowful, even unto death, and asked them to sit and watch with him while he went apart from them a stone's throw to pray (Lk 22:41). Jesus fell on his face and prayed, **"My Father, if it be possible, let this cup pass from me; nevertheless, not as I will, but as thou wilt"** (Mt 26:36–39). Who overheard the prayer? Perhaps Peter, James, or John did before they fell asleep, but a stone's throw is a long distance. More likely it was young John Mark, who, stirred by his adventure, came close and heard Jesus' prayer. It has been envisioned that in this prayer Jesus foresaw in agonizing detail the suffering he was about to undergo.

2. Jesus returned to the three apostles and found them asleep. Jesus woke them and rebuked them for not watching one hour. He told them to watch and pray not to be tempted (Mt 26:40–41). Jesus went apart and, being reconciled to his fate, prayed, **"If this cannot pass unless I drink it, thy will be done"** (Mt 26:42).

Again, it has been envisioned that in this prayer Jesus saw the sins of the world which he would be asked to bear, all past, present, and future sins, and the weight of sin almost overwhelmed him who had never sinned.

Such a theory would explain how my individual sins have caused Jesus to suffer 2,000 years ago and how I helped crucify him. Whenever I resist sin, I lessen the burden he foresaw and whose weight he felt then. This interpretation is based on a visionary, Anne Catherine Emmerich. There is no possible evidence for or against, but it is an interesting hypothesis.

3. Jesus returned a second time and again found the three apostles asleep. He rebuked them and returned to his prayers (Mk 14:40). He again prayed his acceptance of the Father's will (Mt 26:44). It has been envisioned that in this prayer Jesus foresaw all the sinners who would ungratefully scorn and even denounce his sacrifice for them, adding greater weight to the burden of their sin which he foresaw that he would have to assume. It has also been envisioned that Satan tempted him at Gethsemane, arguing that the burden of all the world's sins was impossible to bear, especially when so many sinners would reject him, and his sacrifice for them would be useless. When Satan left Jesus after tempting him in the wilderness, he departed **"from him until an opportune time."** What could be a more opportune time for Satan's return (Lk 4:13)? When could Jesus have been more vulnerable? The temptation, if it occurred, was successfully resisted.

❖ ❖ ❖

4. Jesus sweated blood (Lk 22:44). Under great emotional stress, capillaries in the sweat glands can rupture and excrete blood, called hemohidrosis. This condition causes the skin to become extremely tender and fragile and enhanced Jesus' suffering from scourging and crucifixion.

❖ ❖ ❖

5. Being outside the grotto, Jesus could not have failed to see the crowd approaching across the narrow Kidron valley. He awaited his "hour." Jesus returned the third time and woke the three apostles just as Judas entered the olive grove, leading a "crowd" (Lk 22:47). The crowd with Judas is variously described as **"a great crowd with swords and clubs, from the chief priests and the elders of the people"** (the Sanhedrin) (Mt 26:47; Mk 14:43) or as **"chief priests and captains of the temple and elders"** (Lk 22:52) or as **"a band of soldiers and some officers from the chief priests and the Pharisees"** or **"the band of soldiers and their captain and the officers of the Jews"** (Jn 18:3, 12). The group included at least one slave of the high priest (Mt 26:51; Mk 14:47; Lk 22:50; Jn 18:10). The "great crowd" included high-ranking temple officials, Pharisees, and some of their servants and slaves. It also included some soldiers, or temple guards, with several of their officers. Some in the crowd were armed with swords and some just with clubs. It seems clear that the soldiers, or temple guards, were there as individuals accompanying the high officials, along with their servants and slaves, rather than as an organized military unit. The temple guards had no jurisdiction outside the temple, and the presence of an organized unit at Gethsemane could have constituted an insurrection. *Acts* shows that it was the Roman troops, not Jewish soldiers (temple guards), who had jurisdiction to preserve order in Jerusalem outside the temple precincts (Acts 21:30–36).

Judas knew where to bring the high priest's men because he knew where Jesus customarily spent the night (Lk 22:39; Jn 18:2). Jesus could have avoided capture that night by staying at a different location. Jesus met them and asked, **"'Whom do you seek?' 'Jesus of Nazareth.' 'I am he.'"** The guards and others drew back and fell to the ground (Jn 18:4–6). Jesus thereby asserted his divinity, "I am," and emphasized that he was not to be killed at the will of his enemies but rather laid down his life voluntarily. Judas recovered and came forward in the deep darkness of the grove to kiss Jesus, that being the sign identifying Jesus for his seizure. Judas said, **"Hail Master"** as he kissed Jesus. Even then Jesus gave Judas a chance to repent, saying, **"Friend, why are you here?"** (Mt 26:49–50). But Judas was not to be deterred. Jesus turned to the guards and said, **"[I]f you seek me, let these men go"** (Jn 18:8).

6. During the Last Supper Jesus told his apostles that one who had no sword should sell his mantle and buy one. They answered that they had two swords available, and Jesus said it was enough (Lk 22:36–38). It appears that at least some of the apostles, including Peter, anticipated an attack on Jesus during the coming establishment of the Messiah's kingdom and were prepared to defend him. Two of the apostles had armed themselves, apparently without Jesus' knowledge, judging from his statement. As the guards and servants of the high priest surged forward to seize Jesus, Peter drew a sword and cut off the ear of one of the high priest's slaves, Malchus (Jn 18:10–11). *John* is the only Gospel which identifies Peter by name as the apostle wielding the sword. The other three Gospels describe the event without naming the apostle who cut off Malchus' ear (Mt 26:51; Mk 14:47; Lk 22:49–50). This strengthens the conclusion that the first three Gospels were written before Peter's death and did not identify him, in order to avoid incriminating him. John's Gospel was written after Peter's death, when he could no longer be harmed by the identification. Jesus ordered the apostles to cease resistance. **"No more of this"** (Lk 22:51).

7. Jesus said to Peter, **"Put your sword into its sheath; shall I not drink the cup which the Father has given me?"** (Jn 18:11; Mt 26:52–54). The apostles then scattered, while the guards snatched at them in the darkness. It was in the melee that a "young man," identified by many writers as John Mark, escaped by slipping out of his tunic, leaving it in a guard's hands as he ran off naked (Mk 14:51–52). I am aware that Papias, writing in the early second century, says that John Mark had not "heard" or "followed" Jesus. I construe this to mean that he had not studied under Jesus or traveled with him. This is not inconsistent with John Mark's having met Jesus in his home.

8. Jesus put out his hand and healed Malchus' ear (Lk 22:51). Why did Jesus tell the disciples to bring swords to Gethsemane, when he had no intention of resisting arrest? He had supernaturally foreseen the event. Malchus was a slave, not just a servant but a slave, of the high priest (Jn 18:10). Since a Jew could not own

another Jew, Malchus was a gentile. Jesus' last miracle before his death was to heal a gentile, and that was precisely what he had arranged. Note that all four Gospels describe the cutting off of the ear of the high priest's slave. It is unusual for all four to describe the same event in such detail, which emphasizes its importance.

❖ ❖ ❖

9. The guards secured Jesus. He was the only one they had orders to arrest; if they had had orders to arrest all the apostles, they would have arrested John when he showed up at Annas' house that night or at the cross (Jn 18:13–15). Jesus was led bound out of the grove, while the apostles scattered in fear.

❖ ❖ ❖

10. Much has been written of the supposed cowardice of the apostles and the supposed bluster of their repeated assertions of willingness to defend him or die with him. At least two, including Peter, went secretly armed to protect him. The apostles resisted at Gethsemane, even to armed resistance against overwhelming odds, until Jesus ordered them to desist and clearly surrendered himself. Then they fled and scattered, leaderless, in small groups. If Jesus had led the apostles in resistance, they undoubtedly would have fought, but he ordered them not to resist. U.S. Army doctrine says that whether men fight, or not, depends on leadership. Travis' men fought to the death at the Alamo, while Fannin surrendered a force more than twice Travis's size, only to be subsequently massacred at Goliad. Leadership is all. The apostles' fear was appropriate; there was much to fear, and Peter's three-fold denial was not the mark of one willing to die. But too much is made of "cowardice" when they did fight until their leader ordered them to stop.

Christ before Pilate, Jacopo Robusti Tintoretto, Schola di San Rocco, Venice

THE SCOURGING AT THE PILLAR

❖

PREFACE TO "THE SCOURGING" AND "THE CROWNING"

In these meditations on the scourging and the crowning with thorns, I am aware that the synoptic Gospels sometimes appear to place these events in a sequence different from that given here. I submit that a careful reading shows that the synoptic Gospels are abbreviated, leaving out many of the events, such as Jesus' being taken initially to Annas' house rather than Caiaphas'. They also, like much of scripture, are not strictly chronological. John, the eyewitness, tells a more nearly chronological tale, taking it step by step. Since he wrote after the other three, it may be inferred that his detailed description of the stages of each event was deliberate in order that the details not be lost. I have therefore generally followed John's chronology, inserting details found in the synoptic Gospels not dealt with by John.

❖ ❖ ❖

1. Jesus was taken bound from Gethsemane to the house of Annas. Annas was father-in-law of the high priest, Caiaphas. Both Annas and other members of his family had been high priests, but his own term of office had expired. He was not of the Levitical priesthood, but rather one of the political appointees of the Herodian dynasty. Scribes and some members of the Sanhedrin had gathered at Annas' house (Mt 26:57).

John followed Jesus and his guard to Annas' house. Since John was known to Annas, he entered the courtyard with Jesus and his guard (Jn 18:15–16). How was John known to Annas? His father, Zebedee, was a Galilean, the owner of fishing boats on Lake Tiberias (the Sea of Galilee).

While it is possible that John's family had social or business connections with the temple hierarchy, it is more likely that he had studied under one or more rabbis in the temple for a period of years and was thereby known to the temple hierarchy. The Jews later lumped John with Peter, "calling both of them 'uneducated, common men'" (Acts 4:13), but they said essentially the same thing about Jesus (Jn 7:15). This meant only that the priests, Pharisees, and rabbis, in their own professional eyes, considered them all to be laymen. We may infer that John did not complete his studies, considering his youth, but he obviously learned much theology at some time, as evidenced by his Gospel. Some amount of temple training also would be consistent with his very Jewish Christian writings. He returned to Galilee to fish, rather than pursue a career in the temple, perhaps because he was not pleased with what he saw of the temple establishment. Some scholars have suggested that John's temple connection was that Zebedee was a priest. I consider it unlikely that a priest could fulfill his duties from Capernaum, necessitating each year six trips to Jerusalem of twenty-three days each.

Peter initially stood outside the door, but John saw him and brought him in (Jn 18:16). It was at the house of the ex-high priest Annas that Peter denied Jesus thrice. The synoptic Gospels all conflate the events at Annas' house with those at Caiaphas' house. They all describe Peter's three-fold denial as occurring at "the high priest's house," not identifying by name which high priest was meant, except in *Matthew 26:57*, which says Jesus was taken to Caiaphas, the high priest, and then places Peter's denial in the "high priest's" house, without mentioning the stop at Annas' house. John, in addition to being the only apostle with temple "connections," is also the only eyewitness of the events at both houses. I conclude that the activities at the houses of Annas and Caiaphas were separate events. John describes Peter's denials and then says: **"Annas then sent him** [Jesus] **bound to Caiaphas, the high priest"** (Jn 18:24).

Annas attempted a little pre-trial discovery in questioning Jesus, but Jesus would not be drawn. He referred Annas to his witnesses (Jn 18:19–21). An officer struck Jesus with his hand. Jesus replied, **"If I have spoken wrongly, bear witness to the wrong; but if I have spoken rightly, why do you strike me?"** (Jn 18:22–23). Thus, this first blow was obviously unlawful. Others mocked him and beat him also (Lk 22:63–65). Having failed to draw Jesus into self-incrimination, Annas sent him bound to Caiaphas, the high priest (Jn 18:24). In order to convene the Sanhedrin for a sunrise trial, Annas undoubtedly sent runners to summon the seventy-one members of the Sanhedrin to meet at Caiaphas' house at first light.

❦ ❦ ❦

2. Under Jewish law, a trial could only be conducted in the daytime. The Sanhedrin assembled at Caiaphas' house at first light so as to be ready to proceed at sunrise. It is significant that they were called to meet at Caiaphas' house instead of in their own council chamber in the temple, even though the temple gates opened at dawn. Annas and Caiaphas sought to keep the public in the dark until presented with a *fait accompli.*

Jesus stood mute and would not testify (Mt 26:63). **"[L]ike a lamb that is led to the slaughter, and like a sheep that before its shearers is dumb, so he opened not his mouth"** (Is 53:7). The witnesses against him did not agree in their testimony, an absolute requirement of Jewish law (Mt 26:59–61; Mk 14:56–59). Jesus still refused to testify (Mk 14:60–61). Caiaphas' prosecution was failing. In frustration, Caiaphas turned to Jesus and demanded to know if he were **"the Christ, the Son of God"** (Mt 26:62; Mk 14:60–61). Caiaphas' inquiry as to whether Jesus was "the Son of God" was clearly understood as being a claim to divinity. Such claims by kings were common in the East—for example, the Pharaohs of Egypt, Alexander the Great's claim to be the son of Amon, and claims to divinity by his successors and, even in the years just previously, by the Roman emperors. Jesus then confessed that he was indeed both the Christ and the Son of God. **"I am, and you will see the Son of Man seated at the right hand of Power, and coming with the clouds of heaven"** (Mk 14:62; Mt 26:64). Whereupon, Caiaphas declared Jesus guilty of blasphemy in the Sanhedrin's own hearing, so that other witnesses were unnecessary. The Sanhedrin voted to find him worthy of the death sentence (Mt 26:65–66; Mk 14:63–64; Lk 22:71). After Jesus' conviction, many members of the Sanhedrin spat on him and slapped and struck him and the guards received him back into their custody with blows (Mk 14:65; Mt 26:67).

3. The Sanhedrin, however, could not execute a death sentence; only the Roman government could now do that. Upon

Jesus' conviction by the Sanhedrin not long after sunrise, he was led bound to the praetorium, then located at the Antonia fortress. The Romans had taken possession of Herod the Great's palace when direct Roman rule was established upon the deposition of Archelaus in AD 6. Herod's palace was the seat of Roman administration and the normal residence of the Roman governor. Some writers claim that Jesus was taken to Pilate at the palace rather than to the Antonia. However, the most dangerous times for a possible insurrection were during the major feasts, when Jerusalem swelled with the crowds of pilgrims. It is highly likely that Pilate, with his household, moved to the Antonia during such times, both for security and to be in direct control of the Roman garrison, which was quartered in the Antonia. Some activities at the praetorium, such as scourging a convict and serving as a jail for two thieves awaiting execution, accord better with a fortress containing barracks than with a residential and administrative palace. The Gospels refer to the praetorium as Pilate's headquarters, but it is likely that the praetorium moved with Pilate.

Pilate is referred to in the Gospels as the "procurator." As is shown by an inscription stone found at Caesarea, Pilate's title was actually "prefect." All governors in Judea held that title until Claudius resumed direct Roman rule in AD 44 after Herod Agrippa's death, when dual jurisdiction with local kings finally ceased, and the governors thereafter were given the title of procurator. The Gospels anachronistically gave Pilate the title of the Roman governor at the time the Gospels were written. As an accommodation to the Jews, Pilate came outside so the Jews would not defile themselves by entering a gentile's house, thereby becoming ritually unclean and unable to eat the Passover (Jn 18:29–31). Pilate asked what the prisoner was accused of. He asked Jesus if he was king of the Jews and Jesus ambiguously affirmed it, but Jesus would not respond to questions from the Jews (Mt 27:11–14; Mk 15:2–5).

Pilate suggested that the Jews judge him by their own law (Jn 18:29–30). The Jews replied that they no longer could execute a prisoner, the crux of their bringing Jesus to Pilate (Jn 18:31–32). They told Pilate that Jesus stirred up the people, teaching from Galilee to Jerusalem (Lk 23:5). As a man who had been exposed to the philosophical education of his day, Pilate had a distaste for what he perceived as the Jews' interminable religious controversies. Pilate immediately sought his way out, for the first time. He asked whether Jesus was a Galilean. When Pilate learned that Jesus was subject to Herod Antipas' jurisdiction, he sent Jesus to Herod Antipas, who was in Jerusalem for Passover (Lk 23:6–7). Herod's Jerusalem residence was the old Hasmonean palace, on what is now David Street, a ten- to fifteen-minute walk from the Antonia.

❖ ❖ ❖

4. Herod Antipas had heard about Jesus' miracles and hoped to have Jesus perform some miracle or magic trick for his amusement. Herod questioned Jesus, but Jesus would not answer, enraging Herod. By way of mocking Jesus' purported claim to be king of the Jews, Herod arrayed Jesus in a robe of royal purple and sent him back to Pilate (Lk 23:8–11). The distances in Jerusalem were short, so Jesus was back at the praetorium less than an hour after he left it.

❖ ❖ ❖

5. When the Jews returned from Herod, Pilate called Jesus into the praetorium and examined him (Jn 18:33). Pilate sensed that the charges against Jesus were driven by malice, and his wife had warned him, **"Have nothing to do with that righteous man, for I have suffered much over him today in a dream"** (Mt

27:18–19). In the privacy of the praetorium, Pilate interrogated Jesus regarding his alleged kingship. Pilate concluded his interrogation, "**So you are a king?**" Jesus answered Pilate, "**You say that I am a king.**" In idiom, that was an affirmative answer. As in, "**Are you the son of God?**" "**You say that I am**" (Lk 22:70). Jesus added that his kingdom was not of this world, but rather that he had come into the world to bear witness to the truth. "**Every one who is of the truth hears my voice.**" Pilate responded with a jaded philosophical inquiry, "**What is truth?**" (Jn 18:33–38). The sophists of his day denied the possibility of knowing the truth. The "leaders" of our own secular culture even deny the existence of objective truth. Today is the age of "my truth" and "your truth" in which all "truths" are relative.

Who was the witness to this dialogue? Perhaps it was the centurion or perhaps it was Pilate's wife; there is tradition that both converted to Christianity. It could have been a Jew, since Romans, like many others, regarded slaves and servants as not being present while their "betters" discussed matters before them. By this time, Pilate had no intention of executing Jesus. Calculating that the strange man before him who had been rapturously received by the crowds only days earlier would be popular with the Jerusalem crowd, Pilate sought a second time to evade responsibility. Pilate announced to the Jews that he found Jesus guilty of no crime deserving death (Jn 18:38; Lk 23:13–16).

❖ ❖ ❖

6. There was a custom at Passover that amnesty would be granted to a prisoner favored by the crowd. Pilate submitted to the crowd a choice between Jesus and Barabbas, a murderer in an insurrection (Mk 15:6–7; Mt 27:20–23; Lk 23:18–25; Jn 18:38–40). Pilate expected Jesus to be favored, but he had not reckoned on the ability of the Sanhedrin to influence their people or on the disillusionment of the crowd with a prisoner whose helplessness obviously proved him to be no Messiah, or on the patriotic sentiment in favor of one who had participated in insurrection against Rome. The crowd vociferously chose Barabbas. Pilate's intent had clearly been to avoid scourging Jesus by having him released under amnesty.

"Barabbas" is actually "bar Abbas," or "Son of the Father." Origen says that some early manuscripts named him "Jesus bar Abbas." The priests and their mob were thus offered a choice between a potential Messiah claimant who kills and a Messiah who suffers.

❧ ❧ ❧

7. The timing of Pilate's release of Barabbas is not clear. *Matthew* definitely describes Pilate's washing of his hands before releasing Barabbas (Mt 27:15–26). *Matthew* sums up by saying that Barabbas was released before Jesus was scourged and crucified (Mt 27:26). *John* is less detailed. He only implies that Barabbas was released at an unspecified time. He follows by saying that Jesus was scourged (Jn 18:39–19:1). *Matthew* is clear that Barabbas was released after Pilate washed his hands "of that righteous man's blood" (Mt 27:24). But, the washing of hands could not have occurred before Pilate pronounced final judgment. Indeed, he was still trying to release Jesus after the scourging. I conclude that Pilate held Barabbas until the affair had played out so that he could change course if the situation changed. He was ultimately released after Pilate had pronounced his sentence and washed his hands. Pilate held to his judgment that he found Jesus guilty of no crime deserving death. But Pilate did order that Jesus be chastised by scourging and then released.(Lk 23:22).

If Pilate thought Jesus was innocent, why did he have him scourged? The answer is that Pilate did not say that he thought Jesus was innocent; he said that he thought Jesus did not deserve death. He found that Jesus was claimed by many of his followers to be the king of the Jews; though Jesus did not make that claim in an earthly sense himself, he had not discouraged it. This did not quite amount to insurrection on Jesus' part, but it fell a long way short of guiltless conduct in Rome's and Pilate's eyes and deserved scourging.

8. Jesus was scourged. Jewish law limited the number of lashes, but Roman law did not. The study of the Shroud of Turin shows that two men, standing behind Jesus and on either side of him, beat him with the *flagrum,* a whip with multiple thongs tipped with bar-bell shaped pieces of lead. Jesus was disrobed for the scourging. According to the Shroud, he received strokes sufficient to inflict more than 100 wounds, each about 2" long.

9. The Shroud of Turin, a linen burial shroud now owned by the Pope, is in the Cathedral in Turin, Italy. It shows the image of a man, front and back, whose injuries are those described in the Gospels. The image is a yellow-brown color, similar to a scorch, whose incredible detail has been gradually revealed by modern technology since 1898, when the first photographs showed that the image is a photographic negative. It contains details no forger could have known; indeed, not one of the many debunkers of the Shroud's authenticity has demonstrated a way to reproduce the image.

While art has generally shown Jesus pierced through the palms of his hands, the Shroud shows him to have been pierced through his wrists. The Greek word used for "hand" extends to, and includes, the wrist. Nails through the palms would not support the weight and would tear loose, while nails through the wrist would not only hold, there was also the additional benefit of inflicting excruciating nerve pain. The nail through the wrists causes the thumb to fold into the palm; the Shroud shows eight fingers, but no thumbs.

Again, the Shroud shows the flow of blood down the forearms is in a zig-zag pattern. A crucified prisoner actually dies from asphyxiation. In order to breath, the prisoner would endure the pain of lifting himself up on his pierced feet or ankles until he could no longer endure the pain and would then sink down again. This rise and fall in his posture affected the angle of his forearms and created a zig-zag pattern of blood flow.

Again, the eyes of the man on the Shroud were covered with small coins. Enhanced photography shows that one of these was minted by Pilate. The coin even misspells the name, in Greek, of Tiberius Caesar. When the debunkers cried, "Aha, a forgery!" six different collectors came forward who had coins struck from the same defective die. I could go on and on, but it is not the thrust of these meditations to prove the authenticity of the Shroud of Turin.

❖ ❖ ❖

10. The first documented exhibition of the Shroud in the West was in 1357 in France in the possession of the widow and young son of a French knight, Geoffrey de Charny (also "Charnay"). Members of his family, including relations by marriage, had participated in the fourth "Crusade" that besieged and sacked Constantinople (now Istanbul) in 1203–1204. Most of the Byzantine Empire was divided into Latin principalities, and his family's members had been involved in various Latin principalities as late as 1313. During the Byzantine revival, his family returned to France. One theory is that the Shroud had fallen into their hands and been passed down for 150 years.

I think that a second theory has recently been proven. In 1205 the Shroud was said to have been taken from Constantinople to Athens and was in the possession of Otho de la Roche, second-in-command of the "Crusade," who received Athens and Thessalonika as his reward. The Shroud was seen in Athens in 1207. De la Roche became Preceptor of the Knights Templar in 1225. In 1306 King Philip the Fair of France, fearful of the Templars' power and independence and covetous of their wealth, began an investigation of the Templars that included charges that they worshiped some sort of picture of a head. In 1307 the Templars were suppressed, and their French property was seized by the crown. In 1314 a Geoffrey de Charny, Templar Master of Normandy, was burned at the stake with the last Grand Master. The Templars' vow of chastity means that the later Geoffrey de Charny was not a legitimate son of the Normandy Master. While a family relationship has not been established, it is obvious that the Geoffrey de Charny whose family produced the Shroud in 1357 had been named for the Templar Master.

The Shroud was in the custody of the Templars until their suppression. The Templars were rich, powerful, and secretive, and it is more likely that the Shroud passed through a succession of its officers rather than through a family of minor nobility. The custodianship by the Templars has recently (2009) been firmly established. The statements taken from Templars during the proceedings to suppress them were found to include the statement of a French Templar, Arnaud Sabbatier, who testified that during his initiation in France in 1287, he was shown a long linen cloth with the figure of a man on it, and he kissed the image of the man's feet three times. Upon the Templars' suppression, the Shroud was kept hidden by the family of the Templar officer who had it last.

What changed between the Templars' suppression in 1307 and the production of the Shroud for public view in 1357? In 1328, Edward III of England claimed the French crown by inheritance through his mother, commencing the Hundred Years War between England and France. In 1346, Edward, Prince of Wales, known as the Black Prince due to the color of his armor, decimated the nobility and chivalry of France at Crecy, France. Worse was to follow. The French King's cousin allied himself with the English, introducing the additional element of civil conflict. In September 1356, the Black Prince destroyed a new French army at Poitiers, France, and captured King John of France, who was held for an enormous ransom.

Geoffrey de Charny was the leading knight of his age, as indicated by King John's selection of him to carry the King's sacred banner, the *"Oriflamme,"* signifying "No quarter." At one point, the King had ransomed him from the English for a large sum. He was killed at Poitiers in 1356 while saving King John's life. He obviously was close to the King. While a pilgrim's medal shows de Charny and his wife exhibiting the Shroud, I believe his presence on the medal is as a memorial to his death at Poitiers, since there is no other evidence of an exhibition before 1357. De Charny's widow exhibited the Shroud, protected from its seizure both by his closeness to the King and the nadir of royal authority. The Shroud's exhibition appears to have been a patriotic act done to elevate French morale in the disastrous aftermath of Poitiers.

Much research has been done on the Shroud during the last thirty years, and surviving documents prove that the Shroud of Turin is the same cloth as the Mandylion, which disappeared during the sack of Constantinople. The cloth at Constantinople is reliably traced back to the Holy Image of Edessa, a cloth found hidden above a gate in

Edessa (near the upper Euphrates River in what is now southeastern Turkey) during repairs after a catastrophic flood in AD 525.

After the discovery of the Holy Image in Edessa, the manner of portraying Jesus changed almost overnight. St. Apollinaris Nuovo in Ravenna, Italy, is typical. On one side of the nave is a mosaic procession in which Jesus appears as a clean-shaven young Greek or Roman; on the other side, modified after liberation of Ravenna from the foreign Arian Ostrogoths by the Roman Emperor in Constantinople in AD 540, Jesus is portrayed as the man on the Shroud.

During the first century, Abgar V (reigned 13–50), the king of Edessa, was converted to Christianity and promoted it in his city. He allegedly was healed by a picture of Jesus brought to him by Addai (Thaddeus). It is reasonable to believe that the Shroud found in the tomb by Peter and John (Jn. 20:4–9) was sent to Edessa in order to move such a valuable relic to safety in a Christian city, probably during the persecution by Herod Agrippa in AD 41–44. After Abgar's death, a successor reverted to paganism after AD 57 and persecuted the Christians. During repairs after the 525 flood, a plain tile over a gate was removed. On the opposite side of the tile was a portrait of Jesus and inside a recess was the cloth. Whoever hid it was unable to return to retrieve it. It is probable that the cloth in the recess was the Shroud, hidden during a persecution after AD 57 and recovered after repairs occasioned by the flood of 525.

Virtually the only basis for disputing the authenticity of the Shroud is the carbon-14 dating done in 1988, which dated the Shroud to the period 1238–1430. This evidence is contrary to all other evidence in the case, other than claims of forgery made a generation after the Shroud's initial appearance in France by a late fourteenth-century bishop who brought forward an artist who claimed to have painted the image on the cloth thirty years earlier. But modern tests on the Shroud have shown conclusively that the image is neither painted nor drawn on the cloth. The image does not penetrate even the top thread of the weave.

Recent work (2007) has shown that the sample cut from the cloth for testing included both the original linen fabric and a mostly cotton patch. The owner of the Shroud, the Duchess of Savoy who died in 1531, bequeathed a sample of the Shroud to her local church. The patch closing the hole made by the gift was woven into the original threads with the same herringbone pattern. Both modern photographic enhancement and examinations by fabric experts prove this. The samples taken for carbon-14 dating supposedly were exclusively from the original linen. Even though one of the three labs doing the carbon-14 testing noticed the presence of threads of red silk and blue velvet, it went forward with burning the sample and testing the ashes anyway. The ages of the cloth given by the three labs differ by almost 200 years. These variances arose from the angle of the cutting of the sample, which gave each lab a different percentage of original cloth and the sixteenth-century patch; the labs with a higher percentage of the original linen gave an earlier date for the cloth.

Even with the support of the carbon-14 dating, it takes an act of faith to believe in the face of overwhelming evidence that the Shroud of Turin is anything other than the burial shroud of Jesus.

Christ before Pilate, Luca Girodano, 1650–1655,
Philadelphia Museum of Art, Philadelphia

THE CROWNING WITH THORNS

1. Having scourged Jesus, the soldiers put the purple robe on him and seated him, as if he were a king. They mocked him, crying, **"Hail, king of the Jews"** and struck him with their hands (Jn 19:1–3). One or more of the soldiers cut a thorny vine and made a crown of thorns (Jn 19:2). The pollen and images of two varieties of thorny vines are found on the Shroud. A honey mesquite's thorns are 1½–2" long; the thorns on these vines are longer. According to the injuries shown on the Shroud, the vine was not shaped into a wreath, but rather was wadded together. When it was pressed down onto Jesus' head, it fit him more like a cap, which was indeed the shape of some Mideastern crowns. The Shroud shows puncture wounds above the forehead, in the scalp and at the base of the back of the neck. The blood on the Shroud from these wounds is vital blood, flowing from a living man, as contrasted with blood from the lance wound inflicted on a dead man.

The Sorrowful Mysteries

❖ ❖ ❖

2. The Sudarium of Oviedo, Spain, is a cloth of common fabric (unlike the fine, expensively woven herringbone-patterned Shroud). It has been extensively studied during the last fifteen years or so, inspired by the Shroud studies. It is the **"napkin which had been on his head,"** referred to in *John* 20:7. Under Jewish law, it was considered that life was in the blood of the man or the animal. The law prohibited eating an animal's blood; hence, kosher regulations on the means of slaughter so as to drain the blood. Ordinarily, a dead man's body was washed for burial, but if the man had died a violent death, the body was not washed, so it could be buried with its blood. The law even went to the extent that, where a violent death caused bleeding onto the ground, earth mingled with blood was dug up and buried with the body.

When Jesus died, a post-mortem flow of blood and pulmonary edema issued from his mouth and nose. Someone took a "napkin," or handkerchief, and held it to Jesus' mouth and nose, pressing tightly with the fingers to staunch the flow. Then the cloth was wrapped partially around his head and pinned in place with thorns, which were readily available. Jesus' head had fallen onto his right shoulder, so that the cloth was pinned to his hair and beard on the right side of his face, wrapped around the left side of his face and head and pinned again to the hair at the right rear of his head.

The blood on the Sudarium from the wounds at the base of the back of the neck is vital blood, unlike blood from the nose and mouth. The wounds correspond with those on the Shroud. There are a total of seventy points of coincidence between the features of the man on the Sudarium and the man on the Shroud. The blood type is the same.

3. The Sudarium surfaced in Jerusalem at some time after Constantine's mother, Helena, made a pilgrimage to Jerusalem during Constantine's reign in the early fourth century. When the Persians threatened Jerusalem in the seventh century, it was moved to Alexandria, Egypt, where it was venerated as the napkin containing Jesus' blood. When the Persians threatened the conquest of Egypt, it was sent to Toledo, Spain, for safekeeping. Its arrival and presence in Toledo in the seventh century is of historical record. As the Moslem conquest of Spain proceeded, the Sudarium was sent north to relative safety. It has been kept at Oviedo Cathedral in northwestern Spain since 761. The chest containing the Sudarium and other relics was opened in the presence of King Alfonso VI in 1075. If the Shroud and the Sudarium were used on the same body, the Shroud cannot be a thirteenth- or fourteenth-century forgery.

The recent study of the Sudarium showing seventy points of coincidence with the Shroud renders it mathematically impossible for the Shroud to have been a thirteenth- or fourteenth-century forgery. The Sudarium had never been described in sufficient detail to have allowed such a forgery, if, indeed, there had been available a forger of sufficient technical proficiency. Even a cursory comparison of the quality and verisimilitude to the human form of the image on the Shroud with artistic renderings of the human form done in the thirteenth and fourteenth centuries shows that no such technically proficient artist existed. The Sudarium's historically proven existence, at least as early as the seventh century, proves the Shroud's existence and authenticity as of the same date, long before the carbon-14 test date.

4. After forcing the crown of thorns down on Jesus' head, the soldiers continued to mock him. They spat on him and, taking the mock scepter or rod from his hands, they struck him with it across the face (Mt 27:30; Mk 15:19). The Shroud shows the broken nose and swollen eye likely caused by the blow.

Some writers think the soldiers were playing a variant of "the game of the king" with Jesus, using the purple robe, crown of thorns, and cane scepter as props. The "game" consisted of choosing a burlesque "king," honoring him as such, and then putting him to death at the end of the game. There are marks in the Lithostrotos, the pavement of a courtyard of the Antonia, presently preserved in the Basilica of the Ecce Homo, which some have interpreted as showing that the game was commonly played there.

5. After Jesus had been scourged and crowned with thorns, he was returned to Pilate, wearing the purple robe. Pilate went outside the praetorium again to address Caiaphas, the other chief priests, elders, and the crowd of Jews (Jn 19:4). Pilate announced his decision to the Jews—that he found Jesus guilty of no crime deserving death (Jn 19:4). Apparently, Pilate thought that the brutal scourging would eliminate Jesus as a political threat and, thereby, satisfy the Jews, so he presented Jesus to them, scourged, crowned with thorns, and clothed in a mocking purple robe. **"Behold the man!"** (Jn 19:5) ("Ecce homo!").

6. Pilate had misjudged the determined intent of Caiaphas and the Sanhedrin. They were not satisfied by the pain and humiliation inflicted on Jesus, even though his public humiliation permanently disqualified him as Messiah for most Jews. They still demanded his life. **"Crucify him."** He must die **"because he has made himself the Son of God"** (Jn 19:6–7). Pilate again took Jesus into the praetorium to examine him outside the presence of the Jews. Pilate was disturbed by being told, for the first time, that Jesus claimed divinity. **"Where are you from?"** (Jn 19:7–9). In a pagan world the gods sometimes appeared and intervened in men's affairs. Compare the treatment of Paul and Barnabas as gods at Lystra (Acts 14:8–18). It was not mere superstition on Pilate's part to be concerned by this information, but rather a simple recognition of the supposed fact of divine appearances. Jesus, however, refused to answer a question which, he rightly perceived, was intended to determine if he were Apollo, Mercury, Bacchus, or any other of the host of pagan gods. Pilate returned to a question based on the reality of the situation. **"You will not speak to me? Do you not know that I have power to release you, and power to crucify you?"** (Jn 19:10). Jesus' answer gave Pilate no comfort, although Jesus pronounced Pilate less guilty than the Jews. **"You would have no power over me unless it had been given you from above; therefore he who delivered me to you has the greater sin"** (Jn 19:11).

7. Pilate therefore, for the third time, sought to evade the execution of Jesus. He and Jesus went back to the Jews outside the praetorium, and Pilate again announced his intent to release Jesus.

This time, Caiaphas and the Sanhedrin made it clear to Pilate that they and their friends in Rome would attack Pilate personally in order to destroy his career or even take his life as one disloyal to the Roman regime. **"If you release this man, you are not Caesar's friend; everyone who makes himself a king sets himself against Caesar"** (Jn 19:12). Their return to the accusation of a political insurrection, together with the threat against Pilate, was successful.

✥ ✥ ✥

8. Pilate's prior announcements of his intent to release Jesus were not binding upon him, because they were, in effect, his personal musings on the subject. Now Pilate acted in his official capacity. He took his place on the judgment seat and condemned Jesus to be executed by crucifixion (Jn 19:13–16).

Some writers have questioned the Gospel accounts that the Jewish leadership could thus coerce Pilate. They cite particularly his willingness to shed Jewish blood profusely in putting down a riot arising from his use of temple funds to build an aqueduct some years previously and his massacre of Samaritans at Mt. Gerizim some years later, which event led to his being relieved. But this fails to take into account many elements of the political equation, most of which are unknown to us. Pilate was an imperial official of sufficient reputation and influence at Rome that he had continued to hold his office, but he did not have enough reputation and influence to get himself transferred or promoted out of one of the least desirable postings in the imperial service. It is true that he put down a riot with bloodshed, but we have seen in our own times how the bloody preservation of order in a foreign land can be used by enemies far away to attack one's reputation at home rather than to strengthen it. You can almost hear the gossip at court: "If he had not mishandled the Jews, none of this would have been necessary." And, ultimately, it was just such an act of violence to preserve order, against the Samaritans, that cost Pilate his post.

Pilate had good reason to fear the connections of the Herodians and the priests at the Roman court. The rulers of the Jews had cultivated friends in Rome for almost a century. Antipater, the chief minister of the ethnarch Hyrcanus and father of Herod the Great, brought a large Jewish army to relieve a besieged Julius Caesar in Alexandria, Egypt, in 48 BC. During the Roman civil war following Julius Caesar's assassination, Herod supported Octavian and Antony against Brutus and Cassius, viewed by the Jews as the successors to Pompey, who had desecrated the temple by entering the Holy of Holies. In the subsequent civil war between Octavian and Antony, Herod initially supported Antony against Octavian but timely changed sides and submitted to Octavian after he defeated Antony and Cleopatra at Actium. Octavian (now called Augustus Caesar) confirmed him as king. Herod and his successors cultivated their Roman connections thereafter. A few years after the Crucifixion, Herod Agrippa, a close friend of Claudius, played a critical role in the latter's elevation to the Imperial purple after Caligula's assassination. Josephus, a generation later, was not the first important Jew to have important friends in Rome. Pilate had no way of knowing how extensive were the Imperial connections of Annas, Caiaphas, and the Sanhedrin, but he was wise to be wary.

We have seen how Pilate twisted and turned to avoid executing Jesus. Let us also examine the jurisdictional issues involved. Pilate, as Rome's governor in Judea, had jurisdiction over everything and everyone in Judea (*in rem* jurisdiction). The Jews resident in Judea, Pilate's subjects, had no authority to execute anyone. The Jews brought Jesus to Pilate because he had such authority. Herod Antipas, as ruler of an independent country, though a satellite of Rome in fact, had *in rem* jurisdiction over his territory and he also had personal (*in personam*) jurisdiction over his subjects, wherever they might be. Since Jesus was his subject, as a resident of Galilee, Herod Antipas had *in personam* jurisdiction over Jesus, including the power to execute him. Within Judea, Herod Antipas' jurisdiction was subject to Pilate's. Caiaphas took Jesus to Pilate rather than to Herod Antipas, although Herod was one of the Jews' own. Pilate voluntarily deferred to Herod's jurisdiction, and Herod could have executed Jesus. Herod declined to take jurisdiction. He had already executed one prophet, John the Baptist, and did not relish executing another. Caiaphas probably had surmised as much, which is why he went to Pilate. When Herod declined to accept jurisdiction, the ball was back in Pilate's court. Only after Pilate was thus compelled to accept jurisdiction did he interrogate Jesus.

9. I have great sympathy for, and empathy with, Pilate. He was Everyman. He was neither the first man, nor the last, to know the correct course of action, even to desire to pursue the correct course, but to lack the courage to do so. How often have I done the same? How often have many of us done so?

10. After Pilate condemned Jesus to execution by crucifixion, he publicly washed his hands, claiming, **"I am innocent of this man's blood; see to it yourselves"** (Mt 27:24–26). He inadvertently performed the same ritual—washing the hands—performed by a priest before killing the Passover lamb.

The Way of the Cross: Station 10, Christ Is Stripped of His Garments,
Giandomenico Tiepolo, Sacristy, S. Polo, Venice

JESUS TAKES UP HIS CROSS

◆

1. After being condemned by Pilate, Jesus joined two other felons, previously condemned and already brought out to be led to execution, and the assembly of Roman soldiers detailed to serve as executioners, together with their guard. Someone took Herod's purple cloak or robe from Jesus and gave him back his own (Mk 15:20). As they stripped the purple robe from him, they re-opened the wounds to which the robe had adhered, inflicting further pain.

The minimum number of soldiers required for a crucifixion was four, including a low-ranking non-commissioned officer as commander of the detail. The fact that a centurion (a company commander) was in charge of the detail on this day indicates the presence of more than the normal number of soldiers. It is apparent that the importance of the prisoner Jesus led Pilate to order a large guard element to discourage any possible attempt at rescue.

The other two prisoners to be executed that day are described in the Revised Standard Version as "criminals" (Lk 23:32, 39) or "robbers" (Mt 27:38), though most English-speaking Christians remember the earlier translation and would say that Jesus was crucified between two "thieves" (Authorized Version Mt 27:38).

Some recent translations describe the two felons as "revolutionaries," thereby displaying a bias in favor of "liberation theology," repudiated by St. John Paul II, which goes well with the "inclusive language" or "gender neutral" mistranslations in some of the same works, even rendering the Psalms gender-neutral in conflict with Jesus' own repeated citations of the Psalms as referring to himself. The Church has authorized preparation of a new lectionary.

Finally, the procession included a cart of some type, with a draft animal and driver, to dispose of the bodies and return the cross beams to the Antonia. Everyone knew that the executions would be faster than usual, since Pilate would not want to offend the Jews by polluting their holy day with executions lasting after sundown.

---

2. What was the nature of the "cross" Jesus carried from the praetorium? It was not the entire cross, as shown by so many artists. Rather, it was the cross-beam, or horizontal beam (*patibulum*). The felon initially was tied to the beam to which he would eventually be nailed. The horizontal beam would be raised and slid onto a permanent standing pole. It had to be of such a thickness either to allow for a hole through it, through which the top of the vertical pole would pass, or to allow it to be slid into some sort of notch in the permanent standing pole. A board 6" in diameter might not be strong enough; one 8" thick would. So the beam was 6"–8" square and at least 5' long. Depending on the type of wood, it weighed 50–100 pounds. The surface was rough-hewn, as abrasions on Jesus' shoulders show on the Shroud. The cross-beam was reusable and was stained with the soaked-in blood of its prior occupants.

Roman soldiers were smart enough to minimize their own labor, as well as to safeguard the usefulness of a large piece of lumber. Rather than nail each felon onto the wood, from which they would later have to extract the nails at some effort to themselves, creating new nail holes with each execution and weakening the beam, they probably drilled holes at an angle into the beam. Then they only had to drive the nail through the felon's wrist, positioned over the drilled hole; later extraction of the nail was simple. The scene shown in Mel Gibson's *Passion of the Christ* would be the result, where the felon's second arm is tugged into position to be nailed over a particular spot of the cross-beam. The pain inflicted on the felon was a bonus.

Some felons were scourged and thereby weakened before crucifixion. They nevertheless continued to be dangerous men until finally secured on their crosses. Since a 100-pound beam on the shoulders and arms of a strong man could become a weapon in his hands, some means was used to control him. Perhaps a rope from the beam to each ankle or perhaps a rope around each hand or ankle, each held by one of the soldiers. To do this, it would have been necessary to assign a detail of four soldiers to each felon. That would result in a detail of twelve soldiers for the three felons, a teamster for the cart, plus the extra guard; hence a centurion as commander.

---

3. Jesus fell the first time. He had been weakened by the scourging, bad enough in itself but even worse due to the hypersensitivity of his skin after he sweat blood the night before. We must visualize a fall in which Jesus was unable to put out his hands to break the fall. With the added weight of the cross-beam, it would have been terrible. The Shroud shows abrasions of knees and shins evidencing the falls. The injury to the nose and right cheek and eye may reflect that he fell on his face in addition to being struck with a rod.

4. Jesus met his mother on the way of the cross. The Bible does not mention it, but how can we imagine that she would not have been there? At this point in time she was still the only person, other than Jesus, who knew what was happening, and why. During the twenty years between Jesus' questioning the rabbis in the temple and the commencement of his ministry, Jesus and Mary lived under the same roof. During these years in which Jesus studied the scriptures and prayed to his Father in order to learn what he was supposed to do, do we really think Jesus and Mary discussed only the carpentry business and the weather? They were the only people who ever lived sinless lives, and they must have discussed the scriptures and prayed to ascertain Jesus' mission. When Jesus comprehended the meaning to him of such scriptures as *Psalm* 22, he and Mary surely discussed it. Mary inevitably met Jesus on his way of the cross in order, if only by a look, to strengthen him in his resolve and to affirm her understanding of his mission and her consent to it. Just as Mary consented to become the mother of the Messiah, she consented now to the immolation of her son, the Son of God. She refrained from interceding with him to spare both of them the pain of his crucifixion.

5. The centurion made the determination that Jesus was too weak to carry his cross. He had his men collar a bystander and compel him to carry it for Jesus. The man so coerced was Simon of Cyrene (Mt 27:32; Mk 15:21). The beam was shifted from Jesus' shoulders to those of Simon, who carried it behind Jesus (Lk 23:26). There was something about his contact with Jesus that caused him to believe the later claim that Jesus had risen from the dead. Simon remained in Jerusalem, and his sons, Alexander and Rufus, were devout members of the church in Jerusalem.

❖ ❖ ❖

6. A woman named by tradition as Veronica ("True Image") stepped forward along the way to wipe Jesus' face. At some stage before his death, Jesus' face had indeed been cleaned. The scalp wounds from the crown of thorns would have bled profusely, as scalp wounds do. However, Jesus' face on the Shroud shows only trickles of blood down his forehead from these wounds. If his face had been wiped clean, he would have suffered thereafter only the diminished flow of blood from old wounds which were beginning to clot.

The story that the form of Jesus' face was transferred to Veronica's cloth or veil, is improbable. One such supposed cloth disappeared during the sack of Rome by Charles V's Protestant German troops in 1527. Such a supposed cloth, perhaps the same one, is housed in Italy, but a comparison of the quality of the image on it with the image of Jesus' face on the Shroud, shows clearly that it is not genuine. In all likelihood, the story of the woman who wiped Jesus' face was conflated at some point with the Holy Image of Edessa, which for a long time was exhibited in a form folded to show only the face.

❖ ❖ ❖

7. Even after being relieved of the burden of his *patibulum*, Jesus had been so weakened that he fell a second time.

Among the crowds along the street who viewed the procession were a group of women disciples from Jerusalem. The men disciples were in fear of arrest and had scattered through the city, sheltered by local disciples. Jesus foretold to the women the siege and destruction of Jerusalem. **"Daughters of Jerusalem, do not weep for me, but weep for yourselves and your children"** (Lk 23:27–31).

❖ ❖ ❖

8. Jesus fell a third time. The Bible is silent, but tradition says so. It is not hard to believe that he could trip and fall at least three times on the rough, uneven pavement, especially in his weakened condition.

When the procession arrived at Golgotha, also called Calvary, Jesus was disrobed; that is, he was stripped naked. For a Jew the humiliation of public nakedness was of an entire magnitude greater than that suffered by most men. The shame of it is still felt, as witness the usual artistic version showing Jesus' modesty preserved by some sort of cloth. The earliest artistic rendition of his nudity of which I am aware, other than Arian renditions intended to deny his divinity by emphasizing his humanity, is Giotto's Baptism fresco in the Scrovegni (Arena) Chapel in Padua, Italy (ca. 1305).

Jesus' nakedness is indicated in the Gospels by descriptions of the soldiers casting lots for his garments (Mt 27:35; Mk 15:24; Lk 23:34; Jn 19:23–24). John is most explicit. The four soldiers who crucified him divided his garments into four parts, one for each soldier; but the tunic was valuable as being without seam, so they cast lots for it. A seamless garment was worn by the priests when they sacrificed.

❖ ❖ ❖

9. In the first century AD, the configuration of Jerusalem differed greatly from the walled city we see today, whose walls were built by the Ottoman Turks. In Jesus' time the wall to the west of the Antonia was much closer to it than either a later Roman wall or today's wall. Once through the gate, walking west, there was a small rise on the side of the road. For some reason, this rise was called Golgotha, "the place of a skull," whether from something in its appearance or in its history, we do not know (Jn 19:17). It then had the advantages of proximity to the gate, so it was not far to take criminals; its proximity to a major road for the effect of terrorizing the hostile natives; its topological prominence, as being a discernable rise above the road; and its ease of access for leading prisoners up a gentle incline to the permanent posts on which they and their crosses would be raised. The total distance from the Antonia to Golgotha is about 1,000 yards. Consequently it was less than fifteen minutes' walk from the Antonia to Golgotha.

When Constantine's church was built, all soil and gravel were cut away, together with a portion of the bedrock, so that the remaining rock column now rises precipitously from the ground within the Church of the Holy Sepulcher. Such a precipitous rise is architectural; it would have made it unusable as a convenient place of execution.

Near Golgotha was an abandoned quarry, its face about twenty-two yards from Golgotha. Three tombs had been carved into it, facing toward Golgotha. Visualize the San Antonio zoo and others backed into old quarries. Since it was unlawful to bury anyone inside the walls, all burials had to be beyond the gates. Tombs located so near a gate as these were unusually convenient and valuable. Hence, only a rich man could afford one of them.

Between the face of the abandoned quarry and Golgotha was a "garden." There is no basis to think that an ornamental garden of plants and flowers had been planted beside the dirty road. Rather, the gravelly ground, conveniently located near the gate, was probably used for cultivation of vegetables and perhaps some fruit trees, and the person who cultivated them, whether as employee or as lessee, was the "gardener." Nearby was an abandoned cistern, which served as a garbage pit.

Both Golgotha and the tombs were later buried under the structure of the Emperor Hadrian's temple of Venus. After Hadrian suppressed the bar Cocheba Revolt of AD 132–135, he had expelled all Jews from Jerusalem and ordered a new city, Aelia Capitolina, built over it. Two hundred years later, Constantine's mother, Helena, came to Jerusalem to find the holy places. Hadrian's temple was removed. The three tombs were revealed. The middle tomb was identified as Jesus' sepulcher. A procession way around it was created by carving a path into the rock which separated Jesus' tomb from the quarry wall, destroying the other two tombs in the process.

How did Helena know which tomb was Jesus'? The Jerusalem church had never ceased to exist, though it had left the walled city before Titus' siege, which culminated in the destruction of Jerusalem in AD 70. We may be confident that the location and description of Jesus' tomb, the holiest spot in the world to Christians, though located under Hadrian's temple, was passed down through generations as the tradition of that parish. Hadrian unintentionally flagged the locations of Golgotha and the tomb by erecting a statue of Jupiter over Golgotha and the altar of Venus over the tomb. Graffiti of the period of Hadrian's temple prove the site was an object of Christian pilgrimage even before Helena.

10. Once Pilate had condemned Jesus, he ordered a placard prepared which identified the charge against him. The wooden placard, or *titulus,* said: "Jesus of Nazareth, the king of the Jews." It was written in Hebrew, Greek, and Latin. It was placed on the cross, as Roman practice was to advertise the criminal's offense (Jn 19:19–22; Mt 27:37; Mk 15:26).

Helena had the old abandoned cistern cleaned out, searching for discarded portions of the cross. The *titulus* was found, along with wood which she determined by a test of faith to be the true cross. The *titulus* was cut up and distributed by Helena among Rome, Jerusalem, and Constantinople. The latter two pieces were destroyed or lost, the Jerusalem piece having been carried into battle by the Crusaders and burned by the Moslems.

A portion of the *titulus* is preserved in the Basilica of Santa Croce in Rome, which is on the site of Helena's palace and chapel. Epigraphical studies and examination of the wood have established that it is of a type of wood found near Jerusalem and that the writing style is appropriate to the first century AD. Only portions of the Hebrew, Greek, and Latin text are on the surviving fragment of the *titulus*. The oddity is that the workman who carved the letters into the wood was obviously a Jew with little knowledge of Greek or Latin. The Greek and Latin inscriptions are carved like the Jewish inscription, from right to left. If it were a forgery, that would be an error obviously avoided. Likewise, if it were a forgery the languages would have been in the order given by John, namely, Hebrew, Latin, and Greek instead of Hebrew, Greek, and Latin (Jn 19:20). If it is genuine, as I believe, it shows the hasty work of a Jewish workman far down the pay scale, the sort one would expect to have been given this particular task.

Crucifixion, Pietro Annigoni, 1983,
Chapel of Blessings, Basilica of Saint Anthony, Padua

THE CRUCIFIXION

⋄

1. At the place of execution the prisoner was thrown to the ground and held down by two men, while one held the arm in place and the fourth drove the nail. When both wrists were nailed to the cross-beam, the total weight of the beam and man was about 200–275 pounds. There is no basis for assuming that a crane was used, so lifting the cross-beam into place was done by hand. It required four soldiers to lift the beam and the man nailed to it and to place them it on the vertical pole. To do so meant that they lifted the beam no more than two to three feet above their own shoulders; after lowering the cross-beam into position on the pole, the felon's feet were only a foot or eighteen inches above the ground, not high in the sky as usually portrayed. Since the prisoner was only a short distance above those standing on the ground, there was no problem in speaking to him or, as with the Sudarium, reaching up to pin a cloth around his head.

Once the cross-beam was in place, it was necessary to secure the feet. What was the position of the feet, and how many nails were used? There is a graffito exhibited in the museum on the Palatine Hill in Rome, mockingly showing "Alexamenos worships his god." It is a rough drawing of a man with the head of a jackass on a cross, standing on a level object of some sort. His feet are apart and obviously are nailed separately. The artistic tradition usually shows Jesus with one foot nailed on top of the other. The Shroud shows the left leg bent in rigor mortis, so perhaps one leg was nailed in position higher than the other. But consider the execution from the standpoint of the soldier. Anyone who has driven a nail through any object that does not have a firm base behind it knows that it would be harder to drive a nail through one foot or ankle into another foot or ankle than into wood.

From the soldier's standpoint, it would be safer and easier to use two nails than one. There was always the possibility of an effort by the felon to inflict injury on his executioners. The safest course would be for one soldier to hold one leg, another the other leg, another to hold a foot in place, and the fourth to drive the nail through a single foot into either the vertical pole or, more likely, a short bottom horizontal beam attached to it, in order to preserve the strength of the vertical member. The Russian cross shows precisely such a lower cross-beam. When large numbers were crucified, any type of a "cross" would do, even a real tree. Josephus wrote that those who were crucified were nailed in different ways. Apparently, much leeway was granted for the executioner's sadism or whimsy (Josephus, *Wars,* Book V, Ch. 11). But the vertical members of these crosses were permanent; there were probably a half dozen or so on Golgotha to accommodate periodic executions. No soldier who had to dig a post-hole in solid rock would weaken the integrity of the wood with unnecessary nails. He might be the one to replace it! Perhaps one nail was used to save nails when there were numerous crucifixions, as after one of the periodic Jewish insurrections, when 2,000 were crucified. But two nails would be the norm. The ankle of a Jew crucified during the first century AD was initially thought to show one nail through both ankles, but is now known to show one nail through only one ankle.

We cannot say with assurance how Jesus' feet were nailed. The open end of the Shroud was at his feet, and there is only a partial print of the left foot. Blood appears to originate at both heels but does not indicate how his ankles were nailed.

We can notice that the convenience, or necessity, of having four soldiers for each of these operations corresponds with the number of four given in John's Gospel as dividing Jesus' garments (Jn 19:23–24). Four soldiers crucified Jesus and probably a different four soldiers for each of the thieves (Mt 27:38; Mk 15:27). The guard watched to prevent disorder. The cart with its driver was parked off the road, probably on the side of Golgotha away from the gate to avoid congestion. The centurion oversaw the work of his soldiers, who were not doing this operation for the first time.

---

2. A crowd watched the prisoners being raised and nailed onto their crosses. In addition to the soldiers and travelers entering or exiting the city at the gate, there were "chief priests," "scribes," and "elders" (Mt 27:39–41). The "chief priests" necessarily included Caiaphas and perhaps Annas. Enough "elders," members of the Sanhedrin, attended so that the presence of Joseph of Arimathea and Nicodemus among them would not have been remarkable. Some writers have credited Caiaphas with the patriotic motive of trying to preserve his people, based on his statement that, **"It is expedient for you that one man should die for the people, and that the whole nation should not perish"** (Jn 11:49–50), fearing that Jesus as a purported Messiah would raise an insurrection and bring the power of Rome against Judea. However, Caiaphas' motivation by malice was shown by his mocking Jesus on the cross. **"He is the king of Israel; let him come down now from the cross, and we will believe in him. He trusts in God; let God deliver him now, if he desires him; . . . "** Mt 27:41–43). His motivation was primarily the preservation of his own power and that of his class, as collaborators of the Romans, rather than the welfare of his people.

Among the disciples of Jesus present were, foremost, his mother Mary, Mary Magdalene, and Mary, the wife of Cleophas, Mary's "sister" (Jn 19:25). Also present was Salome (the daughter of Mary, wife of Cleophas), the mother of James and John, along with **"many women, looking on from afar, who had followed Jesus from Galilee, ministering to him"** (Mt 27:55–56; Mk 15:40–41). **"All his acquaintances and the women who had followed him from Galilee stood at a distance and saw these things"** (Lk 23:49). Who were the "acquaintances"—men as juxtaposed with the women—who stood at a distance? They did not include the apostles from the Last Supper, who two nights later still barred the doors for fear of the Jews (Jn 20:19). They probably included some of those from Galilee who had come to Jerusalem for Passover but did not consider themselves as targets for an arrest warrant. Tradition is clear, as well as John's Gospel, that the only one of the twelve apostles present at the Crucifixion was John (Jn 19: 26; 19:35; 21:24), who had stayed near Jesus since his arrest.

After he had been nailed to the cross, Jesus said, **"Father, forgive them; for they know not what they do"** (Lk 23:34). This saying is placed in the narrative immediately after Jesus was nailed to the cross and prior to the descriptions of the "rulers" and soldiers mocking him. Whether the narrative is strictly chronological, Jesus' forgiveness extended to all those who would repent, whether then or later.

The legend of Dr. Faustus is that he sold his soul to the Devil in exchange for omniscience. There have been interpretations of the Faustus legend which would affirm Faustus' fear that, having made his pact with the Devil, he could not save his soul. Such an interpretation is itself inspired by the Father of Lies. For Faustus, and for each of us, it is the Devil himself who seeks to convince us that it is too late for repentance. If Jesus sought Judas' repentance even at Gethsemane in the very act of betrayal, he will not withhold his forgiveness from anyone who repents. The parable of the laborers in the vineyard makes this very point. Those who repent in the last hour receive the same reward as those who do so early in the day (Mt 20:1–16). It, fortunately, is not justice that God offers us, but rather mercy, if only we seek it.

❖ ❖ ❖

3. Jesus was crucified between two thieves. The first picked up the mocking refrain of the chief priest and reviled him. The second thief rebuked the first: **"Do you not fear God, since you are under the same sentence of condemnation? . . . This man has done nothing wrong"** (Lk 23:39–42). Then the second thief turned to Jesus and said, **"Jesus, remember me when you come into your kingdom"** (Lk 23:43). There was something in the second thief that convinced Jesus of his deep repentance. Jesus responded, **"Truly, I say to you, today you will be with me in paradise"** (Lk 23:43).

In saying that Jesus "has done nothing wrong," the second thief implicitly confessed his own wrongful conduct. In hearing his request for Jesus to "remember me," Jesus heard the implied repentance and act of contrition, and Jesus forgave his sins. In his dying repentance and forgiveness, the second thief was spared purgatory, so that he went straight to heaven in the spirit, together with other saints. The second thief sought, and was granted forgiveness of sins which the "chief priests, scribes, and elders" were too proud to seek at the hands of a Galilean carpenter.

4. "When Jesus saw his mother, and the disciple whom he loved standing near, he said to his mother, 'Woman, behold your son!' Then he said to the disciple, 'Behold your mother!' And from that hour the disciple took her into his own home" (Jn 19:26–27). The disciple was John. Mary lived with him until she died, and his Gospel reflects in part what he learned from her during that close relationship.

Many modern writers claim that Jesus' "brothers" mentioned in the Gospels were younger sons of Mary and that her virginity was not life-long (Jn 7:3–5, 10; Mt 12:46; Mk 3:31–32; Lk 8:19–20). Jesus' entrustment of Mary to John is fatal to such an argument. The next oldest son would have had the rights and obligations of a Jewish *pater familias*, and it would have been he who made such a determination about the care of their mother following Jesus' death.

5. "'I thirst.' They filled a sponge with sour wine, put it on hyssop and put it to his mouth" (Jn 19:28). In the Passover ritual, hyssop is used to smear the lamb's blood on the door frame. In almost every age there have been those who could not accept the incarnation, the idea that a holy god would dirty himself with material flesh. Since the writings of some of the Greek philosophers, there has always been the temptation to say the mind or the spirit is good, but the flesh or the material world is evil. The Gnostics were, and are, only one group of such folk. Various heretical theories were advanced in the first centuries of the Christian era, arguing that God only seemed to inhabit human flesh. God did not suffer on the cross; only the man did so, or even that the man

Jesus was a phantom. The early church condemned these heresies as they arose. For the scandalous proposition is a fact; God dwelt in our flesh, suffered, and died. This statement, "I thirst," arguably is evidentiary against these claims.

❖ ❖ ❖

6. "My God, my God, why hast thou forsaken me?" (Mt 27:46; Mk 15:34). **"It is finished"** (Jn 19:30). **"Father, into thy hands I commit my spirit"** (Lk 23:46).

The first of these is the opening line of *Psalm* 22, which describes and forecasts the Crucifixion as it was clearly so understood by Jesus. It also describes the psychological pain experienced by Jesus as he assumed and propitiated the sins of the whole world, past, present, and future. It may well have been his foretaste of this burden at Gethsemane that caused him to sweat blood. He who had never experienced sin himself and its concomitant guilt and grief, had taken on himself all sins of all people of every age. **"For our sake he made him to be sin who knew no sin. . . . "** (2 Cor 5:21). Consequently, for at least part of his time on the cross, he separated himself from the Father more completely than any sinful man has ever done. He was, in actual fact, forsaken by the Father during this process, because he did not pretend to be sinful; he became sin.

Yet, as he felt death approach, he knew that the process of perfect sacrifice and propitiation was coming to a close upon his death, and he could truthfully say, "It is finished." Upon his death the sacrifice and propitiation were complete, and his separation from the Father would end.

Finally, as he felt death coming upon him, he said, "Father, into thy hands I commit my spirit." He, thereby, evidenced his absolute faith in the Father, believing that his own resurrection would be the next act of the drama of reconciliation of God with man.

7. When did Jesus die and how long was he on the cross? The synoptic Gospels agree that he died at the ninth hour; beginning the time at sunrise; that would be about 3:00 p.m. The synoptic Gospels also agree that a great darkness covered the area between the sixth and ninth hours, from about noon to about 3:00 p.m. (Mt 27:45–50; Mk 15; 33–37; Lk 23:44–46). John is silent as to the hour of death and the preceding darkness.

The length of the crucifixion is more complicated. Matthew and Luke are silent as to when Jesus was nailed to the cross. Mark says, **"It was the third hour when they crucified him"** (Mk 15:25). John says, **"It was about the sixth hour"** when Pilate officially condemned Jesus (Jn 19:13–14). How does one reconcile these times? First, there were sundials but no clocks in the Roman world with rare exception, such as the water clock in Athens, a large structure. There is no evidence of any such device in Jerusalem. Second, daytime was divided into four segments between sunrise and the third, sixth, and ninth hours, and sunset. As the time of year changed, the duration of these segments of the day varied. At the time of the Crucifixion, it was shortly past equinox, so each segment would indeed have been three hours in this case. Assuming sunrise was at 6:00 a.m., how would one describe the time of an event that took place four, four and a half, or five hours after sunrise? When does "at the third hour" become "about the sixth hour?"

Because of the short distances involved, it is possible to compress the events between convocation of the Sanhedrin at sunrise and Pilate's condemnation into only three hours, but everything has to go smoothly and swiftly to do so. Likewise it is possible to compress the events between Pilate's condemnation and Jesus' death into three hours, but again everything has to go smoothly and swiftly. The time of Jesus' death cannot be extended to leave much less than three hours till sunset and still allow time for the events between Jesus' death and entombment, nor can the Sanhedrin have legally convened before sunrise. The time compressions are resolved and the problem solved by concluding that Pilate condemned Jesus around 10:00 a.m., and Jesus was crucified about an hour later. Both Mark and John correctly estimated the time of both events as between the third and sixth hours.

The Jews had asked Pilate, at some time not specified, to have the felons killed and removed before sunset so as not to have an execution on the sabbath, which was also a "high day" (Jn 19:31). Sometime after Jesus had died at about 3:00 p.m., the centurion took steps to assure that the felons would be dead and removed before sunset. He ordered their legs broken, which would hasten asphyxiation. The soldiers broke the legs of the two thieves, but when they came to Jesus, they saw he was already dead. Roman executioners knew how to be sure that a prisoner was in fact dead rather than feigning death. One of them thrust his spear into Jesus' right side, through his right lung and into his heart (Jn 19:32–34). The Gospels do not say which side was pierced. However, most artistic renderings correctly show it as the right side, rather than the side on which the heart is located; this information probably came from examination of the Shroud, which clearly shows the wounds as described. In the Passover ritual, no bone of the lamb may be broken.

When the spear pierced Jesus, out flowed "blood and water" (Jn 19:34). Within 30–45 minutes after death, the serum in the blood separates as a clear liquid. When the heart was pierced, it would have flowed out as a clear liquid, appearing to be water. To avoid compression of the events then following, it seems likely that "the ninth hour" could well have been 2:30 or even 2:00 p.m., rather than 3:00 p.m., since the spear thrust had to take place at least thirty minutes later than death for the serum to have separated.

At the ninth hour on the Day of Preparation for the Passover, the priests in the temple sacrificed the Passover lamb. The same hour is that given as the time of the death of Jesus, the Lamb of God.

❖ ❖ ❖

8. "Now there was a man named Joseph from the Jewish town of Arimathea. He was a member of the council, a good and righteous man, who had not consented to their purpose and deed, and he was looking for the kingdom of God. This man went to Pilate and asked for the body of Jesus" (Lk 23:50–52). Joseph was the owner of one of the tombs carved into the face of the quarry a short distance away from Golgotha; the owner of a tomb in such a location necessarily was a rich man (Mt 27:57). He was a "respected member" of the Sanhedrin (Mk 15:43). He was "a disciple of Jesus, but secretly, for fear of the Jews. . . . " (Jn 19:38) (Mt 27:57–58; Mk 15:42–43; Lk 23:50–52; Jn 19:38).

As Jesus was on the cross, Joseph of Arimathea approached John, the only man in the group attending Jesus. He told John of his ownership of the nearby tomb and offered it to Mary for Jesus' burial. Under Roman law, an executed criminal's family had the right to receive his body. John gently approached Mary with the offer, and she gratefully accepted it. Thereafter, Joseph acted as her legal agent to obtain the body upon Jesus' death. John would have confirmed this agency to the centurion.

If Jesus died at 3:00 p.m. and was pierced by a spear at 3:45, Joseph could have been at the Antonia by 4:00. If those who argue that the praetorium was at Herod's palace are correct, the distance was about the same. If, as we have seen, Jesus' death was thirty minutes or even an hour before 3:00, then Joseph had more time, but whether Jesus died at 3:00 or at 2:00, there was sufficient time for the deposition and entombment to have taken place as described in the Gospels.

Pilate questioned whether Jesus was already dead, since the time on the cross seemed too short to have caused death. Pilate summoned the centurion, who assured him that Jesus was already dead (Mk 15:44–46). Pilate's messenger could have walked from the Antonia to Golgotha and returned with the centurion in less than thirty minutes. Thereupon, Pilate granted the request of Mary, acting through Joseph of Arimathea (Mt 27:58; Mk 15:45; Jn 19:38). Joseph probably returned to Golgotha with the centurion in order to tell Mary and Jesus' friends that her request had been granted and in order to delegate responsibilities among those friends. By now, it was approaching 5:00 or perhaps a little earlier.

Joseph of Arimathea was unlike most other members of the Sanhedrin, not only in being a secret disciple of Jesus, but in being willing to make himself ritually unclean, or "defiled," so that he could not celebrate the Passover. Unlike the large group of Jews who would not go in to Pilate, necessitating Pilate's coming outside to them, Joseph obviously did enter under Pilate's roof (Jn 18: 28–29). Joseph further was about to touch a dead man, likewise "defiling" himself.

One must reflect a moment to understand exactly what Joseph was about to do to his life when he decided to help Mary and Jesus' friends in this fashion. His actions were tantamount to a public declaration of his theretofore secret belief in Jesus. Why had he considered it necessary to keep this a secret? **"[M]any even of the authorities believed in him, but for fear of the Pharisees they did not confess it, lest they should be put out of the synagogue: for they loved the praise of men more than the praise of God"** (Jn 12:42–43). Even the poor and unimportant were to suffer the same penalty. The parents of the blind man healed by Jesus would not acknowledge the cure to the Pharisees **"because**

they feared the Jews, for the Jews had already agreed that if any one should confess him to be Christ, he was to be put out of the synagogue" (Jn 9:22). Any member of the Sanhedrin who professed a belief that Jesus was the Messiah stood in jeopardy of being ejected from the Sanhedrin as well as from the fellowship of the synagogue, to which every Jew was entitled. On the day that Joseph found that he could no longer endure to keep his belief a secret, he walked away from "the praise of men." He walked away from his seat in the Sanhedrin. He would be ejected from the synagogue. He would endure social ostracism. His business would suffer and his finances would be attacked.

Having provided the tomb for Jesus, Joseph disappears. There is one, and only one, subsequent tradition regarding him. What is certain is that the founding of Glastonbury Abbey in Somersetshire in southwestern England has always been credited to Joseph of Arimathea and to no one else. It is the only church or monastery in Britain to claim a first-century foundation. Excavations have proven the existence of a few Roman-era remains, indicating importation of goods from the Mediterranean. By the fifth century, a wattle church attributed to Joseph of Arimathea was the holiest site in Britain. The pagan English overran most of the Christian Britons during the period 577–584, but even then the area around Glastonbury held until 658, by which time the English had been evangelized by Augustine, who arrived at Canterbury in 596. Glastonbury was the only British monastery to change over to an English monastery without interruption. Eventually Joseph's wattle church was enclosed in a wooden building to protect it. Both were destroyed by fire in 1184 during the reign of Henry II.

Glastonbury's unique importance was acknowledged by the burial there in the mid-fifth century of "King Arthur," the Romanized, Catholic claimant to imperial dignity who defeated the pagan German invaders and preserved a Romanized Catholic Celtic Britain for another 125 years. Artorius was his name. Rigotamos was his British title, "Kingmost," or Emperor, Latinized as Riothamus. He adopted the heavy cavalry favored by the Roman emperors to fight the German infantry. He so decisively defeated the pagan Angles, Saxons, and Jutes that they were confined to small fringes of territory in the southeast and East Anglia and presented no threat for a century, while the Britons fell to warring against each other, as Celts are wont to do. Having pacified Britain south of Hadrian's Wall, about AD 469 Artorius led an expeditionary force to the Continent in a grand alliance with the Western Empire's Emperor Anthemius; Aegidius, the ruler of an independent Roman Gallic territory; and the Catholic Burgundians against the pagan Saxons and the Arian Visigoths. He was mortally wounded and brought home to South Cadbury Castle, not far from Glastonbury. It was one of many old Celtic hill forts that was reoccupied and refortified during the fifth century wars with the Germans, but it was the only one whose outside wall was refaced in stone. It also contained the foundations for a church in the shape of a Greek cross which, had it been built, would have been the largest structure built north of the Alps in the fifth century. That such a man was buried at Glastonbury speaks volumes regarding its importance.

Did Joseph of Arimathea found a Christian community at Glastonbury? Why not? By professing his belief in Jesus, he had destroyed the prior form of life he had led. What was to hold him in Jerusalem? While direct Roman rule prevailed in Judea, the Christians were comparatively safe and the Church grew in some semblance of peace despite the hostility of the Pharisees and other temple parties. The execution of Stephen was an exception to the rule, done during an interregnum between Roman governors. This period of safety ended in AD 41, when Judea was given by the Emperor Claudius to Herod Agrippa, who sought the favor and support of the Pharisaic party and commenced a severe persecution. He executed James, son of Zebedee, in August 41 and imprisoned Peter during the same persecution. Peter would have been executed but for his miraculous escape (Acts 12:1–17). All the apostles still in Jerusalem dispersed as a result of Herod Agrippa's persecution, and it is likely that many other leading Christians who are not named in the records did the same. The persecution continued until Herod Agrippa's death in AD 44, followed by the resumption of direct Roman rule.

It would have been a reasonable time for Joseph of Arimathea also to depart. We do not know the nature of his business activities, but many types of business would have allowed him to move west, perhaps to Rome. If he went to Rome, a Christian community was already there in sufficient numbers to cause such conflicts within the larger Jewish community that Claudius ordered all Jews (including Christians in his thinking) out of Rome in AD 49. Claudius had invaded Britain in 43 and, by 49, Britain south of the Severn River, including the area of Glastonbury, was both conquered and secure. During the 50s, Britain, and especially the southwest, experienced a boom in both mining and agriculture that led to an increase in population in the southwest, estimated at over 100,000 additional inhabitants. Several years' residence in Rome would have allowed a businessman to become familiar with the Roman west. If one had to leave Rome, why not go where business was good? Did Joseph finance the flight of a group of Christian refugees from Rome to Britain in AD 49? There is absolutely no proof and no way of ever proving where Joseph was between the Crucifixion of Jesus and the time he is reputed to have founded a Christian community at Glastonbury.

I consider it not only possible, but likely, that Joseph of Arimathea founded a Christian community at Glastonbury, probably following the expulsion of the Jews and Christians from Rome in AD 49, at a time when Joseph likely was not yet an old man. We have come through a time during which the intelligentsia of the West have disregarded traditions not backed up with documentation. But discoveries such as finding the bones of St. Peter under the high altar of St. Peter's Basilica and finding the bones of the Romans, Saints John and Paul, buried illegally within Rome's walls by bricking up their bodies under the stairway of their house, over which the church named for them was erected, should encourage us to pay more heed to tradition's versions of the facts. The tradition of Joseph's founding of Glastonbury and the facts supporting that tradition are too strong to be ignored.

9. When Joseph of Arimathea returned from Pilate, there remained about an hour or a little longer until sunset; it was necessary to work swiftly. Since Jesus was to receive a proper burial, the centurion gave orders to deal with his body first. The nails had to be pulled from his feet. Then it took four soldiers to lift the cross-beam with its dead weight up and off of the pole and lay them on the ground. Then they could easily remove the nails from the wrists. The *titulus* that had hung on the top of the pole was tossed into the nearby cistern, used as an accustomed garbage pit.

The centurion indicated to Joseph that he could, then, take charge of the body. Jesus was laid on his back. The blood from the wound in his side ran down his right side and "puddled" in the small of his back. The Sudarium was re-pinned so as to go all the way around Jesus' head, now that it was no longer resting on his right shoulder.

Having tended to Jesus, the centurion had the soldiers assure themselves that the two thieves were dead, presumably in the manner used on Jesus. They were taken down, and their carcasses and cross-beams were placed in the cart to dispose of the bodies and return the cross-beams to the Antonia before sunset.

Another member of the Sanhedrin, a Pharisee, had also stayed until the end. Nicodemus came forward to assist Joseph of Arimathea. He earlier had come to Jesus by night, secretly, in order to speak with him, obviously sharing with Joseph the same fear of expulsion from the Sanhedrin and the synagogue if he were thought to be a believer. While Nicodemus clearly was no disciple of Jesus at the time of this encounter, he nevertheless was seeking a deeper knowledge of Jesus, and his search ripened into faith by the time of the Crucifixion (Jn 3:1–15). He had still earlier protested in the Sanhedrin against the Pharisees' plotting against Jesus. **"Nicodemus . . . said to them, 'Does our law judge a man without first giving him a hearing and learning what he does?' They replied, 'Are you from Galilee too?'"** (Jn 7:50–52). The threat in the Pharisees' response is barely veiled. Like Joseph, Nicodemus also defiled himself by handling a dead body and was unable to keep the Passover (Jn 19:39–40). We do not know what became of Nicodemus, but it is obvious that he suffered the consequences of his public kindness to Jesus' mother and friends.

Prior to Jesus' crucifixion, both Joseph of Arimathea and Nicodemus had been afraid to be publicly associated with Jesus. To all reasonable observers, Jesus' humiliating death put an end to his claims to be the Messiah, much less the Son of God. What caused these two men publicly to become disciples at this time of apparent failure? (1) "Father, forgive them." (2) Jesus' assertion of divinity, even from the cross. "This day, you will be with me in paradise." (3) Two events over which Jesus had no control: presenting him vinegar on a hyssop stalk and not breaking his legs, both associating him with the Passover lamb. (4) Jesus' invocation of *Psalm* 22. As scholars, this would have put them in mind of the prophecies of Isaiah. (6) Increasing darkness until at the time of Jesus' death, "the sun's light failed" (Lk 23: 44–45) and "the earth shook, and the rocks were split. . . . " (Mt 27: 51). (7) Finally, the serenity of Jesus' countenance throughout his ordeal.

Were Joseph of Arimathea and Nicodemus the only Jewish leaders who became Christians? We cannot prove that other members of the Sanhedrin itself joined them, but they were joined by "a great many of the priests" (Acts 6:7). Imagine the price they paid for their faith!

The centurion would not have appreciated the references to, and fulfillment of, Jewish scripture which were apparent to Joseph and Nicodemus. He would have been affected by Jesus' forgiveness of his enemies, his continued assertion of his divinity, the serenity of his countenance, and the radical disturbances of nature that accompanied his death. The centurion concluded not only that Jesus was innocent, but also that he was indeed the son of God (Lk 23: 47; Mt 27:54; Mk 15:39). Tradition asserts that the centurion became a convert to Christianity.

Other disturbances of nature occurred which were not visible at Calvary at the time of Jesus' death. The veil of the temple was torn in two from top to bottom (Mt 26:51; Mk 15:38; Lk 23:45). **"[T]he tombs also were opened, and many bodies of the saints who had fallen asleep were raised, and coming out of the tombs after his resurrection they went into the holy city and appeared to many"** (Mt 27:52–53). These events, both before and after the Resurrection, can be understood only as supernatural events presaging the miraculous resurrection in the case, of the veil of the temple, and underscoring it in the case of the spirits who walked abroad.

Once Jesus' body was safely down, John, Joseph, and Nicodemus carried the body about twenty-two yards from Golgotha across the cultivated area to the quarry's face and Joseph's new tomb, probably to the privacy of the vestibule, in order to put some distance between the group and the activities of the soldiers in finishing off and loading up the carcasses of the two thieves (Mt 27:59–60; Mk 15:46; Lk 23:53; Jn 19:40–42). Then Joseph and Nicodemus went back through the gate. Joseph bought an expensive linen shroud. Nicodemus bought myrrh and aloes; due to their weight (about 100 pounds), he probably had the shopkeeper carry the load for him on his return to Golgotha (Jn 19:39).

Jesus was left with Mary, John, and the others. We can well picture the numerous artistic renderings of the Pieta, which ring true in this case, as Mary held her dead son. Some of the women gathered or purchased flowers as the group waited on Joseph and Nicodemus. The centurion, the executioners, the guards, and the cart all moved away. Jesus and those who stayed with him until the end were finally alone.

10. When Joseph and Nicodemus returned with the necessities for burial, it was about 5:30 p.m. or perhaps a little earlier. There was a need for haste. They spread the shroud on the shelf in the inner room of the tomb on which bodies were to be laid until the flesh decomposed and the bones could be re-interred. The Sudarium was removed and placed in the inner chamber. Jesus was placed on the bottom fold of the Shroud, which was then folded over the top of his head till it reached his feet at the open end. Myrrh and aloes were used as aromatics and to anoint—not to clean—the body, since it could not be cleaned due to the violence of his death and the necessity to leave the blood with the body. Other cloths were used, which are lost or destroyed. One was a chin band, apparent on the Shroud of Turin. There may have been bands to secure his arms against rigor mortis. The women who had obtained flowers laid them inside the Shroud. Faint images of twenty-eight types of plants, including twenty-three flowers, three bushes, and two thorn vines, appear on the Shroud. All of them grow in the area of Jerusalem, some of them grow nowhere else, and twenty-seven of them bloom during March and April.

Shortly before sunset, the group completed their tasks and rolled the heavy stone across the doorway. Jesus was left alone. Only Mary knew what would happen next. The day was probably April 7, AD 30.

THE GLORIOUS
MYSTERIES

The Supper at Emmaus, Jacopo Bassano (Jacopo dal Ponte), c.1538, Kimbell Art Museum, Fort Worth, Texas; Acquired with the generous assistance of a gift from Mildred Sterling Hedrick

THE RESURRECTION

◆

1. The day after the Crucifixion (even though it was the Passover and the sabbath) "the chief priests and Pharisees" went to see Pilate. Presumably Caiaphas was among them, since Pilate necessarily would have been approached upon the authority of the Sanhedrin. They told Pilate that Jesus had said he would rise again after three days and that it would be dangerous if Jesus' disciples stole his body and then told the people he had risen (Mt 27:62–64). In view of the importance of this possibility, why hadn't the rulers of the Jews asked for a guard from the commencement of the entombment? It is probable that this particular teaching by Jesus was not brought to their attention until the day after the Crucifixion. After all, even the disciples themselves had paid little or no attention to this teaching. But the urgency created by this new information led the chief priests to break the Passover and the sabbath to make this request to Pilate. Only the day before, Pilate had shown these men the courtesy of meeting with them outside the praetorium, so that they would not be defiled. Yet here they were, defiling themselves, to conduct business on the sabbath and Passover by seeking another interview with Pilate. What delicious irony!

Pilate's authority as Rome's governor had been compromised by the success of the threat by these same men against him personally only the day before. They now defiled the Passover and themselves by seeking an audience with Pilate on this high holy day. Pilate tested their urgency and need for some action by him by receiving them in his audience hall rather than outside, as he had courteously done the day before. When they further defiled themselves by entering under his roof, his authority—and Rome's—was reestablished.

The Pharisees asked Pilate to authorize a guard to be set at Jesus' tomb. Pilate was not about to use Roman soldiers to guard a dead man, particularly a man he had executed under compulsion by the men standing before him. Pilate replied, **"You have a guard of soldiers; go, make it secure as you can"** (Mt 27:65). Roman soldiers had jurisdiction to act within the city of Jerusalem, as evidenced by the example that it was Roman soldiers who rescued Paul from the mob (Acts 21:27–36). Furthermore, all Judea was under direct Roman government. Pilate's consent was sought and obtained because otherwise only Roman soldiers would have had jurisdiction over the area of the tomb. Pilate, having been coerced into killing Jesus the day before by these same men, took sardonic satisfaction in their consternation and allowed them to get out of their jam as best they could by themselves. Place emphasis on the two "yous" in the above quotation, and the hostility is clear. The guards were temple soldiers under temple authority. They had not fought a foreign enemy for more than a generation. Their job was ceremonial or, occasionally, to intimidate their own people. Their discipline, therefore, was not to the standard of Roman soldiers.

Because the entire purpose of the guard at the tomb was to be sure that Jesus' body could not be removed, we may be confident that the officer of the guard opened the tomb to assure himself that Jesus' body had not been removed before the guard was posted.

No commander in his right mind assumes responsibility for an inventory (of a body in this case) without inspecting it first.

Before the arrival of the women disciples at the tomb, there was a localized earthquake in the area of the tomb, and the stone rolled back. An angel sat upon the stone (Mt 28:1–2). The entry to the tomb is 52" high and 26" wide. The stone that closed the tomb was in the shape of a millstone, which could be rolled to open or close the tomb. The arc of the stone at an elevation of 52" would indicate a stone more than 5' high. In order not to be fragile, its thickness would have been like that of a millstone, about 3"–4" thick. For the angel to have sat on top of a stone 5' in the air would have been undignified. We may therefore surmise that the stone had rolled back and then fell over and the angel was sitting upon the thickness of the stone, about 4" above the ground, or more if the stone fell at an angle.

The guards ascertained that the tomb was empty, probably before the angel's physical appearance. Upon the angel's materialization, the guards trembled and fled into the city. A Roman soldier would have thus deserted his post at the cost of his life, but temple soldiers were of a different caliber. There is no indication that the guards and the women disciples actually saw each other. The recitation of the events places the flight of the guards **"while** [the women] **were going"** to tell the disciples (Mt 28:11), but that is done to make the guards' action introductory to their meeting with the chief priests. It is a more reasonable interpretation, in my opinion, that the guards had fled well before sunrise, before the women arrived, and that they did not see each other.

✦ ✦ ✦

2. "When the sabbath was past," some women disciples bought spices and ointments to anoint (not to clean) Jesus' body

(Mk 16:1; Lk 23:56). The sabbath ended at sunset on Saturday, so the women had procured their materials after sunset. The women gathered and went to the tomb very early on Sunday. The time was **"toward the dawn"** (Mt 28:1) or **"very early . . . when the sun had risen"** (Mk 16:12) or **"at early dawn"** (Lk 24:1) or **"while it was still dark"** (Jn 20:1). What was the time they went to the tomb? "Sunrise" can be the appearance of the sun's disk rather than its complete visibility two minutes later. The degree of darkness of an early dawn will depend on the cloud cover at the time. Do the Gospels describe the light conditions at the moment the women left on their mission, at the time they arrived at the tomb, or at the time they ran to tell the other disciples? The gospels are not meteorological records, and some combination of these circumstances explains the apparent discrepancies. It was very early Sunday morning.

The women who went to the tomb included Mary Magdalene (Mt 28:1; Mk 16:1; Lk 24:10; Jn 20:1). Another was described by Matthew as **"the other Mary"** (Mt 28:1), referring back to his earlier list of the women present at the Crucifixion, naming **"Mary the mother of James and Joseph"** (Mt 27:56). Mark describes the same woman as **"Mary the mother of James"** (Mk16:1), referring back to his earlier list of the women at the Crucifixion, including **"Mary the mother of James the Younger and of Joses"** (Mk 15:40). Luke describes her as **"Mary the mother of James"** (Lk 24:10).

James the Younger, or James the son of Alpheus, is the man who was martyred by the Jews at Jerusalem during a gubernatorial interregnum in AD 62 and was also called the "brother" of Jesus. The Mary who was his mother was, therefore, Mary, the wife of Cleophas, making her children the first cousins or stepcousins of Jesus. She was married to Joseph's brother, causing John to refer to her as the "sister" of Mary.

Since Hebrew and Aramaic had no word for "cousin," Jesus' relationship to James was included in the kinship of "brother."

The belief that Jesus was the only child of Mary, consistent with her perpetual virginity, was held by all the Fathers, as well as all the Reformers of the sixteenth century and was not questioned until the "Enlightenment" of the eighteenth century.

The two Marys were accompanied to the tomb by Salome (Mk16:1), mother of James and John, and Joanna (Lk 24:10), and **"the other women with them"** (Lk 24:10) of an unknown number, but the plural indicates at least two more.

As the women went on their way to the tomb, they worried about how they could roll back the heavy stone (Mk 16:3). They found that the stone had already been rolled back, and an angel was sitting on it (Mt 28:2). Matthew says, **"The angel said to the women, 'Do not be afraid; for I know that you seek Jesus who was crucified. He is not here; for he has risen, as he said. Then go quickly and tell his disciples that he has risen from the dead, and behold, he is going before you to Galilee; there you will see him. Lo, I have told you'"** (Mt 28:5–7).

In *Mark* the women found the stone rolled back. **"And entering the tomb, they saw a young man sitting on the right side, dressed in a white robe; and they were amazed. And he said to them, 'Do not be amazed; you seek Jesus of Nazareth, who was crucified. He has risen; he is not here; see the place where they laid him. But go, tell his disciples and Peter that he is going before you to Galilee; there you will see him, as he told you'"** (Mk 16:4–7).

Luke tells it with significant differences. When the women found the stone rolled away, they went into the tomb but did not find Jesus' body. **"While they were perplexed about this, behold, two men stood by them in dazzling apparel; and as they were frightened and bowed their faces to the ground, the men said to them, 'Why do you seek the living among the dead? He is not here, but has risen. Remember how he told you, while he was still in Galilee,**

that the Son of Man must be delivered into the hands of sinful men, and be crucified, and on the third day rise'" (Lk 24:2–7).

What is common to these three accounts is that the women saw two angels. Matthew's account identifies the person seen as an "angel" and the other two accounts describe the appearance from which the reader should conclude that they were angels. Mark's account says the women actually first saw an angel after they entered the tomb; he was sitting on the right side. This account describes the physical layout of Jesus' tomb. One stoops to enter the first chamber, the vestibule, in which the body would be prepared for burial. A second low entry leads into the second chamber, the sepulcher. On the right side of the sepulcher a shelf was carved out of the living rock, on which Jesus' body was laid. The text does not designate which chamber the angel was sitting in or the location in such chamber. He surely was sitting on the shelf in the sepulcher rather than on the floor of the vestibule.

How does one reconcile these three accounts? There were at least six women at the tomb and perhaps more. No one would have passed an angel seated on the round stone in order to enter the tomb. The angel seated inside materialized and became visible after one or more women had entered the vestibule. At that same instant the angel seated on the stone outside the tomb also became visible to the women who were still waiting to enter the tomb. Both angels rose from their seated positions to address the women. The two angels had different messages for the women. One angel delivered the message quoted in *Matthew* and *Mark* that Jesus had risen and they should tell the other disciples. The other angel drew the didactic conclusion for them, reminding them of Jesus' teaching that he must be delivered into the hands of sinful men, be crucified, and rise (Lk 24:4–7).

When the angels disappeared, the women then ran to tell the other disciples.

3. The Virgin Mary is startlingly absent from all four lists of women going to the tomb early Sunday morning. After she had stayed by Jesus throughout his passion, crucifixion, and entombment, are we to believe that "the poor dear" was just too physically or emotionally exhausted to accompany the other women on Sunday morning? That does not sound like the Virgin Mary we encounter in the Gospels and in subsequent tradition, a strong and determined woman in every good sense.

It is probable that Mary did not accompany the others because Jesus had already appeared to her. There is a tradition that he did so. This tradition is evidenced especially by the existence of a Chapel of the Apparition of Jesus to Mary in the Church of the Holy Sepulcher in Jerusalem. In view of the extraordinarily close relationship between Jesus and Mary, he would have wanted to appear to her first, so as to relieve her grief and fear and, even, doubt as to whether his interpretation of the scriptures regarding himself had been correct.

Jesus' appearance to Mary was no later than about 5:00 a.m., so Mary could excuse herself from going to the tomb. It is likely that Jesus' resurrection was in some manner related to the localized earthquake and rolling back of the stone at the tomb's entrance. Therefore, the timing of Jesus' appearance to Mary places the time of the guards' discovery of the empty tomb and their flight some time earlier.

Mary could not go to the tomb with the other women, pretending not to know what they would find. Nor could she tell anyone, either in advance or thereafter, without depriving the others of the honor of bearing the message of the empty tomb to the men. By not making herself a public witness at that time, Mary also avoided subjecting her own credibility to attack, as was done to all the women who told what they had seen and were disbelieved.

It is significant, and no accident, that Jesus appeared first to women. He, thereby, elevated their status for all time above the place they held in both Jewish and pagan societies. In a criminal proceeding, a woman was not even competent to testify, at least in some cases, as shown in the tale of Susanna and the elders. In all cases a woman's credibility was slight, and there was nothing unusual about the men refusing to believe their incredible message (Mk 16:11; Lk 24:11).

The women had stayed in different lodgings of various disciples scattered over the city, as had the men. One did not then reserve a block of rooms for "the party from Galilee." The women would have returned to different locations. Some told what they had seen and heard and were disbelieved (Lk 24:11). Others, surmising they would not be believed, kept silent and awaited further developments (Mk 16:8).

***

4. Mary Magdalene was one of the women at the tomb. When she left it, she ran to Peter, who was with John. She told them that "we," referring both to herself and the other women, **"do not know where they have laid him"** (Jn 20:2). Mary Magdalene thereby showed a lack of understanding of the significance of what she had seen. If she had believed and understood what the angels had told them—he is risen—she would no longer have been concerned with the body having been taken. Like Thomas, Mary Magdalene continued in this state of incredulity until her own personal epiphany.

Peter and John ran to the tomb. John was younger and arrived first. **"Stooping to look in, he saw the linen cloths lying there, but he did not go in"** (Jn 20:4–5). Mary Magdalene and the one or more other women with her would have run after them, but at a slower pace. John waited for Peter, in deference to him, so that Peter could enter first. John's deference to Peter was in marked contrast to the attempt of James and John, egged on by their mother, to shoulder their way ahead of Peter in the inner circle, which had taken place so short a time before.

"Simon Peter came, following him, and went into the tomb; he saw the linen cloths lying, and the napkin which had been on his head, not lying with the linen cloths but rolled up in a place by itself. Then the other disciple, who reached the tomb first, also went in, and he saw and believed; for as yet they did not know the scripture, that he must rise from the dead" (Jn 20:6–9).

Although Jesus had told the disciples that he must die and rise again, their rejection of this teaching carried over to prevent their comprehension of what had happened, with the exception of John, who "saw and believed."

As previously mentioned, the tomb consisted of two rooms, a vestibule and a sepulcher. The entry to the vestibule, which was closed with the stone, is 26" wide and 4'4" high. The vestibule is 12'8" deep and 11'2" wide. A second entry, aligned with the first, leads from it into the sepulcher, which is 6'10" deep and 6'4" wide. The thickness of the two entries adds to the total depth of the tomb. Almost half the width of the sepulcher is occupied by a ledge 6'10" deep and 3'1" wide, the edge of which is flush with the entry. The entrances face east and would admit the light of the rising sun to illuminate the sepulcher partially.

From the entry before going in, John could see the "othonia," translated as "linen cloths." It would be most unlikely that, even viewed from the most favorable angle, John would have been able to see any burial cloths on the ledge, particularly since it was in the shadow of the wall between it and the vestibule fifteen to twenty-two feet deep into the tomb. The "othonia" were the binding bands for the chin and perhaps the arms, and did not include the "sindon," translated as "shroud." Nor, from the entry, could John see "the napkin which had been on his head," the "sudarion" (Greek), referred to in its Latin translation "sudarium." The implication is that the Shroud and the Sudarium were on the ledge, not visible from the entry. Since the Sudarium was not placed in the Shroud with the body, it had been placed on the ledge to keep the blood in it close to the body. Upon entering the vestibule, Peter could see the Shroud and Sudarium on the ledge, as well as the bands on the floor. There is some disagreement among scholars as to the terminology, and some would include the Shroud as one of the "linen cloths" on the floor, visible from outside the entry, with the "napkin" or Shroud not visible, meaning it was on the ledge by itself. I have chosen the former interpretation, which appears more likely, but I do not see that it makes any difference as to the central fact of resurrection.

John "saw and believed." Since the disciples had not understood Jesus' teaching about being crucified and rising the third day, Peter did not understand that Jesus had risen any more than Mary Magdalene had. "[Peter] **saw the linen cloths by themselves, and he went home wondering at what had happened**" (Lk 24:12). But John "saw and believed." He believed that Jesus had risen, based on what he had heard from Mary Magdalene and then seen for himself. What he saw was the image of Jesus on the Shroud. Peter and John took all the burial cloths with them. Their preservation by the Church was the only reason to describe them in the Gospels in such detail.

5. Seeing the image of Jesus on the Shroud on the morning of the Resurrection, John had the advantage over us of not

being distracted by claims that it was a forgery. The image he saw was breathtakingly realistic and familiar. It is clearest where the fabric touched Jesus' body; there is some distortion where a curved surface is displayed on a flat cloth, the same problem one has in transferring a round globe to a flat map. Even today, the evidence is overwhelming as to the identity of the man on the Shroud, and John certainly had no problem recognizing him.

The image on the Shroud is unique, because it records a unique event, a man dead for about thirty-seven hours returning to life. While those who have seen the Shroud over the last 1,500 years have recognized what the image on the Shroud shows, until 1898 there was little effort to understand how the image was imprinted on it. All efforts to replicate the transfer of such an image to cloth have failed miserably. The detailed data on the Shroud have been revealed due to the scientific advances of our technological age and could never have been detected in earlier times. It is as if the Shroud had been encoded with data that could not be known until our own era and was intended to be a sign to an unbelieving, scientific age.

I have read the different theories of how the image was made on the cloth of the Shroud. One theory makes the most sense to me. We now know that, at a certain level, heat and light are interchangeable forms of energy. A flash of incredibly intense light for an incredibly short period of time theoretically could give off heat to scorch the cloth without destroying it. Such a process would cause the characteristic, previously noted, of a distortion similar to trying to picture a curved surface on a flat sheet.

Therefore, the Shroud of Turin is best understood as a snapshot of the Resurrection. It was laid down 2,000 years ago as a special sign to our own technological age. As is always the case, the Lord not only does not compel belief, but rather he always leaves an escape hatch for unbelievers to justify and remain in their unbelief.

Finally, regarding the Shroud of Turin, its most remarkable feature is the calmness and serenity of Jesus' face, which does not at all accord with the tortures inflicted upon him. We are familiar with the fact that severe trauma or pain before death can cause such irremovable contortions of the facial features that such people have closed-casket funerals. Jesus' face does not reflect such contortions. If he did go through his ordeal while preserving the serenity of his countenance, this would explain how the centurion could recognize that something extraordinary was occurring and conclude, "**Truly, this was the Son of God**" (Mt 27:54).

⸎   ⸎   ⸎

6. When Peter and John left the tomb to return to town, they took the Shroud and Sudarium with them. Mary Magdalene lingered behind (Jn 20:10–11). John describes what happened: "**But Mary stood weeping outside the tomb, and as she wept she stooped to look into the tomb; and she saw two angels in white, sitting where the body had lain, one at the head and one at the feet. They said to her, 'Woman, why are you weeping?' She said to them, 'Because they have taken away my Lord, and I do not know where they have laid him.' Saying this, she turned around and saw Jesus standing, but she did not know that it was Jesus. Jesus said to her, 'Woman, why are you weeping? Whom do you seek?' Supposing him to be the gardener, she said to him, 'Sir, if you have carried him away, tell me where you have laid him, and I will take him away.' Jesus said to her, 'Mary.' She turned and said to him in Hebrew, 'Rabboni!' (which means teacher). Jesus said to her, 'Do not hold me, for I have not yet ascended to the Father; but go to my brethren and say to them, I am ascending to my Father and your Father, to my God and your God'"** (Jn 20:11–17).

Matthew's version appears to differ materially from John's. After describing the women's encounter with an angel, he continues: **"So they** [the women] **departed quickly from the tomb with fear and great joy, and ran to tell his disciples. And behold, Jesus met them and said, 'Hail!' And they came up and took hold of his feet and worshiped him. Then Jesus said to them, 'Do not be afraid; go and tell my brethren to go to Galilee, and there they will see me'"** (Mt 28:8–10).

Mark's version is shorter. **"Now when he rose early on the first day of the week, he appeared first to Mary Magdalene, from whom he had cast out seven demons. She went and told those who had been with him, as they mourned and wept"** (Mk 16:9–10).

John and Mark mention only Mary Magdalene as being present at the tomb on this occasion. Matthew clearly uses the plural, "They took hold of his feet. . . . " (Mt 28:9). The failure of John and Mark to list each person present on each occasion is not significant; the Gospels do not give laundry lists. Mary was accompanied by the woman (women) who went with her to Peter and John. *John*, the most chronological of the Gospels and the most detailed regarding the Passion, clearly places the time of this encounter after Peter and John left the tomb. Matthew conflates the original encounter of the entire group of women at the tomb with the encounter of Mary Magdalene and one or more women with Jesus, not distinguishing between the two occasions. Nor does he mention Peter and John's visit to the tomb. Each Gospel writer tells in as short a space as possible the events that illustrate the points he considers important. Matthew's omission of the intervening events is not significant. Mark clearly distinguishes the morning's first trip to the tomb from its second (Mk 16:1–9). Mary Magdalene was there after Peter and John left.

Why did Jesus speak only to Mary Magdalene? Where was the other woman (women)? After Peter and John left, Mary Magdalene looked into the tomb and saw two angels sitting on the ledge in the sepulcher. Mary and the other woman entered the vestibule and made obeisance, bowing their heads to the ground. After the angels had spoken to them and then disappeared, Mary Magdalene exited the tomb first, and her companion remained inside to marvel and to mourn. Mary spotted the apparent gardener and walked up to him to inquire as to the body's location. The man then identified himself as Jesus. When the other woman exited the tomb, she saw Jesus and Mary and came up to them after Jesus had finished speaking to Mary Magdalene. Not only John, but also Mark, emphasizes that Jesus first appeared to Mary Magdalene (Mk 16:9; Jn 20:16–17). As the two (or more) women worshiped Jesus, holding his feet, he spoke to both of them.

Jesus said to Mary Magdalene, **"Do not hold me, for I have not yet ascended to the Father. . . . "** (Jn 20:17). Yet the women **"came up and took hold of his feet and worshiped him"** (Mt 28:9). In the context of John's Gospel, Jesus told Mary, "Do not hold me" immediately after she recognized him and cried out, "Rabboni!" We can scarcely conceive the rush of emotion that enveloped Mary Magdalene when she recognized Jesus and suddenly realized that he had risen from the dead. This was the same body she had helped entomb only thirty-eight hours earlier. In all probability, she made a motion as if to embrace Jesus. It was this motion toward him that Jesus halted with the admonition, "Do not hold me." His risen body, with its spiritual powers over place and matter, was not to be handled by others. Nowhere in the New Testament is there any indication that anyone did so.

The exception was that Jesus allowed and offered the touching of his five wounds. The women **"took hold of his feet and worshiped him"** (Mt 28:9). In holding his feet, Mary and the other woman could not have failed to touch the nail wounds in his feet as they worshiped him. The feet were the dirtiest part of the body. They were the part washed upon entering a house, and washing the guest's feet was the function of the slave or servant, if there was one. We are reminded of the scene, only six days before the Passover, in which Mary, sister of Martha and Lazarus, had anointed Jesus' feet and wiped them with her hair. Or the scene only sixty hours earlier in which Jesus washed the disciples' feet. For the women to hold Jesus' feet as they worshiped him was an act of service and submission, quite unlike the loving embrace with which Mary Magdalene had sought to greet Jesus. A week later Jesus would offer Thomas the opportunity to handle his other three wounds. It is implied, but clear, that Thomas did not have the temerity to do so, despite artistic renderings to the contrary.

Allowing the touching of his wounds was salvific. Otherwise, Jesus' body was not to be handled during his Resurrection appearances.

Mary Magdalene went to the disciples and told them, **"I have seen the Lord"** and gave them his message (Jn 20:18). Presumably the other woman (women) went with her, and both attested to Jesus' resurrection, as Jesus had instructed them (Mt 28:10). **"But when they** [the disciples] **heard that he was alive and had been seen by her, they would not believe it"** (Mk 16:11). Jewish law required two witnesses' testimony. The two (or more) witnesses were women, and the disciples would not believe what they said. Their subsequent vindication, and the honor accorded to Mary Magdalene as the first disciple to whom Jesus appeared, was the commencement of the elevation of the dignity of women in the eyes of the Christian world.

7. The disciples from Galilee were scattered around Jerusalem in the homes of local disciples. They did not reassemble one by one or one group with the next until later in the day. Obviously, the disciples who disbelieved the witness of Mary Magdalene that Jesus had spoken to her and of the women that had touched his feet did not include John in their group, since John already believed (Lk 24:22–24; Jn 20:8). Peter and John stayed in a place not including other disciples, since it would have been inconceivable that any disciple present with them would not have run to the tomb with them. One group of disciples, including Cleophas and the other disciple who went to Emmaus, did not know what to make of the disappearance of Jesus' body, reported by the women and confirmed by Peter and John (Lk 24:22–24). Almost all of them did not believe the women's report of seeing angels at the tomb. Thomas was elsewhere and did not join the assembly that day. At this point, we only know of John's belief that Jesus had risen (Lk 24:22–24; Jn 20:8).

Two of the disciples, Cleophas and one other, left to go to Emmaus, seven miles north on the road to Galilee. Since Cleophas is not a name frequently encountered, he was probably Joseph's brother, brother-in-law to the Virgin Mary. The theologian Origen, writing in the first half of the third century, identifies the other disciple as Simon, the son of Cleophas and Mary. As the two were on the road, a stranger overtook them and fell into conversation with them. In response to their incredulity at the report of the women, the stranger responded, **"'O foolish men and slow to believe all that the prophets have spoken! Was it not necessary that the Christ should suffer these things and enter into his glory?' And beginning with Moses and all the prophets, he interpreted to them in all the scriptures the things concerning himself"** (Lk 24: 25–27).

"So they drew near to the village to which they were going. He appeared to be going further, but they constrained

him, saying, 'Stay with us, for it is toward evening and the day is now far spent.' So he went in to stay with them. When he was at table with them, he took the bread and blessed, and broke it, and gave it to them. And their eyes were opened and they recognized him; and he vanished out of their sight" (Lk 24:28–31). It was still the week of unleavened bread, so the bread he consecrated was unleavened.

The two disciples had left the gathering in the upper room that morning after the return from the tomb by Peter and John but before Mary Magdalene and the other woman (women) returned after seeing Jesus. They may have returned to their lodgings and/or eaten before getting on the road. They took about three hours to walk to Emmaus, seven miles north of Jerusalem. A U.S. military pace covers 18,000 feet, or 3.4 miles, in an hour, not allowing for periods of rest. Two tired and discouraged men walking in sandals on cobblestones probably made between two and two-and-a-half miles per hour. If the day was "far advanced" but still had enough daylight that the stranger could have gone further, it was around 4:30 p.m. By the time the innkeeper prepared and placed food before them, it was evening, about 5:00 p.m.

The first thing to note is the unusual physical form of Jesus' resurrected body. To Mary Magdalene he first appeared to be a gardener. To these disciples he was a total stranger. When he appeared to the disciples that night, he was instantly recognized. But when Jesus appeared to the disciples on the beach in Galilee, **"none of the disciples dared ask him, 'Who are you?' They knew it was the Lord"** (Jn 21:12). Jesus could come and go, appearing from and vanishing into thin air as he saw fit. He could appear in the form of other men until such time as he chose to make himself known, if he did so choose.

The more important thing to note is the subject matter of Jesus' discourse to his disciples during his Resurrection appearances.

Accounts of most of these appearances give no description of why he came and what he wished to communicate. Yet he was not making these appearances just to prove that he had risen. The account of his conversation with the two disciples is the first describing the substance of his post-Resurrection teaching. The purpose of his appearance was **"to interpret to them in all the scriptures the things concerning himself"** (Lk 24:27). He gave the disciples an exegesis of the "scriptures" (the Old Testament). This exegesis was the basis of Peter's address to the crowd on Pentecost (Acts 2:14–36). Jesus' teaching to the disciples during his Resurrection appearances, for the most part unrecorded in the New Testament, constitutes the foundation of "the Tradition" of the Church and the teaching authority of the apostles and their successors, the bishops.

Once Jesus had blessed and broken the bread, he vanished. The presence of his resurrected body was no longer necessary; he remained with them in the consecrated bread.

The two disciples **"rose that same hour and returned to Jerusalem"** (Lk 24:33). They did not "rise instantly." Presumably they strengthened themselves for the return to Jerusalem by finishing the meal before them, including the consecrated bread. We can picture their haste in the dark along the rough road, aided by the light of a moon a few days past full. Their return journey surely took no more than two hours, returning to the upper room about 7:30 p.m.

"They found the eleven gathered together and those who were with them, who said, 'The Lord has risen indeed, and has appeared to Simon!' Then they told what had happened on the road, and how he was known to them in the breaking of the bread" (Lk 24:33–35). But Mark says, **"After this** [his appearance to Mary Magdalene] **he appeared in another form to two of them as they were walking into the country. And they went back and told the rest, but they did not believe them"** (Mk

16:12–13). The most likely reconciliation of these two accounts is that the disciples were reassembling in the upper room, arriving in groups from around the city. The two disciples returning from Emmaus were greeted by a group of disciples who disbelieved them. Since Cleophas was stepfather of James, son of Alpheus, and the grandfather or stepgrandfather of James and John, it is obvious that none of them were in the group of disciples who refused to believe Cleophas, backed by the testimony of a second witness. Nor was Peter there, since he had seen Jesus himself by that time.

Foreseeing the disciples' disbelief, the Virgin Mary had been absent all day. Peter had been absent and arrived to tell the disciples that Jesus had appeared to him. In all probability, Peter had gone to Mary first in order to relieve her grief, not knowing that Jesus had already appeared to her. Peter also told some disciples, who preceded him to the upper room and told the group assembled there. At this point Cleophas and the other disciple who went to Emmaus were believed. Upon Peter's word, the disciples finally believed. Peter later went to the upper room and told the disciples of his own encounter with the risen Lord. The account in *Luke*, placing the two disciples' relation of their story after being told of the epiphany to Peter, would appear to be inconsistent with the disbelief recorded in Mark, unless we recognize that the Gospels are not strictly chronological.

※　※　※

8. "The Lord has risen indeed, and has appeared to Simon" (Lk 14:34)! Paul said, **"[H]e appeared to Cephas, then to the twelve"** (1 Cor 15:5). Sometime that Sunday afternoon, Jesus appeared to Peter. It seems clear that Jesus accepted Peter's repentance and assuaged his guilt and grief. The fact that the first apostle to whom Jesus appeared was Peter is highly significant.

Jesus thereby recognized, or confirmed, the primacy of Peter among the disciples. Peter was not the first disciple, but he was among the three of the inner circle. Jesus took Peter, James, and John to witness the raising from the dead of the daughter of Jairus. Likewise, he chose the same three to witness his Transfiguration. It was Peter who first publicly confessed Jesus to be the Messiah. Jesus in response had renamed Simon as Peter and stated that he would found his church upon this rock (Petrus) and would give Peter the authority to bind and loose on earth. His primacy among the three is impliedly recognized in the conspiracy of Salome, Zebedee's wife, and especially her older son James, to get Jesus to elbow Peter out of the way to make preferred places for James and John. Again, all three were chosen to accompany Jesus at Gethsemane. The angel at the tomb told the women to "go, tell his disciples and Peter . . . ," singling out Peter (Mk 16:7). In his subsequent Resurrection appearances, Jesus would further grant Peter authority over the other apostles (Jn 21:15–19), but this was the first post-Resurrection recognition of the primacy of Peter.

The first letter of Clement, third Bishop of Rome, written about AD 96 to the Corinthians, displays the early exercise by the successors of Peter of the primacy originally accorded to Peter himself. Clement was himself trained by Peter. A schism had arisen in the church at Corinth. The first time I read this letter, it struck me that it could have come out of the Vatican last week. It interprets and applies scripture at considerable length. Its tone is patient and irenic. But in the end it confidently asserts a position of primacy over Corinth. "[T]**he Lord's name is being blasphemed because of your stupidity, and you are exposing yourself to danger**" (Ch. 47). "**You see, dear friends, how well protected they are whom the Master disciplines. Yes, he is like a good farmer, and disciplines us so that the outcome of his holy discipline may mean mercy for us. And that is why you** who are responsible for the revolt must submit to the presbyters" (Ch. 57). "**If, on the other hand, there be some who fail to obey what God has told them through us, they must realize that they will enmesh themselves in sin and in no insignificant danger**" (Ch. 59). "**[Y]ou will make us exceedingly happy if you prove obedient to what we, prompted by the Holy Spirit, have written, and if, following the plea of our letter for peace and harmony, you rid yourself of your wicked and passionate rivalry**" (Ch. 63) (emphasis supplied). Did Corinth have its own bishop and priests? Of course, unless there was an episcopal interregnum which occasioned the schism. What is clear is that the Bishop of Rome intervened in the internal affairs of a different diocese. He asserted his own special enlightenment by the Holy Spirit and that God addressed the broad Church through himself. Finally, he demanded obedience to his decision. He even referred to himself in the royal "we." The primacy of the See of Peter has been with the Church from the beginning.

Some writers have argued that the letter of Clement was written earlier, before Clement became Bishop of Rome, but the authority claimed and exercised in the letter is that claimed only by the apostles or one having apostolic authority, namely a bishop, and there is no reasonable basis for such a letter otherwise.

❖ ❖ ❖

9. Later in the evening, as the disciples were seated at table, after hearing from the two returned from Emmaus and from Peter, "**Jesus himself stood among them**" (Lk 24:36). Jesus suddenly appeared in the upper room, despite "**the doors being shut where the disciples were, for fear of the Jews. . . .**" (Jn 20:19).

Jesus greeted the disciples, "**Peace be with you**" (Jn 20:19; Lk 24:36). "**But they** [the disciples] **were startled and frightened,** and supposed that they saw a spirit. And he said to them, 'Why are you troubled, and why do questionings rise in your hearts? See my hands and my feet, that it is I myself; handle me and see; for a spirit has not flesh and bones as you see that I have. And when he had said this, he showed them his hands and his feet'" (Lk 24:37–40). John adds that he also showed them the wound in his side (Jn 20:20). There is no indication that anyone stepped forward to "handle" Jesus, and it seems improbable that anyone did so.

Jesus **"upbraided them for their unbelief and hardness of heart, because they had not believed those who saw him after he had risen"** (Mk 16:14). Though Jesus had not been present to see the disciples' response to the women who first returned from the tomb, later to Mary Magdalene and her companion(s) and to the two disciples who returned from Emmaus, he had knowledge of what had occurred. He had the divine attribute of omniscience.

Jesus demonstrated that he was not a ghost by asking for something to eat and then eating a piece of fish in front of the disciples (Lk 24:41–42).

Jesus renewed his teaching of the disciples. **"'These are my words which I spoke to you, while I was still with you, that everything written about me in the law of Moses and the prophets and the psalms must be fulfilled.' Then he opened their minds to understand the scriptures, and said to them, 'Thus it is written that the Christ should suffer and on the third day rise from the dead, and that repentance and forgiveness of sins should be preached in his name to all nations, beginning from Jerusalem'"** (Lk 24:44–47). This is a more detailed description of the same teaching he gave the two disciples on the road to Emmaus.

At the time selected by himself, Jesus vanished, as he had on the earlier epiphanies.

Thus, on that Resurrection Sunday Jesus was seen on five separate occasions, first presumably by Mary, then by Mary Magdalene and her companion(s), then by Cleophas and one other disciple on the road to Emmaus, then by Peter, and then by ten of the eleven apostles and the disciples gathered with them.

❖   ❖   ❖

10. "[S]ome of the guard went into the city and told the chief priests all that had taken place. And when they had assembled with the elders and taken counsel, they gave a sum of money to the soldiers and said, 'Tell people, his disciples came by night and stole him away while we were asleep. And if this comes to the governor's ears, we will satisfy him and keep you out of trouble.' So they took the money and did as they were directed; and this story has been spread among the Jews to this day" (Mt 28:11–15).

Doubtless, many Jews of the time were successfully misled, to their great cost. Indeed, one even encounters this story of the purloined body among unbelieving writers down to the present day. The weakness in the story is that a guard who sleeps on duty, especially if his default results in the precise harm the guard was posted to prevent, as here, is subject to extreme punishment, including death. That would be true even in a lax, ceremonial unit like the temple guards. Yet the guards were not punished but were bribed to tell a lie which, if true, would subject them to such punishment. If they had refused to accept the bribe to lie and had told the truth, they would have been charged with sleeping on duty and punished for covering it up. It is a transparent lie, indeed. The claim to have slept through the noise of rolling back the stone makes the lie even more preposterous.

As for the offer to protect the soldiers from Pilate's wrath, that was a cheap offer. Pilate had no interest in the dereliction of duty of the temple guards in performing a task set by temple officials rather than by himself. The fact that the soldiers reported to the temple authorities and that the temple authorities assured them of protection from Pilate proves that the soldiers were temple guards, rather than Roman. Caiaphas had no authority to protect Roman soldiers from their own Roman governor, and Caiaphas would have subjected himself to severe risk if he had bribed Roman soldiers to lie to their commander.

The temple hierarchy sought to protect their own particular interest by subverting the gospel. They were the first in a long line of such folk. Beginning with the Gnostics, we have all those who literally rewrite scripture to promote their own interests. Recent examples include Jehovah's Witnesses and those who mistranslate the scriptures in order to further their own agendas. There are those who create new scriptures, such as the Mormons. All these and many others are the proud descendants of Caiaphas and Annas.

Ascension of Christ, Benvenuto Tisi Garofalo, Galleria Nazionale d'Arte Antica, Rome

THE ASCENSION

❖

1. The apostle Thomas was not present when Jesus appeared to the disciples the night of his Resurrection. When the others told him, he responded, **"Unless I see in his hands the print of the nails, and place my finger in the mark of the nails, and place my hand in his side, I will not believe"** (Jn 20:25).

The following Sunday, the disciples again were gathered in the upper room. This time Thomas was with them. We may reasonably assume that after the Resurrection the disciples gathered daily to pray in the hope of seeing Jesus again. The group would have included the eleven apostles and numerous other disciples, including the women, most notably the Blessed Virgin Mary. Jesus postponed his next appearance an entire week to allow the disciples time to digest the enormity of what had happened.

"The doors were shut, but Jesus came and stood among them, and said, 'Peace be with you.' Then he said to Thomas, 'Put your finger here, and see my hands; and put out your hand, and place it in my side; do not be faithless, but believing'" (Jn 20:26–27). The disciples were still in fear of the Jews and had locked the door. Jesus again exercised his power of appearing out of thin air. And he called Thomas on the violence of his statement of disbelief, having divine knowledge of it without having been present.

Thomas' response states the conclusion he had previously drawn, which was the basis for his disbelief. Thomas had concluded that only God could rise from the dead, not a Messiah. Jewish monotheism argued against Jesus being God; how could it be that a man could be God alongside Yahweh? Since only God could rise again, therefore, thought Thomas, Jesus had not risen. Thomas probably did not step forward to feel Jesus' wounds; that would have been to doubt his senses and again offend Jesus. When Thomas saw that Jesus had indeed risen, he accepted the logical consequence of his reasoning.

"Thomas answered him, 'My Lord and my God!'" (Jn 20:28). Thomas was the first person publicly to state this conclusion. Jesus was not only the Messiah. He was divine. It took the next 350 years to work through to an understanding of how this can be so, when God is One. Thomas deserves the credit for starting that process.

Until the Resurrection, the disciples recognized Jesus as the Messiah promised to Israel. Many of them, perhaps most, recognized him as "someone" more than the Messiah. Jesus was called "Kyrios" on a number of occasions. After the great draft of fish that preceded Simon's call, Simon said, **"'Depart from me, for I am a sinful man, O Lord'"** (Lk 5:8). On this and other occasions when a disciple calls Jesus "Lord," the word used is "Kyrios." Kyrios is best translated as a term originally akin to the feudal meaning of "lord," one having ownership or rule of an area and all the property and people in it. It did not denote "deity," though under Christian usage it has come to do so. The disciples also sometimes acknowledged Jesus as "the Son of God" (e.g., Mt 14:33). Such a person would be one specially favored by God but not actually divine. Jewish monotheism was the primary characteristic which separated the Jews from rest of the world, and the Jewish people hugged it to themselves as their national identity.

"Jesus said to him [Thomas]**, 'Have you believed because you have seen me? Blessed are those who have not seen and yet believe'"** (Jn 20:29). Thomas' test would have limited Christianity to a handful, who would soon die out. But Jesus does not leave us dependent on naked belief, or fideism. During his Resurrection appearances, he taught his disciples, rather than relying just on the impact of their having seen him. Today Catholics still rely on both faith and reason.

---

2. The disciples went to Galilee after that appearance on the second Sunday.

In *Matthew* and *Mark* an angel told the women at the tomb, **"[H]e is going before you to Galilee; there you will see him"** (Mt 28:7; Mk 16:7). *Acts* says Jesus **"charged them not to depart from Jerusalem, but to wait for the promise of the Father"** (Acts 1:4). This second instruction was clearly referable to the time between the Ascension and the Descent of the Holy Spirit at Pentecost. In *Luke*, Jesus instructs the disciples to **"stay in the city, until you are clothed with power from on high"** (Lk 24:49). Jesus told the disciples this just before the Ascension, likewise referable to the time before the Descent of the Holy Spirit.

Matthew describes only one post-Resurrection appearance after the appearance to the women at the tomb, that being the appearance to the disciples on a "mountain" in Galilee. He compresses all teaching and an unidentified post-Resurrection appearance into five verses, in the first of which he says that **"the eleven disciples went to Galilee"** (Mt 28:16–20). He does not mention either of the two appearances to the disciples in the upper room in Jerusalem on two successive Sundays.

Mark conflates the first and second Sunday night appearances in the upper room but then compresses all subsequent teachings and the Ascension into six verses, not mentioning where any of this occurred. He describes no appearances after that on Easter Sunday night and the subsequent Sunday night (Mk 16:15–20).

Luke likewise compresses all post-Resurrection teaching and the Ascension into ten verses, not mentioning any appearances after the first Sunday night's or where any event occurred (Lk 24:44–53).

Only John describes the second appearance in the upper room and a detailed account of his appearance to the fishing disciples on the shore of Lake Tiberias, but he describes no other appearances (Jn 20:26–29; 21:1–25), though he clearly implies that there were such. **"Now Jesus did many other signs in the presence of the disciples which are not written in this book; but these are written that you may believe that Jesus is the Christ, the Son of God, and that believing you may have life in his name. . . . But there are many other things which Jesus did; were every one of them to be written, I suppose that the world itself could not contain the books that would be written"** (Jn 20:30–31; 21:25).

It is clear that the disciples stayed in Jerusalem until at least the Monday morning following the second Sunday night appearance in the upper room. It is also clear that they went to Galilee and saw Jesus there. They returned to Jerusalem and saw him in Jerusalem, at least on the occasion before and during his Ascension.

It is about 120 miles from Jerusalem to Capernaum. Because there were so many men in the group, they could travel the direct route through Samaria, rather than the longer, safer route east of the Jordan. With women in the group, they probably made about twenty miles a day, or a six-day journey, not counting any sabbath.

Counting from Easter Sunday, the fortieth day, Ascension Day is on a Thursday. If Jesus so instructed the disciples on that second Sunday night, they could have left Jerusalem on Monday, the ninth day. They would have arrived at Capernaum on the fifteenth day, since they would not have traveled on Saturday. If they left Capernaum to return to Jerusalem on the thirty-third day, a Thursday, not traveling on Saturday, they would have arrived in Jerusalem on the day before the Ascension. That would have given them seventeen full days in Capernaum. Obviously, if they left Jerusalem later or returned earlier, it would shorten the time in Galilee.

I suggest that the maximum time in Galilee should be considered. The statement of the angel to the women at the tomb points in that direction. Furthermore, Jerusalem was a dangerous place for the disciples, since they lived and moved so close to the temple and its informers. Galilee was much safer. Finally, most of Jesus' work was done in Galilee, and there the disciples would have the most believers and sympathizers.

❖   ❖   ❖

3. Having arrived in Galilee, the disciples waited for Jesus' appearance. While they waited, Peter decided to go fishing, and James, John, Thomas, Nathanael, and two other disciples accompanied him one night but caught nothing (Jn 21:1-3). **"Just as day was breaking, Jesus stood on the beach; yet the disciples did not know that it was Jesus. Jesus said to them, 'Children, have you any fish?' They answered him, 'No.' He said to them, 'Cast the net on the right side of the boat, and you will find some.' So they cast it, and now they were not able to haul it in, for the quantity of fish. That disciple whom Jesus loved said to Peter, 'It is the Lord!' When Peter heard that it was the Lord, he put**

on his clothes, for he was stripped for work, and sprang into the sea. But the other disciples came in the boat, dragging the net full of fish, for they were not far from the land, but about a hundred yards off" (Jn 21:4–8). Even though the disciples were expecting Jesus to appear, they did not recognize him on the beach. This was not due to their being one hundred yards distant or to the early morning light. When they were face to face with him, they still were not sure (Jn 21:12). It was John who identified him, perhaps from his having addressed them as "children" and the reenactment of the great draft of fish that had triggered the discipleship of Peter, Andrew, James, and John (Lk 5:4–11).

"**When they got out on land, they saw a charcoal fire there, with fish lying on it, and bread. Jesus said to them, 'Bring some of the fish that you have just caught.' So Simon Peter went aboard and hauled the net ashore, full of large fish, a hundred and fifty-three of them; and although there were so many, the net was not torn. Jesus said to them, 'Come and have breakfast.' Now none of the disciples dared ask him, 'Who are you?' They knew it was the Lord. Jesus came and took the bread and gave it to them, and so with the fish. This was now the third time that Jesus was revealed to the disciples after he was raised from the dead**" (Jn 21: 9–14).

❖ ❖ ❖

4. After breakfast, Jesus took Peter aside and walked apart. John followed them at a distance, but apparently within hearing range, since he reported the conversation (Jn 21:20). "**When they had finished breakfast, Jesus said to Simon Peter, 'Simon, son of John, do you love me more than these?' He said to him, 'Yes, Lord; you know that I love you.' He said to him, 'Feed my lambs.' A second time he said to him, 'Simon, son of John, do**

you love me?' He said to him, 'Yes, Lord; you know that I love you.' He said to him, 'Tend my sheep.' He said to him the third time, 'Simon, son of John, do you love me?' Peter was grieved because he said to him the third time, 'Do you love me?' And he said to him, 'Lord, you know everything; you know that I love you.' Jesus said to him, 'Feed my sheep. Truly, truly, I say to you, when you were young, you girded yourself and walked where you would; but when you are old, you will stretch out your hands, and another will gird you and carry you where you do not wish to go.' (This he said to show by what death he was to glorify God.) And after this he said to him, 'Follow me'" (Jn 21:15–19).

The first two times that Jesus asked Peter, "Do you love me," he used the word for the *agape* form of love, used in describing a religious or divine form of love. Both times Peter replied that he loved Jesus using the word for the *phileo* form of love, a brotherly love for family and close friends.

The third time Jesus asked Peter if he loved him with brotherly love. That is why Peter grieved, because Jesus' third question had underscored Peter's lesser form of love for Jesus, while Jesus wanted the *agape* love. Peter had answered Jesus truthfully and admitted that Jesus knew that Peter was not yet capable of giving Jesus *agape* love, rather than *phileo* love. Peter's subsequent career showed that his love for Jesus deepened into the *agape* form, which Jesus foreknew would occur.

Every distinction in the Gospel has a purpose. It is no slip of the tongue that Jesus directs Peter to look after both his lambs and his sheep. The lamb is the offspring of the sheep. The distinction drawn is between Jesus' "sheep," the apostles, their successors, the bishops, and their agents, the priests and deacons, and their offspring, the laymen. Jesus directed Peter to feed both the lambs and the sheep, but to "tend" the sheep. His first duty is to "feed," to nourish with his teaching office, both clergy and laity. His next duty is to give direction, to "tend," the bishops and other clergy. Jesus gave Peter his Petrine ministry and primacy on the beach by the Sea of Galilee.

The word play between *phileo* and *agape* does not exist in Aramaic, nor does it in English. It is startling to realize that this conversation between Jesus and Peter was held in Greek. For Jesus to make his point, it had to be. This underscores that in "Galilee of the Gentiles" the population were largely bilingual. This also underscores that the Gospels, written before the destruction of Jerusalem, were already for a mostly Greek-speaking church, although it was still largely Jewish.

⸻

5. "For I delivered to you as of first importance what I also received, that Christ died for our sins in accordance with the scriptures, that he was buried, that he was raised on the third day in accordance with the scriptures, and that he appeared to Cephas, then to the twelve. Then he appeared to more than five hundred brethren at one time, most of whom are still alive, though some have fallen asleep. Then he appeared to James, then to all the apostles. Last of all, as to one untimely born, he appeared also to me" (1 Cor 15:3–8).

It was possible in Galilee to assemble 500 people to hear Jesus. It would not have been safe to do so in Jerusalem. In order for the disciples to have assembled a crowd of 500 to see and hear Jesus, Jesus must have given the apostles a time and place that he would appear. Not knowing of any appearance in Galilee between the encounter on the beach and the appearance to the 500, Jesus presumably did so during the breakfast on the beach. It is reasonable to surmise that Jesus sent them to Galilee, not only for safety, but also to make an appearance to a crowd so large as to disprove claims of a conspiracy hatched among a handful of disciples to lie about his Resurrection.

Paul says Jesus appeared to "five hundred brethren at one time." Where? This almost assuredly was the appearance referenced in *Matthew*: **"Then the eleven disciples went away into Galilee, to the mountain which Jesus had appointed for them"** (Mt 28:16). It is most likely that this was the same "mountain," or "hill," near Capernaum that is also the traditional location of the "Sermon on the Mount," a location well-known to Jesus' disciples in Galilee. It was an identifiable location to which the apostles could have urged his disciples to go at the specific time designated in advance by Jesus.

The most likely spot for this appearance was an uninhabited, uncultivated, rocky hill, or "mountain," called Et Tabgha, about two miles outside of Capernaum. In the fourth century, after the legalization of Christianity under Constantine, three churches were built on the site, commemorating the Sermon on the Mount, the Multiplication of Loaves and Fishes, and the Apparition of Jesus to the Apostles. It currently is the location of the Church of the Beatitudes. It is highly likely that the appearance to the 500 occurred on this hillside, which would have been already identified with Jesus' ministry.

Jesus obviously appeared in his recognizable form. In a gathering of 500, every person could see Jesus and the marks of his Passion; there could be no argument about who it was. The fact, as Paul wrote, that most of the 500 were still alive gives assurance of the accuracy of Paul's account.

"Now the eleven disciples went to Galilee, to the mountain to which Jesus had directed them. And when they saw him, they worshiped him; but some doubted" (Mt 28:16–17). Those who doubted were among the 500, not among the apostles. As Jesus foretold in the parable of Lazarus and Dives, **"If they do not hear Moses and the prophets, neither will they be convinced if some one should rise from the dead"** (Lk 16:19–31). The Lord does not compel belief, but always leaves a means to justify disbelief in order to preserve free will. Even some of those who saw the resurrected Jesus did not believe.

❖ ❖ ❖

6. Jesus appeared to James (1 Cor 15:7). We know nothing more. But Jesus thereby accepted James' repentance and absolved him of any lingering guilt remaining from the effort to shove past Peter, for which James bore primary responsibility with his mother.

This James was James, the son of Zebedee and Salome, the elder brother of John, "James the Greater," rather than James, son of Alpheus, "James the Less." He was the first apostle to be martyred, during the persecution by Herod Agrippa in August, AD 41.

❖ ❖ ❖

7. Jesus instructed the disciples to return to Jerusalem. We do not know when he did so; it could have been part of the original direction to go to Galilee or any appearance thereafter. In all likelihood he timed their arrival in Jerusalem to be on the day before he planned to ascend, so as to minimize risk. As shown by Jesus' elaborate precautions to protect the Last Supper, minimization of risk, rather than foolhardy bravado, was Jesus' style.

❖ ❖ ❖

8. The disciples again assembled in Jerusalem, probably in the upper room at John Mark's home. They included not only the eleven apostles, but also **"the women and Mary the mother of Jesus, and with his brothers"** (Acts 1:12–14). The apostles were all staying there at the time of Pentecost, ten days later (Acts 1:13). It seems likely that they stayed there together on the night they returned from

Galilee and, following Jesus' instruction before the Ascension to remain in Jerusalem, they continued there together until Pentecost.

The different Gospels usually conflate Jesus' post-Resurrection teachings, sometimes into a single passage. I have previously indicated those passages which most likely occurred during the earlier appearances. It is reasonably apparent that certain of Jesus' teachings occurred upon the return to Jerusalem.

"**'All authority in heaven and on earth has been given to me. Go therefore and make disciples of all nations, baptizing them in the name of the Father and of the Son and of the Holy Spirit, teaching them to observe all that I have commanded you; and lo, I am with you always, to the close of the age'**" (Mt 28:18–20).

"**'Go into all the world and preach the gospel to the whole creation. He who believes and is baptized will be saved; but he who does not believe will be condemned. And these signs will accompany those who believe: in my name they will cast out demons; they will speak in new tongues; they will pick up serpents, and if they drink any deadly thing, it will not hurt them; they will lay their hands on the sick, and they will recover'**" (Mk 16:15–18).

"**'[R]epentance and forgiveness of sins should be preached in his [Christ's] name to all nations, beginning from Jerusalem. You are witnesses of these things. And behold, I send the promise of my Father upon you; but stay in the city until you are clothed with power from on high'**" (Lk 24:47–49).

"**To them [the apostles] he presented himself alive after his passion by many proofs, appearing to them during forty days, and speaking of the kingdom of God. And while staying with them he charged them not to depart from Jerusalem, but to wait for the promise of the Father, which, he said, 'you heard from me, for John baptized with water, but before many days** you will be baptized with the Holy Spirit.' So when they had come together, they asked him, 'Lord, will you at this time restore the kingdom to Israel?' He said to them, 'It is not for you to know times or seasons which the Father has fixed by his own authority. But you shall receive power when the Holy Spirit comes upon you; and you shall be my witnesses in Jerusalem and in all Judea and Samaria and to the end of the earth'" (Acts 1:3–8).

It is possible that Jesus appeared to the disciples in the upper room on one occasion and led them to Mount Olivet on a separate occasion, but security argues against this. Jesus would not want the temple hierarchy to interfere with his farewell address and Ascension, so it is probable that he led the apostles to Mount Olivet after he had appeared and instructed the disciples as a group. The appearance was during daylight hours.

There are themes common to these accounts. The disciples are to proclaim the gospel to "all nations" and to the end of the earth. It is a comfort to me, when I have trouble acting upon the unambiguous teaching of scripture and the Church, that the disciples had trouble also. For example, even after Jesus' teaching to take the gospel to all nations, Peter's vision of being ordered to eat unclean animals was necessary to prompt him to act on Jesus' unambiguous teaching (Acts 10:1–48).

An even more striking example of the difficulty of accepting what one has heard lies in the question, "Lord, will you at this time restore the kingdom to Israel?" (Acts 1:6). While the descriptions of what Jesus taught in his post-Resurrection appearances are skimpy, it is clear that Jesus **"interpreted to them in all the scriptures the things concerning himself"** (Lk 24:27). **"Then he opened their mind to understand the scriptures, and said to them, 'Thus it is written, that the Christ should suffer and on the third day rise from the dead. . . . '"** (Lk 24:45–46). During the forty days, Jesus appeared to the disciples "speaking of the kingdom of God" (Acts 1:3–4).

We are so accustomed to the Christian gloss on the Old Testament, such as interpreting *Psalm 22* as a prophecy of Jesus' crucifixion, that it requires effort to envision the time before Jesus applied the Old Testament to himself. Up until the Resurrection, none of the apostles so interpreted scripture. That is why Peter remonstrated with Jesus when he foretold his death. Even John the Baptist did not understand scripture as prophesying a Messiah other than one who would restore the kingdom, at least until Jesus referred him to other passages—wherein the blind see, etc. (Mt 11:2–6). Only Simeon, with his prophecy of the sword piercing Mary's soul, and at least two of the Magi read the scriptures correctly (Lk 2:34–35). After Simeon and the Magi, only Jesus understood the scriptures correctly, sharing his learning with Mary. Even after being taught the proper interpretation by the resurrected Jesus, some apostles still asked him when he will act like the real Messiah, the man on a white horse. Since Jesus experienced this from the men who had been with him for two to three years, I may reasonably ask for Jesus' forgiveness of my own stubbornness and difficulty in turning loose of my own preconceptions.

Another theme is that, upon converting persons of all nations, they are to be baptized in the name of the Father and of the Son and of the Holy Spirit. This is the outward and visible sign of conversion. One who hears the gospel and is unwilling to make a public confession of his faith, ordinarily is condemned to live outside the faith. All forms of non-trinitarianism are neatly dealt with in this instruction.

Another theme is that Jesus will accompany the apostles and their converts, in order to protect them. **"Lo, I am with you always. [T]hey will pick up serpents, and if they drink any deadly thing, it will not hurt them"** (Mk 16:15–18). Paul unintentionally picked up a viper in a bundle of sticks but was not harmed (Acts 28:3–6). Some people have practiced snake-handling, intentionally subjecting themselves to possible snakebite as a proof of their faith. But the scripture says that God will protect the believer from mishap, not from intentionally testing God. Jesus condemned an act designed to put God to the test, when he himself had refused to test God by leaping from the pinnacle of the temple (Mt 4:5–7).

Finally, there is the theme that the disciples should stay in Jerusalem to await some great event. "Stay in the city until you are clothed with power from on high." "I send the promise of my Father upon you." "Wait for the promise of the Father." "You shall receive power when the Holy Spirit comes upon you."

9. Jesus appeared to the disciples and taught them in a secure place, probably the upper room at John Mark's home. Jesus, in one of his nonrecognizable forms, led the apostles through the streets of Jerusalem, out the gate, across Brook Kidron, and up the Mount of Olives, a total of less than a mile.

"So then the Lord Jesus, after he had spoken to them was taken up into heaven, and sat down at the right hand of God" (Mk 16:19). **"Then he led them out as far as Bethany, and lifting up his hands he blessed them. While he blessed them, he parted from them, and was carried up into heaven"** (Lk 24:50–51). **"And when he said this, as they were looking on, he was lifted up, and a cloud took him out of their sight"** (Acts 1:9). **"And then they returned to Jerusalem from the Mount called Olivet, which is near Jerusalem, a sabbath day's journey away"** (Acts 1:12).

Where did the Ascension take place? Luke says, "He led them out as far as Bethany," 1.8 miles east of Jerusalem and about a mile beyond the Church of the Ascension. *Acts*, written by the same author, is more specific; it says the site was "a sabbath day's journey" from Jerusalem. Since the Ascension was on a Thursday, this description is given as a measurement of distance, rather than as a limitation on Jesus' choice of a site. A sabbath day's journey, the distance a Jew could travel without violating the sabbath, was 2,000 cubits, or about 1,550 yards. The Church of the Ascension falls within that distance, while Bethany far exceeds it.

The Church of the Ascension is on the way to Bethany. The first surviving written identification of the site was in AD 333, and the first church on the site was built by AD 387. As was the case with the location of the sepulcher and Calvary, the local church had preserved the memory of the location of the major events in the life of Jesus. On balance, it is probable that *Luke* should be construed as indicating a site on the way to Bethany, since *Acts* is more specific and agrees with tradition.

Who was present? Mark describes Jesus as appearing to "the eleven," and all his subsequent references are to "them" and "they" (Mk 16:14–19). Luke describes Jesus' appearance to "the eleven who were gathered together and those who were with them, . . . " and all his subsequent references are to "them" and "they" (Lk 24:33–53). John repeatedly describes Jesus' appearances as being to "the disciples" (Jn 20:18; 20:19; 20:20; 20:26; 20:30; 21:1; 21:2; 21:8; 21:12; 21:14). *Acts* describes Jesus' appearances to "the apostles whom he had chosen," and most subsequent references are to "them" and "they" (Acts 1:2–11). The angels addressed the group as "men of Galilee" (Acts 1:11). *Acts* states that the eleven apostles, naming them, returned to Jerusalem from the Mount of Olives and "went up to the upper room" (Acts 1:12–13).

The statement that Jesus appeared to "the eleven" does not preclude the presence of other disciples at the group appearances the two Sunday nights in Jerusalem, just as the statement that

Mary Magdalene went to the tomb does not preclude the presence of other women (Jn 20:1). Luke specifically says that other disciples were present in the upper room with the eleven. When one considers the religious fervor and emotion which Jesus' post-Resurrection appearances inspired, it is impossible to envision the eleven apostles excluding the other disciples from their gatherings and thereby from Jesus' appearances to the group. Numerous disciples, such as the Blessed Virgin Mary, Cleophas, Mary Magdalene, Mary the wife of Cleophas, and others who figure in the accounts of Jesus' crucifixion and resurrection, were undoubtedly present.

The Ascension is different. Jesus led the group through Jerusalem, which would have limited its size for security reasons. *Acts* is clear that only the apostles were present on this occasion. Though Luke had expressly described the earlier group as "the eleven and those who were with them" (Lk 24:33), in *Acts* he refers to the group at the Ascension as "apostles" and "men of Galilee" and specifically names those who returned to Jerusalem. It seems unlikely that the eleven, either on their own initiative or on direction from Jesus, would have excluded the other disciples from seeing Jesus in the gathering that day in the upper room, especially after they had just spent seven days walking from Galilee, arriving in Jerusalem only the night before. It is, however, clear that Jesus then called out the eleven apostles to accompany him to the Mount of Olives. By calling them out by name to accompany him, he thereby emphasized their uniqueness and authority.

When Jesus had led the apostles out on the road to Bethany to the Mount of Olives, he led them a little way off the road into an open area. He blessed them, and as he blessed them, he began to ascend. **"As they were looking on, he was lifted up, and a cloud took him out of their sight"** (Acts 1:9). Jesus ascended of his own volition at a time and place of his own selection. He was not taken up into heaven by intervention of the Father, as Elijah was taken up by a chariot in the whirlwind (2 Kings 3:11–12).

The best description of the Ascension is in *Acts*: **"He was lifted up, and a cloud took him out of their sight"** (Acts 1:9). He ascended in their sight until he was obscured by a cloud. The ascent probably was not into a high cloud formation, so that Jesus would have become a tiny figure in their sight; rather it was probably into a low cloud formation so that Jesus was recognizable to them until their vision was blocked by the cloud.

❖ ❖ ❖

10. "And while they were gazing into heaven as he went, behold, two men stood by them in white robes, and said, 'Men of Galilee, why do you stand looking into heaven. This Jesus, who was taken up from you into heaven, will come in the same way you saw him go into heaven'" (Acts 1:11).

The description of the two angels accords with what has been described earlier. Just as the apostles were astonished by Jesus' ascension, they were reassured by the angels. As was their wont, the angels vanished after delivering these comfortable words.

Pentecost Window, Max Svabinsky, 1933–1935,
St. Vitus Cathedral, Prague

PENTECOST: THE DESCENT OF THE HOLY SPIRIT

1. The eleven apostles returned to Jerusalem from Mount Olivet with great joy (Lk 24:52; Acts 1:12). **"They went up to the upper room, where they were staying, . . . "** (Acts 1:13). **"All these** [the eleven apostles] **with one accord devoted themselves to prayer, together with the women and Mary the mother of Jesus, and with his brothers"** (Acts 1:14). The entire group totaled about 120 (Acts 1:15). The apostles were together at all times, since the eleven were staying in John Mark's home. Most of the rest were lodged with disciples scattered throughout Jerusalem.

2. Because Jesus had told the disciples that they should stay in Jerusalem and that he would send the promise of his Father to them, they assembled daily in the upper room to pray (Lk 24:49; Acts 1:4, 14). We may readily conclude that these prayers, performed away from public view, included prayers for the coming of the Lord's promise. In addition, the disciples **"were continually in the temple, blessing God"** (Lk 24:52). These temple prayers were the general prayers of devout Jews. There is no indication that the disciples began to proclaim Jesus' Resurrection before Pentecost. To prevent interference with the gift promised to the disciples, it is likely that Jesus' instructions to them included an admonition not to do so.

* * *

3. During the interval between the Ascension and Pentecost, Peter proposed the selection of a twelfth apostle, in order to bring the number back to the number Jesus had selected, twelve, also the number of the tribes of Israel. Peter thereby commenced the role given him by Jesus, to "tend my sheep" (Jn 21:16).

Peter proposed selection out of **"the men who have accompanied us, beginning from the baptism of John until the day when he was taken up from us—one of these men must become with us a witness to his resurrection** [an apostle]" (Acts 1:15–22).

There apparently were a number of disciples, in addition to the eleven, who had faithfully followed Jesus throughout his ministry without being enrolled by Jesus in the twelve-man core leadership. **"And they put forward two, Joseph called Barsabbas, who was surnamed Justus, and Matthias"** (Acts 1:23). Peter having proposed the appointment of a new apostle, he conferred with the other ten apostles and let them nominate two candidates.

One candidate, Joseph Barsabbas, was the son of Alpheus and Mary. His brother, James, son of Alpheus, was already an apostle. Salome was the mother of two apostles, James and John, and she was the daughter of Mary, probably by Alpheus but possibly by Cleophas, so she was the sister or half-sister of James and Joseph. These three apostles were Jesus' kinsmen by blood or by marriage. The selection of Joseph Barsabbas would have given greater weight to Jesus' family in the inner circle of the infant Church. The apostles prayed and cast lots, and the lot fell on Matthias, who was enrolled as the twelfth apostle.

Pentecost: The Descent of the Holy Spirit

4. The fiftieth day after Passover is Pentecost; that year and thereafter in the Christian calendar, unlike the Jewish calendar, it is always on a Sunday. **"You shall hold a holy convocation; you shall do no laborious work; it is a statute forever in all your dwellings throughout your generations"** (Lv 23:15–21). The disciples assembled in the upper room for their own "holy convocation." **"When the day of Pentecost had come they were all together in one place"** (Acts 2:1). The entire community of 120 persons was present, most notably the Blessed Virgin Mary (Acts 1:14; 2:1).

5. **"And suddenly a sound came from heaven like the rush of a mighty wind, and it filled all the house where they were sitting"** (Acts 2:2). It was not a mighty wind that filled the house, but rather a "sound . . . like the rush of a mighty wind." A powerful wind would have blown the robes of the disciples and distracted them, as they tried to preserve the decor of their attire and their modesty. At some point someone undoubtedly looked outside and announced that there was no wind outside that they were hearing.

6. **"And there appeared to them tongues as of fire, distributed and resting on each one of them. And they were all filled with the Holy Spirit and began to speak in other tongues, as the Spirit gave them utterance"** (Acts 2:3–4).

The "tongues" resting on each disciple were not of fire, but rather were "as of fire," something that appeared similar to fire.

One thinks of some sort of electrical display, since God uses his miraculous manipulation of existing material elements to show forth his power, as when Jesus ordered the wind and waves to be still. The coming of the Holy Spirit, accompanied by a sound like a mighty wind, manifested itself, as it was granted to each disciple, in some form of aura, likely electrical, that rested on each one's head.

The Blessed Virgin Mary herself received the Holy Spirit, along with the other disciples. What perfection! And, what was it like for Mary to receive her son's body and blood in the eucharist for the rest of her life?

---

7. **"Now there were dwelling in Jerusalem Jews, devout men from every nation under heaven. And at this sound the multitude came together, and they were bewildered, because each one heard them speaking in his own language. And they were amazed and wondered, saying, 'Are not all these who are speaking Galileans? And how is it that we hear, each of us in his own native language? Parthians and Medes and Elamites and residents of Mesopotamia, Judea and Cappadocia, Pontus and Asia, Phrygia and Pamphilia, Egypt and the parts of Libya belonging to Cyrene, and visitors from Rome, both Jews and proselytes, Cretans and Arabians, we hear them telling in our own tongues the mighty works of God' and all were amazed and perplexed, saying to one another, 'What does this mean?' But others mocking said, 'They are filled with new wine'"** (Acts 2:5–13).

The gift of tongues in this case was the gift of existing languages not known to the speaker. It is different from the glossolalia referred to elsewhere in the New Testament (1 Cor 14:1–19). Speaking in nonexistent languages is a characteristic of "speaking in tongues" as is sometimes experienced today, though some current "speaking in tongues" is speech in an existing language not known to the speaker, as occurred at Pentecost.

Once again, the Lord did not compel belief. The unbelievers attributed what they saw and heard to "new wine," though it was only 9:00 a.m. (Acts 2:13). No matter what the proof, even an encounter with the risen Jesus by the 500, the unbeliever can always find a means to justify his unbelief.

◆ ◆ ◆

8. The noise "like the rush of a mighty wind" had drawn a crowd outside John Mark's home. Standing with all eleven of the other apostles, Peter again took the lead and addressed the crowd (Acts 2:14–42). This first sermon evidences the success of Jesus' post-Resurrection teaching. For the first time a teacher other than Jesus interpreted the Old Testament scriptures in a new way, showing how they foretold the life, death, and resurrection of Jesus.

Peter first cited *Joel* as foretelling the coming of the Holy Spirit that day. **"'I will pour out my Spirit upon all flesh'"** (Acts 2:16–21). Peter then cited *Psalm* 16 as foretelling the Messiah's resurrection. **"'For thou wilt not abandon my soul to Hades, nor let thy Holy One see corruption'"** (Acts 2:25–31).

As to the truth of Jesus' Resurrection, Peter asserted the Church's claim forevermore: **"This Jesus God raised up, and of that we all are witnesses"** (Acts 2:32). While *Acts* mentions only the other eleven apostles as standing with Peter, about 120 had been in the upper room and received the Holy Spirit. We may be confident that they had streamed out of the house behind Peter, no longer fearful of the Jews and hiding behind locked doors, but filled with the Holy Spirit and confidence flowing from it. When Peter said, "[W]e are all witnesses," he doubtlessly gestured toward the entire Church of 120 persons.

Finally, Peter cited *Psalm* 110, as David's foretelling that the Messiah would ascend into heaven. **"'The Lord said to my Lord, sit at my right hand, till I make thy enemies a stool for thy feet'"** (Acts 2:34–35).

It was in this fashion that the early Church preached, to the Jews especially, as Jesus had taught them in his post-Resurrection appearances.

⁌ ⁌ ⁌

9. Many of those who heard Peter were **"cut to the heart, and said to Peter and the rest of the apostles, 'Brethren, what shall we do?' And Peter said to them, 'Repent, and be baptized every one of you in the name of Jesus Christ for the forgiveness of your sins; and you shall receive the gift of the Holy Spirit'"** (Acts 2:37–38). About 3,000 received his word and were baptized that day (Acts 2:41).

These 3,000 new members of the new Church are described as foreign Jews "dwelling" in Jerusalem. The word used for "dwelling" refers to permanent residents, not to pilgrims in town for the feast of Pentecost (Acts 2:5, 14). Such a large number of converts, who were permanent residents of Jerusalem, immediately constituted part of the core group for the new Church and gave it a character different from the Judean Jewish establishment of priests, Pharisees, Sadducees, temple guards, and all those bureaucrats on the payroll of the temple. Since they heard the apostles speaking in their native tongues from the entire Eastern world, those foreign tongues were their native languages.

They were Jews of the diaspora. The lingua franca of the diaspora was Greek, and we can safely assume that most of them spoke Greek as their second tongue, though many of them probably also spoke Aramaic either before or after they had moved to Jerusalem. Furthermore, the Galileans especially, but also many Judeans, spoke Greek as their first or second language. Knowledge of Greek was not limited to the upper classes but was found in all classes, especially in Galilee and the diaspora. Two of the apostles, Andrew and Philip, had Greek names, as did Jesus' uncle, Cleophas. At least one synagogue in Jerusalem conducted its services in Greek. The point is that the Church from its first day was heavily Hellenized. The Galileans themselves were looked down on in Jerusalem because they came from Galilee "of the Gentiles" and were likewise to some degree Hellenized. Witness particularly Jesus' wordplay between *agape* and *phileo* with Peter, which works only in Greek and puzzles those who read it in English without further instruction. Such partial Hellenization does not imply that they were less devout than the Jews of Judea. Rather, many of them doubtlessly had moved to Jerusalem because they were especially devout. Indeed, it was Jews of the diaspora who instigated the killing of Stephen, the first martyr (Acts 6:8–12). The New Testament was written in Greek (with the exception of Matthew's Gospel), not just for the Gentile converts but also for the Hellenized Jews who were a large, and perhaps even a majority, element in the Church even before the Gentiles were evangelized. Pentecost was "the birthday of the Church." The 3,000 joined the 120, and suddenly there was a critical mass of disciples to spread the gospel rapidly, "beginning from Jerusalem."

---

10. "And they [the entire Church] **devoted themselves to the apostles' teaching and fellowship, to the breaking of bread, and the prayers"** (Acts 2:42).

The apostles "taught" the Church. That has always been the first and most important office of the bishop. And what did they teach? They taught from the Old Testament and from the life and teachings of Jesus, as transmitted by him to the disciples both before and after his Resurrection. By AD 50 or 51, Paul would refer to the teachings regarding Jesus as "the traditions which you were taught by us, either *by word of mouth* or by letter" (emphasis supplied) (2 Thes 2:15). Where was *sola scriptura* in the primitive Church, which was the purported model of "the reformers" of the sixteenth century? What we now recognize as the New Testament would be written over a forty-year period following Jesus' death.

The earliest surviving list of the New Testament canon is the Muratonian Fragment, probably prepared in Rome in AD 180–200. It omits *James, Hebrews, 1 and 2 Peter* and *1 John;* it includes the *Apocalypse of Peter,* now rejected. Origen (AD 185–250) says that *James, 2 Peter* and *2 and 3 John* are disputed in parts of the Church. Eusebius (AD 270–340), writing after the triumph of Constantine, says that *James, Jude, 2 Peter, 2 and 3 John,* and *Hebrews* are disputed in parts of the Church. During the early fourth century *Hebrews* was generally rejected in the West but accepted in the East, and the *Apocalypse of John (Revelation)* was generally accepted in the West but rejected in the East. At Constantine's request, Eusebius drew up a list of what he proposed as a canon of the scriptures, which were subsequently translated into Latin by Jerome (AD 345–420), known as the Vulgate. In AD 393, a council of all the bishops in the Roman province of Africa (roughly, modern Tunisia) was held under the direction of Augustine of Hippo. It proposed these same books as the canon of scripture, subject to ratification by Rome, which was given by Pope Innocent in AD 405.

There was no *scriptura, sola* or otherwise, accepted throughout the Church until after Constantine's final triumph in AD 323, or until AD 405 if one is Catholic. The entire Reformation edifice (other than the Anglican) is built upon the written word, as recognized in the primitive Church, as the sole source of religious authority. At what date is the "primitive Church" thus defined? What *sola scriptura* as of that date? All Protestant churches (other than the Anglican) argue that the primitive Church had been irremediably corrupted no later than the reign of Constantine (AD 312–337). There was no general agreement as to the composition of the canon before that date, so which part of the *sola scriptura* does which Protestant want to throw out? Luther wanted to start with *James*. Who else? What else?

The scriptures do not describe the liturgy encompassed in the phrase, "the prayers." Clearly is meant a definite set of prayers, mostly taken from the then-scriptures, the Old Testament. It is clear that individually made-up prayers, varied at the whim of the celebrant, would not be described as "the prayers."

The Church "devoted themselves . . . to the breaking of bread. . . . " The ceremony thus referred to was the re-presentation of the sacrifice of the Last Supper. **"And he took bread, and when he had given thanks he broke it and gave it to them, saying, 'This is my body which is given for you. Do this in remembrance of me.' And likewise the cup after supper, saying, 'This cup which is poured out for you is the new covenant in my blood'"** (Lk 22:19–20). Within twenty-five years Paul could describe the act of consecration which was clearly well established before AD 55: **"For I received from the Lord what I also delivered to you, that the Lord Jesus on the night when he was betrayed took bread, and when he had given thanks, he broke it, and said, 'This is my body which is for you. Do this in remembrance of me.' In the same way also the cup, after supper, saying, 'This cup is the new covenant in my blood. Do this, as often as you drink it, in remembrance of me.' For as often as you eat this bread and drink the cup, you proclaim the Lord's death until he comes"** (1 Cor 11:23–26).

Note that scripture, whether *sola* or otherwise, does not say that the primitive Church devoted themselves to the "breaking of bread" annually, quarterly, or monthly. When they met, "They devoted themselves to the apostles' teaching and fellowship, to the breaking of bread and the prayers" (Acts 2:42). The mass was an integral part of the service from the beginning.

The Assumption of the Virgin, attributed to Paolo Veronese, c. 1548, The David and Alfred Smart Museum of Art, The University of Chicago; Gift of the Samuel H. Kress Foundation

THE ASSUMPTION OF THE BLESSED VIRGIN MARY

1. "In the sixth month the angel Gabriel was sent from God to a city of Galilee named Nazareth, to a virgin betrothed to a man whose name was Joseph, of the house of David; and the virgin's name was Mary. And he came to her and said, 'Hail, full of grace, the Lord is with you.' But she was greatly troubled at the saying, and considered in her mind what sort of greeting this might be. And the angel said to her, 'Do not be afraid Mary, for you have found favor with God. And behold, you will conceive in your womb and bear a son, and you shall call his name Jesus'" (Lk 1:26–31).

Many characters in the Old Testament had "found favor with God," but only Mary was addressed as "full of grace."

The trinitarian God is holy. No Person of the Trinity may be infected in any way by sin. The Second Person, Jesus, could not be God and yet be guilty of any sin, whether committed by himself or imputed to him through the fall of Adam as original sin. Hence, it was necessary that the chain of original sin stretching back to Adam, "human nature," be broken before it affected his own birth. Therefore, it was necessary that the vessel of the incarnation, the God-bearer, be free of sin herself. This was done, not through her own merit, but through the merit of her son.

"We declare, pronounce and define that the doctrine which holds that the most Blessed Virgin Mary, in the first instant of her conception, by a singular grace and privilege granted by Almighty God, in view of the merits of Jesus Christ, the Savior of the human race, was preserved free from all stain of original sin, is a doctrine revealed by God and therefore to be believed firmly and constantly by all the faithful" (Pius IX, *Ineffabilis Deus,* December 8, 1854).

Mary was born free of original sin because God foreknew that she would be the mother of Jesus. Mary's Immaculate Conception had nothing to do with the spiritual condition of her mother, Anne, so it was not necessary that Anne be free of sin, personal or imputed.

The Church has never taught that the Immaculate Conception resulted from a miraculous birth, like that of Jesus. Mary was conceived in the usual way by concourse between Anne and Joachim. Some artists have sought to show the Immaculate Conception visually as resulting from a kiss when Anne and Joachim were reunited after appearances of an angel to them separately. Such works include the cycle on the life of Mary done by Giotto in Padua, Italy's Scrovegni (also called the Arena) Chapel and by the unknown artist of the cycle in the choir of Orvieto Cathedral, Italy. These works of art should always be understood as intending to show the immaculate nature of Mary's conception symbolically. Those who think that the dogma of the Immaculate Conception was a late invention by a "reactionary" Pope, are answered by Giotto's kiss between Joachim and Anne, symbolic of the Immaculate Conception, which was painted in 1305.

Mary was not only born free of original sin but, by God's grace, lived her entire life free of actual sin. The Eastern churches call her "Panagia," the "All-Holy."

While God foreknew that Mary would live free of sin and would become the mother of the Second Person of the Trinity, Mary nevertheless had free will and could have sinned but, by God's grace, chose not to do so. Similarly, she had free will that would have allowed her to decline to bear the Son of God. Mary was not excepted from the mysterious tension between God's foreknowledge and our free will.

2. "When Jesus saw his mother, and the disciple whom he loved standing near, he said to his mother, 'Woman, behold your son!' Then he said to the disciple, 'Behold your mother!' And from that hour the disciple took her into his own home" (Jn 19:26–27). Thus, from the cross Jesus provided for the future care of his mother.

If Joseph had been alive, there would have been no necessity for this; Mary would have gone home to Joseph. The passage confirms that the proper construction of all four Gospels' failure to mention Joseph during Jesus' ministry, is that Joseph had died sometime between Jesus being found in the temple at age twelve and the commencement of his ministry at age thirty-two or thirty-three.

If Mary had had other children besides Jesus, her proper caretaker would have been one of them, and Jesus would actually have infringed on the rights of a younger brother or sister by commending Mary to the care of John. Even the sixteenth-century reformers did not claim that Mary had other children. Only after the "Enlightenment" had worked corrosively for decades did writers begin to suggest the contrary.

3. Where did John live during the years following the Crucifixion? As long as Jerusalem was ruled directly by Rome, the Church was relatively safe from the temple establishment. (An exception was the stoning of Stephen, which occurred during a gubernatorial interregnum, when the Jews acted while Roman power was in abeyance.) However, in January, AD 41, Caligula was assassinated and Claudius was made Emperor. Claudius made a grant of Judea and Samaria to Herod Agrippa, a grandson of Herod the Great, who already had ruled Galilee and much of Herod the Great's other territory. Herod Agrippa was known to favor the Pharisees, and it was believed that he would persecute the Church to curry favor with them. Only James the Greater, son of Zebedee, Peter, and James the Less, the son of Alpheus, remained in Jerusalem. James the Greater was beheaded on Herod Agrippa's orders in August, AD 41 Peter was imprisoned, intended for execution, which was prevented by his miraculous escape described in *Acts* 12.

We may be sure that John, with Mary, lived elsewhere, but we do not know where with any certainty. Since John was a young, unmarried man without a household of his own, his domicile was with his parents. It seems likely that, after Pentecost, he moved his permanent residence back to Capernaum and that he and Mary lived with his parents. Salome and Zebedee were kinsmen, by Joseph, to Mary and in a financial position to afford her friendly, comfortable, and safe accommodations, particularly while John was out of town on his evangelical missions. In Capernaum Mary was surrounded by relatives, friends, and fellow Christians. Capernaum was also a safer place of residence for Mary than Jerusalem.

Herod Agrippa died in AD 44. Judea was again brought under direct Roman rule. It became safe to hold the Council of Jerusalem there in AD 48, which John attended. There is a story, perhaps rising to the level of a tradition of unascertained antiquity, that Mary lived in Jerusalem and daily made the rounds of the holy places, a version of the Way of the Cross. In view of the danger to Mary of living in Jerusalem through the killing of Stephen and the persecution by Herod Agrippa, I give little credence to such a story. Other than this, I have found no tradition as to the location of John and Mary's residence from Pentecost in AD 30 until the AD mid-50s, but I submit that the home of Salome and Zebedee was the most likely location. Salome, at least, was younger than Mary, and Zebedee had financially supported Jesus' ministry.

John is recorded at some point in time as having been in Jerusalem and been sent by the apostles from there to evangelize in Samaria (Acts 8:14). John also accompanied Paul and Barnabas to Cyprus, the first leg of Paul's first missionary journey, probably in AD 46, but John returned to Jerusalem from Cyprus instead of accompanying them into Asia Minor (Acts 13:5, 13). It seems likely that the Judaizers in Jerusalem asked John to go with Paul for a prolonged look at his teaching, since Paul had taught the church in Antioch for a year sometime prior to the Council of Jerusalem. Paul's teaching that it was not necessary for the Gentiles to be circumcised and to follow the law of Moses brought the conflict with the Judaizers to a head and resulted in the Council of Jerusalem, which ruled in Paul's favor. At the Council of Jerusalem in AD 48, James, Peter, and John agreed that they would evangelize among the Jews, while Paul and Barnabas would evangelize among the Gentiles (Gal 2:6–9). The Johannine corpus—that is the *Gospel of John, Epistles of John,* and *Book of Revelations*—is considered to display a very Jewish outlook. It is likely that John spent the period between AD 30 and the mid-50s working mostly in Judea, Samaria, Galilee, and the adjoining areas containing heavy Jewish populations. Upon these assumptions, I submit that John's base was his parents' home in Capernaum, where Mary also lived, and that he worked out of it. I am aware that some writers believe that

John may have worked among the Jewish diaspora in Asia Minor before the late 50s, but I am not so persuaded.

❖ ❖ ❖

4. At about AD 49, two streams of tradition diverge. One has Mary dying in Jerusalem sometime beginning as early as AD 49 or into the 50s and being buried in a tomb next to Gethsemane. The other has Mary living with John in Ephesus and, perhaps, dying there. On balance, it seems most likely to me that Mary and John did live for a time in Ephesus but that she returned to Jerusalem.

John and Mary moved to Ephesus. We do not know with certainty when they did so. It was not before AD 57, when Paul called the elders of the church at Ephesus to meet him in Miletus, as he was making his last trip to Jerusalem (Acts 20:17–38). Until that time, Paul had the apostolic oversight of Ephesus, whose church he had founded and nurtured, actually living in Ephesus from AD 52 until AD 55. At the time Paul arrived in Jerusalem in AD 57, the only apostle in Jerusalem was James, son of Alpheus. Paul was imprisoned for two years, briefly in Jerusalem and thereafter at Caesarea, commencing in AD 57, before he was sent to Rome.

Eusebius says that Timothy was the first bishop of Ephesus. That is probably correct. It is likely that Paul had Timothy go to Ephesus when he was first imprisoned. However, Timothy was still quite young and under Paul's authority, as indicated by *1 Timothy*, written probably in the fall of AD 55, only one-and-a-half years prior to Paul's arrest. **"Let no one despise your youth, but set the believers an example in speech and conduct, in love, in faith, in purity. Till I come attend to the public reading of scripture, to preaching, to teaching. . . . Do not rebuke**

an older man but exhort him as you would a father; . . . " (1 Tm 4:12–5:1). One must allow sufficient time for Paul to realize the indefinite term of his imprisonment, to direct Timothy to go to Ephesus and for Timothy to have done so.

Ephesus was the largest and richest city between Italy and Antioch. Its church was too important to leave indefinitely without apostolic supervision. When it became apparent that Paul's incarceration might be long-term, it was probably at that time that an apostle of John's stature was sent.

John and Mary probably went to Ephesus in AD 59, after Paul was sent to Rome. Mary would have been about seventy-nine years old, assuming Jesus' birth in December 7 BC It is likely that, at or before this time, Zebedee had died and the income from his business operations had ceased. The household which had been Mary's shelter may have needed to be broken up.

There is a strong local tradition that the Church of the Virgin Mary in Ephesus was built on the site of the house where Mary lived with John. A second-century structure used as a church was rebuilt as the Church of the Virgin Mary in the fourth century. In AD 431, the Ecumenical Council of Ephesus was held in that church to decide the status of Mary. Unquestionably, Ephesus was selected as the site of the Council in order to influence the outcome. The Council declared Mary to be Theotokos, not just the mother of Jesus' humanity but rather the God-bearer, the Mother of God.

The current ruins are those of the structure rebuilt at least twice after AD 431. Nevertheless, the tiered seating extending the entire arc of the apse is an unusual design found also in the Basilica of St John in Ephesus, built in the sixth century, and a few other places of similar antiquity. It is, therefore, possible that during the re-buildings of the church, the seats of the Council were preserved, and that these are the very seats of the memorable Council. When their decision was announced, the joyful crowd carried the bishops on their shoulders through the city in a torch-lit procession.

Luke's Gospel was written between AD 57 and AD 60, or a little later, following John A. T. Robinson's *Re-Dating the New Testament* (1976). Luke obviously interviewed Mary, since she was the only witness, or the only surviving witness, to many of the events described by him. The Revised Standard Version, 2nd Catholic Edition, footnotes Luke 1:5–2:52: "The 'infancy gospel,' as it is called, is written in a markedly Semitic style, which differs from that of the rest of the Gospel. It appears to be based on the reminiscences of Mary." It is likely that Luke's interview of Mary took place during her residence in Ephesus. It is unlikely that Luke wrote the "infancy gospel" in a Greek which had a Semitic style. It is more likely that Mary had written her account in Greek or, if in Aramaic, that Luke translated it into a Greek that preserved the Semitic style. Thus the "infancy gospel" is probably the verbatim account of Mary herself.

What did the early Christians know of the "infancy gospel" prior to publication of Luke's Gospel? From Pentecost on, the Church taught that Jesus was divine, the Son of God. The early Christians necessarily wondered how God could be born of a woman, and an answer was necessary. The first answer was that given by Matthew in the earliest Gospel: **"[T]hat which is conceived in her is of the Holy Spirit; . . . "** (Mt 1:20). Matthew told the story from Joseph's point of view, in order to protect Mary.

Where did Matthew get his information? He necessarily received Joseph's story as told probably to Cleophas and then passed on by Cleophas to the apostles and other disciples after Jesus' Ascension and the Descent of the Holy Spirit.

✦ ✦ ✦

5. In AD 64, during Nero's reign, much of Rome burned. He eventually tried to place the blame on the Christians, and the Neronian persecution began in late AD 64 or, more likely, in early AD 65. The shock to the Christian communities was tremendous. Theretofore, Roman rule and law had always been the protector of the Christians against the Jewish persecutions, as reflected by most of the New Testament. While the Neronian persecution was not carried out throughout the empire, word of the actions in Rome would have traveled swiftly to Ephesus, capital of the province of Asia. The church in Ephesus had good reason to fear the possibility of governmental persecution and also attacks from the Jews and the silversmiths, using the persecution in Rome as a pretext (Acts 19:24–41). The mother of Jesus would have been an attractive target in either case, with the added temptation of trying to extract from her, under torture, a denial of her son's divinity. The risk to her would have been increased by the prior publication of Luke's Gospel.

John obviously would have adopted measures to protect Mary. A German visionary, Anne Catherine Emmerich (1774–1824), described a vision of a house in which Mary had lived and died. Though she had never been to Asia Minor nor had any of those around her, she described the house and its surroundings in great detail. In 1891 Lazarists from Smyrna, following the published account of her visions, found the ruins of a small building which had been part of a small monastery. The building originally was a house, which was converted into a house church during the first century. It is located on the slope of a mountain five miles outside of Ephesus, well off of the main road in an isolated situation. It would have been unnoticed, but still accessible by John from Ephesus. A church was built nearby in the fourth century. Popes Paul VI, St. John Paul II, and Benedict XVI have all visited the shrine built over the ruins of the house.

Other than Emmerich's vision, the tradition has been that Mary spent her last days in Jerusalem, as attested by apocryphal writings from as early as the third century, which place her death and burial in Jerusalem. St. Brigid of Sweden had her own vision, while in Jerusalem, in which Mary appeared to her and told her that she had been buried in the tomb in Jerusalem and had been assumed from it. I am inclined to follow the traditions that place Mary in Jerusalem in her last days. Nevertheless, Emmerich's vision offers a compelling description of the manner in which John fulfilled his obligation to protect Mary during their residence in Ephesus.

6. If we follow the tradition that Mary died in Jerusalem, John took Mary to Jerusalem from Ephesus. There is a narrow window of time during which this could have occurred. The full fury of the Neronian persecution subsided by the end of AD 65 after a popular revulsion set in. The Jewish Revolt began in Jerusalem in the summer of AD 66. Mary's return to Jerusalem must be dated to AD 66 after commencement of the sailing season that spring allowed her and John to take a ship from Ephesus to Caesarea, the closest major port to Jerusalem. Mary was about eighty-six years old.

To those who think people did not live so long "back then," we can point to Anna, who was eighty-four when Jesus was presented in the temple. Average ages are unimportant; those who survived childhood lived a goodly span, expecting to live to "three score and ten," or more. The main threat to women's longevity was childbirth, which Mary did not experience after the birth of Jesus. Furthermore, living a life entirely free of sin would cause one to avoid many bad habits which can shorten a life span.

7. Mary's arrival in Jerusalem would have caused quite a stir in the church there. She had not been in Jerusalem for at least eight or nine years, since she went to Ephesus with John. Many members of the church had never seen her, and they would have thronged to see her and to ask her about Jesus.

Why did she return to Jerusalem? She would have wanted to see those disciples still alive, men and women, with whom she had associated during Jesus' ministry. Apostles and disciples who knew her would have traveled to Jerusalem to bid her farewell. She probably also wanted to see again the places sanctified by her work and that of her son. She undoubtedly would have pointed out such places in Jerusalem and Bethlehem for the benefit of the new Christians.

Since *Luke* was written and published about AD 57–60, or soon thereafter, many Christians then learned for the first time the details of the conception and birth of God as a man. It is entirely likely that many Christians questioned the authority of Luke. It may well be that one reason for Mary's return to Jerusalem was to affirm publicly the accuracy of *Luke's* account.

The tradition that Mary left this world in Jerusalem is very strong. In addition to apocalyptic writings dating from the third century, there is the location of her "tomb." It adjoins the olive grove and grotto at Gethsemane, the owner of which was clearly a disciple of Jesus, since he allowed Jesus and his disciples to use the property regularly. He, or his heir, likely owned the connecting tract on which Mary was said to have been buried. A church was built over the tomb in the fifth century, probably inspired by the Council of Ephesus and perhaps to assert the claim of Jerusalem to have been her final resting place.

It can be argued that the publication of Luke's Gospel would not have occurred until after Mary's death, because it raised her profile and made her a more obvious target, if she were still alive. If Luke's Gospel was written between AD 57 and AD 60, or shortly after, this argument would indicate that Mary died in Jerusalem between AD 49 and the AD mid-50s or that she moved to Ephesus and died there before the Neronian persecution. It may equally be argued that Mary willingly undertook the risk in order to satisfy a widely felt need for more knowledge of the manner in which God became man. Her withdrawal to the country outside Ephesus was a response to the increased risk.

The tradition of Mary's residence in Ephesus is very strong. The strongest evidence is the tradition of the Church of the Virgin Mary having been built on the site of her residence, strengthened still more by the implicit recognition of that claim in setting the Council of Ephesus in that church on the issue of Mary's status. The vision of Anne Catherine Emmerich uncannily described the location of a place she, and anyone else around her, had never seen, and the authenticity of her vision is, at least, impliedly supported by three recent papal visits to that shrine. While there is much learned dispute about the date of Mary's death, a later date seems probable, because she could not have gone to Ephesus with John before AD 57.

There is a tradition that the Church of the Dormition in Jerusalem is on the site of the house in which Mary lived. That is possible. But the site may be that of the house in which she lived at the time she departed this life. It need not have been the site of a long-term residence in Jerusalem, which I believe unlikely.

It should be apparent to the reader that efforts to determine the movements and residences of John and Mary are based on extremely thin evidence. The inferences must be spun out more than is the case with any other subject of these meditations. Despite all the difficulties, the course which appears to me to be the most likely is that John and Mary moved to Ephesus in AD 59; they remained in the city until the winter of AD 64–65, at which time John moved her to "the house of Mary" outside of Ephesus; they returned to Jerusalem in the spring of AD 66; and Mary left this earth in Jerusalem sometime before the commencement of the Jewish Revolt in the summer of AD 66.

8. Following the dominant tradition, Mary spent her last days in Jerusalem. She either died or went to sleep. In either case, she left this earth from Jerusalem.

The Eastern tradition is that Mary went to sleep (the Dormition of the Virgin Mary). The Western tradition is not so clear. Most Western theologians say that Mary died. A minority agree with the Eastern tradition. What the entire Roman and Eastern Churches agree on, is that Mary's body was physically assumed into heaven. In support of this, there have never been any relics of the Blessed Virgin Mary, nor has any one ever claimed to have any such.

9. "[W]e pronounce, declare, and define it to be a divinely revealed dogma: That the Immaculate Mother of God, the Ever-Virgin Mary, having completed the course of her earthly life, was assumed body and soul into heavenly glory" (Pius XII, *Munificentissimus Deus,* November 1, 1950).

The dogma of the Assumption of the Virgin Mary carefully leaves open the question of whether Mary died or fell asleep before being bodily assumed into heaven.

A primary argument supporting the dogma is that, what son having the power to do so, would not bring his mother back to life and into paradise and spare her the corruption of her body? Since Jesus had the power to do so, he would have exercised it.

"[T]he bodies of even the just are corrupted after death, and only on the last day will they be joined, each to its own glorious soul. Now God has willed that the Blessed Virgin Mary should be excepted from this general rule. She, by an entirely unique privilege, completely overcame sin by her Immaculate Conception, and as a result she was not subject to the law of remaining in the corruption of the grave, and she did not have to wait until the end of time for the redemption of her body" (Pius XII, *Munificentissimus Deus*, 1950).

For Mary to have been assumed was appropriate to her Immaculate Conception, her sinless life, and her divine motherhood, coupled with her life-long virginity. The privilege of assumption in order to avoid bodily corruption is consistent with these other privileges. I find this argument also implicitly supports the Eastern position. These privileges point also to Mary's having been excepted from the human necessity of death. As is argued in favor of Jesus' allowing his mother to avoid corruption after death, what son, having the power to do so, would not spare his mother the pain and pangs of death itself?

---

10. Some theologians cite *Psalm* 131 in support of this dogma. "Arise, O Lord, into your resting place: you and the ark, which you have sanctified" (Ps 132:8). Mary has been considered the true ark, the ark of the Incarnation, who contained the true God.

Revelation speaks to this imagery of Mary as the ark. "Then God's temple in heaven was opened, and the ark of his covenant was seen within his temple; there were flashes of lightning, voices, peals of thunder, an earthquake and heavy hail. And a

great portent appeared in heaven, a woman clothed with the sun, with the moon under her feet, and on her head a crown of twelve stars; she was with child, and she cried out in her pangs of birth, in anguish for delivery" (Rv 11:19–12:2).

What Jew, reading this for the first time, would not have gasped? In Solomon's temple the ark was placed in the Holy of Holies. The ark had been taken from Solomon's temple by Jeremiah and hidden. It had never been found. In both the second temple and Herod's temple, the Holy of Holies was empty. In John's vision, the Ark of the Covenant is in God's temple in heaven. But instead of an elaborate box containing the tablets of the Ten Commandments and a sample of manna, the Ark of the Covenant is a pregnant woman, obviously Mary. *Revelation* was written in AD 68–70, after Mary's assumption and before the fall of Jerusalem.

It is possible to read this passage as describing two separate visions. However, bearing in mind that the original text was not divided into chapters and verses, it is more reasonable to construe the second vision as a continuation of the first. Otherwise, what is the point of saying that the ark is in heaven, and stopping?

"[I]t is reasonable and fitting that not only the soul and body of a man, but also the soul and body of a woman should have obtained heavenly glory. Finally, since the Church has never looked for the bodily relics of the Blessed Virgin nor proposed them for the veneration of the people, we have a proof on the order of a sensible experience. . . . It is our hope that belief in Mary's bodily assumption into heaven will make our belief in our own resurrection stronger and render it more effective" (*Munificentissimus Deus*).

Coronation of the Virgin, Fra Angelico, c.1450, Museo di S. Marco, Florence

THE CORONATION OF THE BLESSED VIRGIN MARY

1. "The Lord God said to the serpent, 'Because you have done this, cursed are you above all cattle, and above all wild animals; upon your belly shall you go, and dust shall you eat all the days of your life. I will put enmity between you and the woman, and between your seed and her seed; he shall bruise your head, and you shall bruise his heel'" (Gn 3:14–15).

From the earliest days, the Church has considered this passage as "the proto-evangelium." The first Eve brought sin and death into the world through her disobedience. Mary is the second Eve, who brings salvation into the world through her obedience, in the form of "her seed," Jesus, and sin and death will be overthrown. The earliest Fathers called Mary "the New Eve." "The former [Eve] was seduced to disobey God, but the latter [Mary] was persuaded to obey God, so that the Virgin Mary might become the advocate of the Virgin Eve. As the human race was subjected to death through a virgin, so was it saved by a virgin, and thus the disobedience of one virgin was precisely balanced by the obedience of another" (Irenaeus, *Against Heresies,* Book V).

The hymn "Adam lay ybounden" expresses this concept. "Ne'er had the apple taken been, ne'er had Our Lady been heavenly Queen. Blest be the time that apple taken was. Therefore moun we singen, *Deo gratias.*" I have sometimes questioned the theology of blessing The Fall. St Augustine calls The Fall, "O happy fault." I suppose, if the theology didn't bother him, it shouldn't bother me. But there is no question regarding the blessing of the world's redemption through Mary's obedience.

---

2. Mary was the first to believe the gospel, and she is preeminently the greatest of the believers in the gospel. As discussed in the meditation on the Annunciation, Mary believed the words of the angel announcing, **"[Y]ou will conceive in your womb and bear a son, and you shall call his name Jesus. He will be great and will be called the Son of the Most High, and the Lord God will give to him the throne of his Father David. . . . "** (Lk 1:31–32). While Mary asked to know how this was to be done, wholly without the participation of her espoused husband, Joseph, her belief had already been given. She requested and received the angel's explanation of how this would occur: **"The Holy Spirit will come upon you, and the power of the most high will overshadow you; therefore the child to be born will be called holy, the Son of God"** (Lk 1:35). This was the decisive moment in human history. Mary, through exercise of her free will, could have declined the risk of accepting a pregnancy without knowing Joseph's reaction, possibly even suffering death as the result. God's plan for the world's salvation hung on her response. **"And Mary said, 'Behold the handmaid of the Lord; be it unto me according to thy word'"** (Lk 1:38). The Incarnation could occur only after Mary's belief gave rise to her consent. In a sense, Jesus was conceived in Mary's mind before he was conceived in her womb.

Elizabeth had prayed for six months to know the identity of the Messiah whose way was to be prepared by her son, John. Instantly recognizing Mary as the mother of the Messiah, Elizabeth exclaimed, **"Blessed is she who believed that there would be a fulfillment of what was spoken to her from the Lord"** (Lk 1:45).

In her *Magnificat*, Mary responded to Elizabeth, **"For behold, henceforth all generations shall call me blessed"** (Lk 1:48). Mary's faith and consent commence the New Covenant between God and man. But for Mary's faith and consent, God's plan to reverse the fall brought about by Eve's disobedience, would not have occurred, at least at that time.

Before adoption of the Gregorian calendar, the new year began with Lady Day, March 25, the Feast of the Annunciation, the conception of Christ, instead of on January 1.

❖   ❖   ❖

3. Mary is the Mother of God, as recognized dogmatically at the Council of Ephesus. From the instant of conception, Mary carried the Second Person of the Trinity within her womb.

How could this be? God blessed the material world as being "good," and he has never hesitated to cause the material world to behave in a manner contrary to the normal rules in order to accomplish his own purposes. Such examples come to mind as the parting of the Red Sea, stopping the sun during the fall of Jericho, Jesus' stilling the wind and waves, and the "dancing" of the sun at Fatima.

The chromosomes of Mary obviously were affected in some manner to produce a male child. But there had to be a change, since Mary's ovum, by itself, could only produce a female child. Indeed, in some lower forms of life, reproduction can occur through parthenogenesis, whereby a female of the species can reproduce without being impregnated by a male; but, because the female carries only the female chromosome, only female issue can result. If the impregnation of Mary had occurred by some form of parthenogenesis, only a female child could have resulted. Does God the Father have chromosomes and DNA? It seems unlikely. More likely is a hypotheses that Mary was impregnated through a miraculous working on her own chromosomes to change one female chromosome to a male chromosome and thereby allow chromosomal division and reproduction to produce a male child without the action of a male sperm. With the necessity for miraculous action being confined to those changes necessary to produce a male child, then we may conclude that in every other respect Jesus was the child of Mary. If we want to know what Mary looked like, feminize the features of Jesus on the Shroud of Turin, and one will see a portrait of Mary.

Mary was the Mother of God, as Jesus grew in her womb, nurtured from Mary's body. At Jesus' birth, Mary suffered the pangs of childbirth, as foretold in the proto-evangelium and as described in *Revelation,* and Jesus was born in the usual way. There is a tradition in the Eastern Churches that Jesus was born without disturbing Mary's hymeneal virginity, which is also accepted by many in the West. I recognize that such a doctrine is explained as a consequence of Mary's eternal virginity. The *Catechism* should not be read as confusing the substance of Mary's virginity with the form of it. The *Catechism* says the Church confesses "Mary's real and perpetual virginity even in the act of giving birth. . . . " One could also say that the Church confesses Mary's virginity even as her figure altered as Jesus grew in the womb. The physical changes in her body do not affect the fact of her "real and perpetual virginity." The *Catechism* leaves the details open, without dogmatic interpretation, just as the doctrine of the Assumption leaves open the question of whether Mary died or fell asleep. I do not consider it wise to pile miracle upon miracle, when one miracle will suffice.

Such a doctrine is like the story about the cherry tree bending down to Mary so she could pick its fruit. Such stories are efforts to explain symbolically the underlying truth, but the embellishments weaken the credibility of the underlying truth, and are therefore inadvisable, particularly in our scientific age.

The theory that Jesus was born without disturbing Mary's hymeneal virginity, indeed even without causing her pain, is akin to the various heresies based on the idea that God is pure and therefore cannot be besmirched by the dirt and messiness of humanity. The great heresies, in a way, are variations on this theme. Jesus was God and could not suffer, so he was a phantom. Or, he was pure as God is pure, so he could not be made of materialistic flesh and blood, because the material world is evil and only the spiritual world is good. Or, the greatest heresy of all, since Jesus did suffer and die, he was not divine. The application of this concept to Mary is what we are dealing with. As early as Irenaeus, writing in the second half of the second century, this idea was circulating among the Gnostics. Irenaeus refutes those Gnostics who claimed that "[Jesus] had passed through Mary like water through a tube. . . . " (Irenaeus, *Against Heresies,* III, 11). That is an apt description of the effect of the theory we are discussing. If Jesus passed through Mary like water through a tube, he would not break her hymen. Nor would her belly have swelled. Nor would all the complex physical changes that accompany pregnancy have occurred. Nor would she have lactated after he was born. Unless Jesus was born accompanied by his mother's afterbirth and covered in her blood, he was not a man, and some of the heretics were right. But they were not.

Mary nursed Jesus with milk produced in the usual way from her body, likewise without affecting her "real and perpetual virginity." She ministered to him in changing him, cleaning him, feeding him, and clothing him. He was in every sense a human being. Yet, from conception, he was also God.

Being God does not mean that Jesus was omniscient as an infant and as a child. When he was taught to read, he really learned to read and was not play-acting that he was learning something he already knew. When he studied the scriptures and prayed to learn how they applied to him, he was not pretending to learn something he already knew. The hypostatic union of God and man in Jesus developed his knowledge of his identity and mission over time, and even then the Father sent Moses and Elijah to Jesus to strengthen his conviction of the accuracy of his interpretation of the scriptures, so as to fortify him for the ordeal to come.

❖ ❖ ❖

4. Mary was the first and best taught of the disciples. When she gave her fiat to the angel, she began her discipleship.

We do not know precisely when Joseph died. It is clear from the Gospels that he was alive when Jesus stayed in the temple at age twelve and that he had died before Jesus' ministry began at age thirty-two or thirty-three. We know that he lived long enough to train Jesus in his own trade as a carpenter and that Jesus made his living in that trade, presumably inheriting Joseph's tools and carpentry establishment. From this we may infer that Joseph lived long enough to help raise Jesus to maturity, at least until he was approximately twenty, or older. This inference is supported by the Father's gift of Joseph to Mary and Jesus as their guardian and provider, a mission which he performed exceptionally well. It is therefore probable that Joseph survived until Jesus was at least twenty.

After Jesus had been fully trained as a carpenter by Joseph and was old and skilled enough to support himself and Mary, it is reasonable to believe that the Father allowed Joseph to die so as to give Jesus and Mary time to themselves as Jesus sought to learn the nature of his ministry. Mary and Jesus were the only two sinless human beings since The Fall. Over a course of years, Jesus undoubtedly discussed with Mary his interpretation of the scriptures concerning himself. She was, therefore, the best-taught and most knowledgeable of the disciples.

In the Protestant churches, Mary virtually disappears after Jesus' twelfth year. In fifty-eight years as a Protestant, I remember only one sermon on Mary, and it began with disclaimers. The scriptures are not silent about Mary's discipleship. She is present at the wedding at Cana, and her intercession commences Jesus' performance of miracles and confirms his disciples in their belief that he is the Messiah. Mary and his "brothers" (cousins) join him at Capernaum (Mt 12:46–47). Mary is expressly present at the foot of the cross. She is expressly present at Pentecost. The specific enumeration of times of her presence indicates that she was also present in the interstices—that is, throughout most of his ministry. Her failure to accompany the women to the tomb was so unusual that it raises the probability that she already knew he had risen, because the risen Jesus had appeared to her first.

Mary was preeminently the greatest of the disciples.

---

5. Mary is the co-operatrix with Jesus in the work of salvation. This title takes nothing away from Jesus' uniqueness and divinity, since her cooperation was always in aid of his mission. Even as she cooperated by consenting to bring the Son into the world, she also consented to the immolation of the sacrifice she had brought forth. She suffered in union with him.

6. Mary is the Mother of the Church.

The Gospels are not chronologies, so it is difficult to determine the timing of the events of Jesus' ministry, or even the order in which they occurred. *John* is the most nearly chronological, once the theologically related passages concluding with the wedding at Cana have been covered. A likely sequence is that, following his baptism by John (Mt 3:13–17; Mk 1:9; Lk 3:21; Jn 1:29–34), Jesus withdrew into the wilderness to pray (Mt 4:1–11; Lk 4:1–13). **"And Jesus returned** (from the wilderness) **in the power of the Spirit into Galilee, and a report concerning him went out through all the surrounding country. And he taught in their synagogues, being glorified by all"** (Lk 4:14–15).

During this period of teaching "in their synagogues," Jesus called the first of his disciples, probably Andrew, Simon Peter, James, John, and Philip (Mk 1:16–20; Lk 5:1–11; Jn 1:43–51). These are the first five disciples according to Pope Benedict XVI, relying on Mark and Luke. John's account gives Andrew, Simon Peter, Philip, and Nathanael of Cana as the first four. (The omission of James and John in *John* probably arises from John's policy of not naming himself in his own Gospel.) It may well be that Nathanael Bartholomew of Cana had become a disciple before the miracle at the wedding; it is equally reasonable to conclude that his discipleship, like that of Simon the Cananaean, resulted from the miracle.

Jesus preached in the synagogues of Galilee. He and his first disciples went to the wedding in Cana, where they met Mary and his "brothers" (cousins), who were also guests. It was there that he performed his first miracle, "the first of his signs" (Jn 2:11). If *John's* list of the first disciples is more accurate, it is likely that Jesus' cousins, the brothers James and John, saw the miracle and were influenced to become his disciples after the wedding, as *John* indicates.

"**After this** [the wedding in Cana] **he went down to Capernaum, with his mother and his brothers and his disciples; and there they stayed for a few days**" (Jn 2:12). This is the first mention that Mary accompanied Jesus and the disciples. Then follows a series of healings in Capernaum (Lk 5:12–26).

"**And he came to Nazareth, where he had been brought up; and he went to the synagogue, as his custom was on the sabbath day. . . . And he said to them, 'Doubtless you will quote to me this proverb, "Physician, heal yourself; what we have heard you did at Capernaum, do here also in your own country."' . . . And they rose up and put him out of the city, and led him to the brow of the hill on which their city was built, that they might throw him down headlong**" (Lk 4:16–30).

From this sequence of events it appears that, up until the wedding at Cana, Jesus and the initial group of four or five disciples were not accompanied on their perambulations by women disciples. Indeed, it would have appeared scandalous to do so. Mary joined the group after the wedding at Cana. Her presence with Jesus and his entourage would have become permanent either before, or certainly no later than, Jesus' ejection from Nazareth. It is inconceivable that she would have continued to live in such a hostile environment after that event, which occurred early in Jesus' ministry.

It was the presence of Mary with Jesus' entourage which made it possible for other women to join the group and travel with men unrelated to them.

"**Soon afterward he went on through cities and villages, preaching and bringing the good news of the kingdom of God. And the twelve were with him, and also some women who had been healed of evil spirits and infirmities; Mary, called Magdalene,** from whom seven demons had gone out, and Joanna, the wife of Chuza, Herod's steward, and Susanna, and many others, who provided for them out of their means"** (Lk 8:1–3). Thus is described the nucleus of the women disciples, who accompanied the men, ministered to them, and provided financial support.

Mary was effectively the chaperone who made this possible. She was probably older than the other women. She undoubtedly served as advisor and comforter to them, leading the women disciples and functioning as their mother. And because she was Jesus' mother, the men also would have treated her with special deference and love. As the disciples at that time regarded Jesus as the Messiah and expected him to become king, they regarded Mary as the Queen Mother, like Solomon's mother, Bathsheba, a position of great honor, dignity, and power in Jewish history.

"Then his mother and his brothers came to him, but they could not reach him for the crowd. And he was told, 'Your mother and your brothers are standing outside, desiring to see you.' But he said to them, 'My mother and my brothers are those who hear the word of God and do it'" (Lk 8:19–21). Or in *Matthew*, even more vehemently, Jesus responds to the notice: **"Stretching out his hands toward his disciples, he said, 'Here are my mother and my brothers! For whoever does the will of my Father in heaven is my brother, and sister, and mother'"** (Mt 12:46–50; Mk 3:31–35). If Jesus' disciples are his brothers and sisters, his mother is likewise their mother.

A similar point is made: **"[A] woman in the crowd raised her voice and said to him, 'Blessed is the womb that bore you, and the breasts that you sucked!' But he said, 'Blessed rather are those who hear the word of God and keep it!'"** (Lk 11:27–28). Only one person could receive the blessing bestowed by the woman in the crowd, but all people can receive the blessing described by Jesus.

These passages have been misconstrued by some as Jesus' rejection of his mother and "brothers" or even that Mary and his brothers had come to take their lunatic kinsman home. Jesus' deliberate expansion of the definition of those who could claim kinship to him had a purpose. Since his disciples expected Jesus to restore the Davidic kingdom and reign as its king, they expected high government positions for themselves. Among his own kinsmen, the belief was strong that they should receive positions nearest the throne, as shown by the request of Jesus' cousin, or step-cousin, Salome and her sons, James and John, that they should receive precedence over Peter. If Jesus had created a new dynasty, there would have been nothing surprising in this. The Hasmonean dynasty created by the Maccabees was an example within living memory.

Jesus was determined that his Church would not be a dynastic organization, dependent on ties of kinship rather than holiness. Even so, the early Church walked a tightrope as to whether Jesus' kin supported the Church or ran it. Seven kinsmen were members of Jesus' entourage: his mother Mary, Cleophas' wife Mary, her two sons, James and Joses, and her daughter, Salome, and her two sons, James and John. Three apostles, James the son of Alpheus, James, and John, were first cousins or first cousins once removed, by blood or marriage. Step-cousin Joses (Joseph) Barsabbas was one of two nominees for selection of a replacement for Judas Iscariot; had he been selected, it would have made four out of twelve apostles kinsmen, instead of three. Cousin, or step-cousin, the apostle James, son of Salome and Zebedee, was a leader of the church in Jerusalem at his martyrdom in August AD 41. He was succeeded by step-cousin and apostle James, son of Alpheus, as the head of the church in Jerusalem, and cousin Simon succeeded him as its first bishop until his martyrdom not long before the Jewish insurrection in AD 66. The church in Nazareth was led by descendants of his cousin Jude. The presence in his entourage of so many of Jesus' kinsmen indicates the likelihood that Joseph, with the agreement of Mary, at some point in time had told his brother Cleophas the secret of Jesus' birth, and Cleophas passed this information within his family at some appropriate time. It was a close call, even in the face of Jesus' admonition that all believers would be his brothers and sisters, but the New Israel was not to have a new royal dynasty.

In giving Mary to John as his mother, Jesus from the cross appointed her as Mother, not only to John, but to all the Church.

※ ※ ※

7. The Blessed Virgin Mary is the model of Christian chastity.

Let us be clear about our definitions. Virginity is a technical physical condition, which may be entirely unrelated to chastity. Chastity is a state of the spirit, which may be recovered even by a former prostitute, such as Mary Magdalene is said by tradition to have been.

Virginity at marriage and chastity thereafter have been considered essential in almost all societies throughout history, because the woman's failure in either respect could burden her husband with a child, and heir, not his own. Consequently, the sanctions have usually been Draconian. An example is the "honor killing" among the Moslems. Even today in many Moslem nations the father or brother of a woman guilty of sexual intercourse outside of marriage may kill her, even if it resulted from rape. Some Moslem immigrants to the United States have brought this pleasant cultural practice with them.

The teachings regarding chastity appear to be related to the status of women generally. In much of the Moslem world, women are sequestered literally or by their dress. The Hindu practice of suttee, burning the living wife of the dead husband on his funeral bier, was halted only in the nineteenth century by the British imperialists. "Our custom is to burn our widows." "Yes, and our custom is to hang the men that do it." Even today, the Indian government lacks the will, or perhaps, desire to halt or punish the Hindu custom of "dowry killings." In Japan, the wife is generally not included in the social activities of the men, even at high levels of society, though the Emperor has recently sought to change this.

The Christian view of virginity and chastity is radically different, as is the resultant status of women. **"He who looks on a woman to lust after her has already committed adultery in his heart"** (Mt 5:27–28). Jesus places the burden of protecting a woman's chastity primarily on the man. The woman is not relieved of responsibility, though Jesus mitigated the punishment for her error in dealing with the woman caught in adultery (Jn 8:2–11). There is no comparable teaching on this subject in non-Christian religions.

"Husbands, love your wives, as Christ loved the Church and gave himself up for her, that he might sanctify her, . . . that she might be holy and without blemish. Even so, husbands should love their wives as their own bodies. He who loves his wife loves himself. . . . ; for this reason a man shall leave his father and mother and be joined to his wife, and the two shall become one flesh" (Eph 5:25–31). **"Love is patient and kind; love is not jealous or boastful; it is not arrogant or rude. Love does not insist on its own way; it is not irritable or resentful; it does not rejoice at wrong, but rejoices in the right. Love bears all things, believes all things, hopes all things, endures all things. Love never ends; . . . "** (1 Cor 13:4–8). I have read, in translation, the major writings of all the major classical authors, Greek and Roman. There is absolutely nothing in classical literature that remotely approaches these Christian teachings. Those who say that their author, Paul, denigrated women merely disclose their own abysmal ignorance of the world in which he worked.

The Church's teaching on this subject has not been perfectly followed during the last 2,000 years of Western Civilization. None of the Church's teachings have been perfectly followed; sin is always present in the world. Nevertheless, women's elevated status in Christian nations, and in only those nations, is attributable to the veneration of Mary and the Church's teachings on the status of women. Chivalry toward women is solely a Christian concept, and its primary basis is also the veneration of Mary. Modern radical feminists, in insisting that there is no difference between men and women, attack all remaining vestiges of chivalry. They are offended even when a man opens a door for a woman. Where there is no place for chivalry, there is less likely to be a place for the veneration of Mary.

This is not to say that the pagan world had no regard for virginity and chastity other than as property rights. But there is a cold savagery attached to the instances in which they are held in high regard as virtues. Witness the manner in which Artemis had Acteon's dogs kill him, even though he had stumbled upon her in her bath wholly unintentionally. Witness female circumcision still practiced in Africa, done for the purpose of protecting chastity by removing from women the pleasure of sexual intercourse, another lovely custom now found in the United States and in Europe. I do say that the principal draw of pagan religion was, and is, its sexual excitement, not the recitation of bowdlerized myths about the gods. From temple prostitution to the self-castration of the rites of Attis to the Bacchanalian revels to innumerable other pagan religious rites, the sexual element was paramount. And not just between men and women. Sex between men, sex between women, sex between men and both adolescent and pubescent boys, sex between men or women and beasts—all approved at one or many times and places in the pagan world in which the early Church arose. How modern it all sounds!

The Catholic Church has had its share of recent scandals of a sexual nature, particularly of a homosexual nature, but its doctrinal condemnation of such actions has never been compromised. As Pope Benedict XVI said, even now the Church is cleansing "the filthiness" which had infected a portion of it. Pope Francis has continued and increased that "cleansing" of the Church.

But in many of the non-Catholic ecclesial organizations, which threw out Mary with the "Reformation," something different is stirring. In organizations such as the United Church of Christ, the Evangelical Lutheran Church of America, the Presbyterian Church of the U.S.A. and The Episcopal Church, together with several others, homosexual conduct even by the ministry, to say nothing of the laity, is not only tolerated, but approved, *de jure*. In many other ecclesial organizations it is approved *de facto*, at least on a "local option" level.

As is rapidly becoming evident, approval of homosexual activity is not the end of the line. Nor is the approval of homosexual marriage. How much longer can we discriminate against our Moslem immigrants and indigenous "fundamentalist" Mormons whose religions allow for multiple wives or our African immigrants whose modesty demands female circumcision? On what basis do we oppose the demand of North American Man-Boy Love Association (NAMBLA) that we should not discriminate against adolescent and pubescent boys by denying them the opportunity to experience and learn homosexual love? Note the widespread movement, particularly in Europe and Canada, to lower the age of consent for boys to fourteen, as a first step. Those non-Catholic ecclesial organizations, such as The Episcopal Church (I single it out, because I know it well), which have approved homosexuality among their bishops and priests, *de jure,* have declared black to be white. They are driven by sexual excitement in doing so and, by doing so, have rejoined the pagan swamp from which the Church separated itself. One may see it on the floor of The Episcopal Church's General Convention, passing resolutions endorsing abortion at any stage of pregnancy, prohibiting participation at General Convention by an organization dedicated to assisting homosexuals to practice abstinence or even to be cured and revert to heterosexuality and kissing the same sex on the mouth on the Convention floor.

❖ ❖ ❖

8. Mary intercedes for us, upon our request, with the Son. The model of her intercession is the wedding at Cana. Protestants insist that they have a relationship directly with God and may pray directly to him. So they do, and so they may. But the same man who insists that he prays only to God and does not need to pray to Mary, or any of the saints, for intercession, sees nothing inconsistent with asking friends, ministers, or even strangers to pray for him or his family. Consider the prayer chains in many churches that pray for the sick. Protestants find no problem in requesting intercessory prayers from the living, even from strangers. So it is not intercession that is the problem.

The problem is an insufficient understanding of "the communion of the saints," which most Protestants acknowledge in their creeds. The communion of the saints is the community of the entire Church. It includes the "Church Militant," living on earth today. It also includes the "Church Triumphant," composed of those already in heaven. The living may speak to the dead in their prayers. There seems little reason to think that those already in heaven, partaking of the joys and powers of eternity, cannot hear our intercessory prayers to them and do not have the charity to want to intercede for us with God, in whose presence they stand.

If we may speak in our prayers to the saints in heaven, and if it is all right to request intercession, why on earth would we not request intercession from the only mortal who ever led a sinless life, Mary, the Mother of God? Many Protestants confuse prayer for intercession to Mary, or to the saints, and the respect or veneration paid to them, with worship, which is due only to God. Again, Cana is the model. Mary tells the servants, "Do whatever he tells you." She points them to obedience to Jesus, to God. That is the same function Mary, and all the saints, perform when we venerate them and seek their intercession. They point us toward obedience to Jesus, to God.

Mary also is active in another form of intercessory activity. She appears from time to time to humans to ask them to intercede on behalf of someone. The best documented example of this nature is the series of apparitions to the shepherd children at Fatima, Portugal. Mary asked the children to tell the faithful to pray the rosary for the conversion of Russia. She promised to send a sign that would make their witness to the apparitions credible to others. Thousands saw the sun "dance" on October 13, 1917, including Marxist atheists many miles away.

In addition to the apparitions which have been investigated and declared authentic by the Church, Mary sometimes appears to those who derive comfort and inspiration from her apparition but, for one reason or another, do not seek the laborious and often controversial investigation by the Church. Nevertheless, there seems little reason to question that there have been more apparitions of Mary than those officially acknowledged by the Church.

9. "And a great portent appeared in heaven, a woman clothed with the sun, with the moon under her feet, and on her head a crown of twelve stars; she was with child and she cried out in her pangs of birth, in anguish for delivery. And another portent appeared in heaven; behold, a great red dragon, with seven heads and ten horns, and seven diadems upon his head. His tail swept down a third of the stars of heaven, and cast them to the earth. And the dragon stood before the woman who was about to bear a child, that he might devour her child when she brought it forth; she brought forth a male child, one who is to rule all the nations with a rod of iron, but her child was caught up to God and to his throne, and the woman fled into the wilderness, where she has a place prepared by God, in which to be nourished for one thousand two hundred and sixty days . . . And when the dragon saw that he had been thrown down to the earth, he pursued the woman who had borne the male child. . . . Then the dragon was angry with the woman, and went off to make war on the rest of her offspring, on those who keep the commandments of God and bear testimony to Jesus" (Rv 12:1–6, 13, 17).

There have been interpretations of this passage which strain to apply it to anyone except Mary. Nevertheless, the vision is clearly applicable to Mary. The dragon, like the serpent of the proto-evangelium, refers to Satan, and the woman in travail with the birth of her male child, is clearly Mary. Just as the dragon seeks to devour her child, so did Herod seek to destroy Mary's son, Jesus. Jesus, like the woman's child, was protected by God. As Mary, Joseph, and Jesus fled into the desert on their flight to Egypt to escape Herod, so the woman flees into the desert and finds refuge there for three and one-half years ("one thousand two hundred and sixty days"), the length of time between the flight to Egypt and the return from Egypt. The dragon, having failed to devour the woman's son, makes war on the rest of her offspring, defined as "those who keep the commandments of God and bear testimony to Jesus." Thus it is foreseen that Satan will make war upon the Church and its individual members, the children of Mary, Mother of the Church..

Our generation has again witnessed the truth of this vision, having seen the Church assailed from without by Marxists, Nazis, fundamentalist Moslems, and, now, "totalitarian relativists" (cf. Benedict XVI) and from within by men and women who have sought to redefine evil so as to accommodate their own immoral lifestyles.

10. "[A] woman clothed with the sun, the moon under her feet, and on her head a crown of twelve stars. . . . " (Rv 12:1). **"And God made the two great lights, the greater light to rule the day, and the lesser light to rule the night; he made the stars also. And God set them in the firmament of the heavens to give light upon the earth, to rule over the day and over the night, and to separate the light from the darkness. And God saw that it was good"** (Gn 1:16–18). In John's vision, Mary is clothed with the glory, beauty, and brilliance of heaven. The twelve stars in her crown symbolize the twelve tribes of the Old Covenant and the twelve apostles of the New Covenant.

No serious person claims that Mary, in heaven, wears a material crown like the crown of an earthly queen. Her crown is the Church. The twelve stars with which she is crowned in the vision constitute a portion of the glory of heaven with which she is clothed, as well as the Church. Mary is portrayed artistically as being crowned, but this is artistic imagery, an effort to show visually what cannot really be portrayed.

Mary, a created being like ourselves, is the only one of us already to be physically, as well as spiritually, present in heaven. She is the token, and promise, of our own resurrection. She has therefore been clothed and crowned with the glory of heaven.

Pray for us, O Holy Mother of God, that we may be made worthy of the promises of Christ. Amen.

SELECTED BIBLIOGRAPHY

Alcock, Leslie. *Arthur's Britain: History and Archeology, AD 367–634*. New York: Penguin, 1989.

Antonacci, Mark. *The Resurrection of the Shroud*. New York: M. Evans, 2000.

Ashe, Geoffrey. *The Discovery of King Arthur*. New York: Doubleday, 1985.

Ashe, Geoffrey. *King Arthur's Avalon: The Story of Glastonbury*. London: Collins, 1957.

Ashe, Geoffrey, Leslie Alcock, C. A. Ralegh Radford, Philip Rahtz, and Jill Racy. *The Quest for Arthur's Britain*. New York: Praeger, 1968.

Athanasius. *On the Incarnation*. New York: St. Vladimir's Press, 1996.

Bagatti, B. *Excavations in Nazareth, Vol. I*. Jerusalem: Franciscan Press, 1969.

Bauckham, Richard. *Jesus and the Eyewitnesses: The Gospels as Eyewitness Testimony*. Grand Rapids, MI: Erdmans Publishing, 2006.

Belloc, Hilaire. *The Great Heresies*. Rockford, IL: Tan Books, 1991.

Benford, M. Sue and Joseph G. Marino. "Discrepancies in the Radiocarbon Dating Area of the Turin Shroud." *Chemistry Today*, Vol. 26, 4 (July–Aug. 2008). www.ohioshroudconference.com/papers/p09.pdf.

Bennett, Janice. *Sacred Blood, Sacred Image: The Sudarium of Oviedo*. Littleton, CO: Libri de Hispania, 2001.

The Book of Common Prayer, 1928 ed. New York: The Church Pension Fund, 1945.

Carroll, Warren H. *The Founding of Christendom*. Front Royal, VA: Christendom Press, 1985.

Catechism of the Catholic Church, 2nd ed. Citta del Vaticano: Libreria Editrice Vaticana, 1997.

Claude E. Phillips Herbarium. *The Botany of the Shroud of Turin: A Floral Crime Scene Investigation*. Dover, DE: Delaware State University, 2004.

Clifford, Ross, ed. *Leading Lawyers Look at the Resurrection*. Claremont, CA: Albatross Books, 1991.

Eusebius. *The History of the Church*, trans. G. A. Williamson, rev. ed. London: Penguin Books, 1989.

Finegan, Jack. *Handbook of Biblical Chronology*, 4th ed. Peabody, MA: Hendrickson Publishers, 1998.

Hahn, Scott. *Hail, Holy Queen*. New York: Doubleday, 2001.

Hahn, Scott. *The Lamb's Supper: The Mass as Heaven on Earth*. New York: Doubleday, 1999.

Harding, Catherine D. *Guide to the Cappella del Corporale of Orvieto Cathedral*. Orvieto, Italy: Opera del Duomo di Orvieto, 2004.

Hardon, John A. *On the Real Presence of Jesus Christ in the Eucharist.* Naples, FL: Sapientia Press, 2000.

Hoade, Eugene. *Guide to the Holy Land.* Jerusalem: Franciscan Press, 1984.

Holy Bible, Authorized Version (King James Version). New York: Thomas Nelson.

Holy Bible, Revised Standard Version, Catholic Edition, 2nd ed. San Francisco: Ignatius Press, 2006.

Hughes, David. *The Star of Bethlehem: An Astronomer's Confirmation.* New York: Simon & Schuster, 1980.

Humber, Thomas. *The Sacred Shroud.* New York: Pocket Books, 1963.

Iannone, John C. *The Mystery of the Shroud of Turin.* New York: Alba House, 1998.

Josephus, Flavius. trans. William Whiston. *The Wars of the Jews.* New York: A. L. Burt.

Kondor, Louis, ed. *Fatima in Lucia's Own Words.* Still River, MA: Ravengate Press, 2003.

Mary's House: All Are Invited. Mary's Media Foundation.

Meagher, James L. *How Christ Said the First Mass.* Rockford, IL: Tan Books, 1906.

Morris, John. *The Age of Arthur: A History of the British Isles from 350 to 650.* New York: Scribners, 1973.

Moscini, Marcello. *Guide to St. Christina's Basilica, Bolsena.* Bolsena, Italy: 1991.

Nasuti, Nicola. *The Eucharistic Miracle of Lanciano.* Lanciano, Italy: Litografia Botolini, 1988.

The New Oxford Annotated Bible. New York: Oxford University Press, 1977.

Newman, John Henry. *An Essay on the Development of Christian Doctrine.* Foreword by Ian Ker. Notre Dame, IN: University of Notre Dame Press, 1989.

O'Connor, Rev. James T. *The Hidden Manna: A Theology of the Eucharist.* San Francisco: Ignatius Press, 1988.

Odell, Catherine M. *Those Who Saw Her: Apparitions of Mary.* Rev. ed. Huntington, IN: Our Sunday Visitor, 1995.

Pernoud, Regine, trans. Henry Taylor. *The Templars: Knights of Christ.* San Francisco: Ignatius Press, 2009.

Perrotta, Louise Bourassa. *St. Joseph: His Life and His Role in the Church Today.* Huntington, IN: Our Sunday School Visitor, 2000.

Rahner, Hugo, trans. Sebastian Bullough. *Our Lady and the Church.* Bethesda, MD: Zaccheus Press, 2004.

Richardson, Cyril C., ed. *Early Christian Fathers.* New York: Collier Books, 1970.

Robinson, John A. T. *Redating the New Testament.* Philadelphia: Westminster Press, 1976.

Sennott, Thomas. *Not Made by Hands.* New Bedford, MA; Franciscan Friars of the Immaculate, 1998.

Sri, Edward. *Dawn of the Messiah: The Coming of Christ in Scripture.* Cincinnati, OH: St. Anthony Messenger Press, 2005.

Stevenson, Kenneth E. and Gary R. Habemas. *Verdict on the Shroud: Evidence for the Death and Resurrection of Jesus Christ.* Ann Arbor, MI: Servant Books, 1981.

Stravinskas, Peter M. J. *The Catholic Answer: Book of Mary.* Huntington, IN: Our Sunday Visitor, 2000.

Thiede, Carsten Peter and Matthew D'Ancona. *The Quest for the True Cross.* New York: Palway, 2002.

Trouve, Marianne Lorraine, ed. *Mother of Christ, Mother of the Church: Documents on the Blessed Virgin Mary.* Boston: Pauline Books, 2001.

Willam, Franz. *Mary the Mother of Jesus.* New York: Scepter, 2004.

Wilson, Ian. *The Blood and the Shroud.* New York: Free Press, 1998.

ROSARY MEDITATIONS
is available in multiple formats.

Hardcover with dustjacket
(color illustrations)

Printed cover
(color illustrations)

Printed cover
(black and white illustrations)

Paperback
(black and white illustrations)

eBook for Kindle, Nook,
& iBooks

For bulk orders of 100 books or more, please call
(432) 599-3712 or email info@rosarymeditations.com

❦ ❦ ❦

Visit **www.RosaryMeditations.com**
to learn more and order today!

www.ingramcontent.com/pod-product-compliance
Lightning Source LLC
Chambersburg PA
CBHW052130010526
44113CB00034B/1218